JOBS FOR AMERICANS

 The American Assembly, *Columbia University*

JOBS
FOR AMERICANS

Prentice-Hall, Inc., *Englewood Cliffs, New Jersey*

A SPECTRUM BOOK

Library of Congress Cataloging in Publication Data

Main entry under title:

JOBS FOR AMERICANS.

(A Spectrum Book)
At head of title: The American Assembly,
Columbia University.
Background papers for the American Assembly on
Manpower Goals for American Democracy, held at
Arden House, Harriman, N.Y., May 1976.
Edited by E. Ginzberg.
Includes bibliographical references and index.
1. Manpower policy—United States—Addresses,
essays, lectures.   2. United States—Full
employment policies—Addresses, essays, lectures.
I. Ginzberg, Eli (date)   II. American
Assembly on Manpower Goals for American Democracy,
Arden House, 1976.   III. American Assembly.
HD5724.J67   331.1′1′0973   76-40054
ISBN 0-13-510024-0
ISBN 0-13-510016-X pbk.

10 9 8 7 6 5 4 3 2 1

PRENTICE-HALL INTERNATIONAL, INC. (*London*)
PRENTICE-HALL OF AUSTRALIA PTY., LTD. (*Sydney*)
PRENTICE-HALL OF CANADA, LTD. (*Toronto*)
PRENTICE-HALL OF INDIA PRIVATE LIMITED (*New Delhi*)
PRENTICE-HALL OF JAPAN, INC. (*Tokyo*)
PRENTICE-HALL OF SOUTHEAST ASIA PTE., LTD. (*Singapore*)
WHITEHALL BOOKS LIMITED (*Wellington, New Zealand*)

HD
5724
.J67

Table of Contents

Preface   vii

Eli Ginzberg
Introduction: The Purposes of an Economy   1

1   *Moses Abramovitz*
In Pursuit of Full Employment   8

2   *Robert M. Solow*
Macro-policy and Full Employment   37

3   *Arthur M. Okun*
Conflicting National Goals   59

4   *Lloyd Ulman*
Manpower Policies and Demand Management   85

5   *Barbara R. Bergmann*
Reducing the Pervasiveness of Discrimination   120

6   *Andrew F. Brimmer*
Economic Growth and Employment and Income Trends
among Black Americans   142

7   *Robert J. Lampman*
Employment versus Income Maintenance   163

8   *Juanita M. Kreps*
Some Time Dimensions of Manpower Policy   184

Index   206

The American Assembly   211

Preface

The temperature and volume of dialogue on almost any social illness will vary directly with the degree of pain with which the nation is afflicted. It follows, therefore, that the distress of high unemployment will stimulate intense and sometimes loud and heated discussion of its costs, consequences, and possible cures.

The recession of 1974–75 brought with it the highest rate of unemployment since World War II. Measures to ameliorate, if not cure, the disease have been suggested by many, agreed upon by some, but seldom applied. For example, according to learned diagnosticians, one approach to recession is in effect to tolerate unemployment in order to avoid aggravating inflation. An opposite school of thought holds that the nation cannot afford the human waste of unemployment and that more jobs for more Americans should have top priority. The employment picture is further complicated by the effects of discrimination against minorities and women.

This book was written to assess whether full employment is a worthy goal and, if so, to look at the possibility of finding jobs for more people, the costs and difficulties of doing so, and the acceptability of the necessary individual and institutional changes. It was planned primarily for the National Commission for Manpower Policy under the editorial supervision of Dr. Eli Ginzberg, Professor of Economics at Columbia University and Chairman of the Commission. It is published by The American Assembly because it served as advance background reading for The American Assembly on *Manpower Goals for American Democracy*, May, 1976, at Arden House, Harriman, New York. (The report of that meeting may be had from The American Assembly.)

The Commission supplied some of the funds for the Assembly project, as did the Ford Foundation. But neither is to be associated officially with the opinions herein. The views belong to the authors themselves. And The American Assembly, a national nonpartisan forum, takes no position on matters it presents for public study and discussion.

Clifford C. Nelson
President
The American Assembly

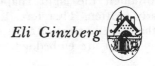

Eli Ginzberg

Introduction:
The Purposes of an Economy

This book has several distinctive features, the identification of which will help the reader follow the individual contributions and the principal themes that tie them together.

To begin with, a word about its origin and sponsorship. The chapters that comprise this book were contracted for by the National Commission for Manpower Policy, a statutory body established under Title V of the Comprehensive Employment and Training Act of December 27, 1973, which charges the commission with the responsibility of advising the President and Congress on a national manpower policy. Recognizing that in fulfilling this assignment it must pay primary attention to employment policy, the commission elicited the cooperation of a distinguished group of academicians. It may be worth noting that each of the contributors has not only left his or her mark on his or her discipline but each has also played a role in the world of policy. The sense of reality that permeates the entire work reflects this experience and accounts for the difference between the present effort and most academic endeavors.

After the preparation of these chapters had been contracted for, the commission was fortunate to arrange with the American Assembly for a national conference at Arden House in May 1976 on *Manpower Goals for American Democracy.* In working out this arrangement both the commission and the American Assembly recognized that the papers in process of preparation would be ideally suited as background readings for those who would attend the national conference.

ELI GINZBERG *is A. Barton Hepburn Professor of Economics and Director, Conservation of Human Resources, Columbia University. He is also Chairman of the National Commission for Manpower Policy and Chairman of the Board of the Manpower Demonstration Research Corporation.*

Although the eight chapters deal with weighty subjects, they are clearly written. Therefore, I, as editor, see no need to summarize each of the contributions. Rather, I will deal briefly with the three principal themes that are embedded in the eight chapters.

— What is the responsibility of the federal government in the arena of job creation and how can it better discharge this responsibility?
— To what extent must governmental and nongovernmental policy be shaped to eliminate serious malfunctioning of the labor market particularly with respect to women, minorities, and other disadvantaged groups whose participation is hobbled by history, tradition, and prejudice?
— What are the limits to which an expanded job program can be pushed, and to what extent must an affluent society resort to other devices such as income transfers and adjustments in work scheduling to enable people to enjoy a more satisfactory life with a wider range of options?

In discussing each of the foregoing themes I will call attention to some of the considerations that surfaced in the early work of the commission as it attempted to meet its assignment of outlining the elements of a national manpower policy.

On the critical issue of a national employment policy, it is clear that three decades after the passage of the Employment Act of 1946 the country has not yet moved up to the starting line. As late as December 1970, President Nixon vetoed new manpower legislation because, among other reasons, it contained a proviso for a modest job creation program. Several months thereafter, he accepted the Emergency Employment Act because the federally supported jobs were to be "transitional" and the act would expire at the end of two years. And the new CETA legislation (1973) almost foundered because of White House opposition to Title II which provided specific funding for public service jobs. President Ford's veto in February 1976 of the public works bill with its job-generating provisions indicated the continuing lack of consensus about the proper role of the federal government in the arena of job creation.

But another strand to this story must be highlighted. In the fall of 1975, the chairman of the Federal Reserve Board in his speech at Athens, Georgia, advocated that the federal government become the employer of last resort (with jobs paying 10 percent below the minimum wage) and that it set a goal of zero unemployment (no one who is able and willing to work would be without a job).

In March 1976, a revised Hawkins-Humphrey Full Employment Bill was readied and the Joint Economic Committee (Herbert Humphrey, Chairman) after extended hearings around the country held a national conference in Washington to focus attention on the need for a national employment policy.

The first three chapters by Abramovitz, Solow, and Okun provide the reader with a deepened perspective as to the reasons that the federal government was so slow in facing up to the employment challenge. To oversimplify, one can say that in the late 1950s Eisenhower and his advisors were more concerned about the strength of the dollar and the dangers of inflation than about the wastes of unemployment; during most of the 1960s the macroeconomic policies of the Kennedy-Johnson Administrations worked sufficiently well (in light of the later inflation too well) to push the unemployment rate down to a desirable if not optimal point—around 3.5 percent in 1969.

The third period—from 1969 to 1976—saw the economy operating at its lowest level of efficiency in the post-World War II era, suffering at one and the same time from high unemployment and substantial inflation. When neither the classic remedy of forced deceleration with increasing unemployment nor the more unorthodox efforts at price-wage-dividend controls in peacetime succeeded in eliminating the inflationary virus the economy first moved up in 1972–73 and then entered upon the severe recession of late 1974–75 which brought the unemployment rate close to 9 percent. Both the administration and the Congress were sufficiently shaken by the persistent virulence of inflation to avoid radical new approaches to reducing unemployment and opted instead for widening and strengthening the net to support the millions who lost their jobs and needed income support.

In its *First Annual Report to the Congress,* October 1975, the commission recognized that it would not be easy to bring the unemployment rate quickly down to a tolerable level but expressed its dismay with the "widespread belief that the nation must live with this undesirable situation (high unemployment) for several years to come." In this same report the commission took note of the large numbers in the population, not counted as unemployed, who needed employment assistance—those working part-time because they cannot find full-time jobs; those who are discouraged to a point where they no longer are looking for a job; young people out of school but not yet actively in the labor market; sizable numbers of women at home who would welcome an opportunity to work; the physically and emotionally handicapped; older persons with good health forced into premature retirement; and the large numbers of working poor who though they are holding a job do not earn enough to lift their families out of poverty.

The commission believes that no responsible democracy can shirk the responsibility of addressing the need of its citizens for jobs, better jobs, and adequate income without which so many are embittered—not only the counted unemployed, but as the foregoing listing indicates possibly two to three times that number. The commission knows that it will not be easy to develop solutions but it believes that no more time must be lost in placing the job issue at the top of the nation's domestic agenda. The commission has committed itself to forwarding its preliminary recommendations on a national manpower policy to the President and the Congress in the fall of 1976.

There are many who believe that the labor market operates like a commodity market: demand and supply reach an equilibrium through an adjustment in wages or prices. But the contributions of Professors Ulman, Bergmann, and Brimmer indicate otherwise. Each in his or her own way illuminates the extent to which the labor market is characterized by what economists describe as imperfections and that plain-speaking people would recognize as the consequences of powerlessness in which individuals and groups are poorly positioned to compete for jobs—surely the preferred jobs which are always limited in number. The difficulties may stem from their age, sex, race, location, language, educational certification, license, or any other of the supports that facilitate access to desirable jobs. And they may be further disadvantaged—and usually are—by the policies and procedures of employers both in the private and public sector that make discriminations among applicants and employees not in terms of their capacity to perform but on untested assumptions that the young, the less educated, members of minority groups, and females are incapable of performing as well as prototypal white males.

Professor Ulman emphasizes that one of the most important contributions of manpower policies, properly designed and implemented, is to broaden opportunities for those who are particularly disadvantaged in the labor market. While manpower policy must speak to the needs of all workers, Ulman stresses that it is best suited to moderate the special difficulties that the more vulnerable members of the labor force encounter in the struggle for jobs and income.

Bergmann and Brimmer stress that in the face of a continuing imbalance between qualified applicants and good jobs those whom society has as a result of history and tradition singled out as being inferior will generally be at the end of the queue unless two things happen: the economy experiences a long and sustained period of expansion so that the number of preferred job applicants is insufficient and employers are accordingly forced to modify their specifications; and secondly, public policy makes use of the full panoply of instruments at its command— from law to publicity—to reduce, even if it cannot quickly eliminate, discriminatory employment policies and practices.

The last two pieces by Professors Lampman and Kreps address issues that, while centered around work, involve considerations that go beyond. Lampman helps us to understand how far an ambitious and successful national effort in the job arena can go to reduce and eliminate problems faced by individuals and families that now are trapped in poverty. He carries the analysis far enough to make it clear that no matter how successful the nation is in designing and implementing a job creation program for all seasons there would still be a continuing and large need for various forms of income transfers for those unable to work, those who should not be forced to work (mothers of young children), those whose incomes from work would not cover the minimum needs of their large families. The commission has recognized from its initial explorations that a comprehensive manpower policy cannot be concerned exclusively with jobs but must extend its considerations to include the interface between income earned from work and other sources of income, including in particular, income transfers.

It is Dr. Kreps, in the concluding chapter, who reminds the reader that men and women were not put on this earth to work but rather that work should be so structured, assigned, and scheduled as to enhance the lives of people and to improve the quality of their society. Specifically, Dr. Kreps calls attention to the more or less rigid assignments that our society —and most other advanced societies—have developed where work is stage two in the life cycle following upon education and training and preceding retirement. She suggests that it might result in substantial gains to the individual and to the society if much greater freedom were introduced into the timing of work, the extent to which people worked, and how they combined work with education, family responsibilities, and leisure pursuits. No one can read her chapter without recognizing that important as it is to find constructive resolutions to the current and prospective shortage of jobs, there is another bundle of problems and opportunities regarding the role of work that require innovative thinking and innovative solutions.

This introduction carries the title "The Purposes of an Economy" and it is that subject that I want to address in my concluding comments. The nation's bicentennial is a watershed in many regards, not the least in marking the first time in our history when the doctrine of optimal growth has been under serious questioning at the same time that the responsibility of the federal government to assure a continuing high level of employment is moving to the top of the nation's agenda. How can these apparently contradictory values be reconciled and what do they suggest by way of guidance to the American people as it enters upon its third century of development?

Without committing the members of the commission to the following interpretation, I believe that my concluding observations have been informed by our active association over many months. I hope that I speak for the entire commission when I say that we believe that this great nation cannot be true to its aspirations and goals as long as individuals able and willing to work are forced to eat the bread of idleness because of periodic and often prolonged malfunctioning of the economy. There is nothing in the laws of nature or of man that requires that such punishment be inflicted on the innocent who is more frequently the victim than the incompetent or the malingerer.

Next we hold it a violation of the nation's commitment to justice and equity to so distribute jobs and rewards that individuals who differ from the favored prototypes in matters of sex or race or credentials be denied equal opportunity to compete in the labor market. To tolerate discrimination against one's fellow citizen, to take advantage of his weakness, to hold him down by improper means is unworthy of our heritage and our future. We have recognized this and have begun to take corrective action but we must redouble our efforts.

The commission is acutely aware of and disturbed with the bleak prospects that face so many inner city and rural youth who after a constricted and often blighted childhood and adolescence reach working age only to find themselves rejected by employers who have no jobs or more frequently no jobs for youths, as if these young people were to blame for not being older. Many leaders and citizens have been slow to recognize that the violence, alienation, and recklessness that cause so much loss of life and property are directly related to the fact that American society rejects so many young people when they are ready to enter upon work and assume adult responsibilities. For a society to act so destructively toward itself is difficult to understand and impossible to accept.

The commission is aghast that many who advocate a policy of inaction as a response to the unconscionably high unemployment rate of recent years emphasize that with disability payments available to the seriously handicapped, with husbands able to support their wives, and with retirees able to live on their private pensions supplemented by Social Security, the claims of these large groups for part- or full-time work have no urgency. They can be excluded when the total number of potential job claimants are summed.

Nothing can be farther from the truth. If the lives of the handicapped are narrowed and confined by virtue of their disability, they have special need for a job, not only because of the self-esteem that they would gain by being usefully employed, even if less than full-time, but because they have a special need for social support and meaning that is inherent in most work assignments.

The cavalier disregard of the claims of married women to the right to work on the score that their husbands are able to support them is an extreme form of male chauvinism, less justified because only a minority of married men are able by their own work to assure their wives and children a desirable standard of living. But the question of size of the husband's income is largely irrelevant in the face of the wife's right to shape her life according to her own values and goals. Surely no one will wish to argue that by marrying or having children a woman has relinquished her claim on society to provide her the opportunity to work if she desires to do so.

Finally, a society that ignores the desire of many of its older citizens to continue to work, if often on a reduced schedule, is party to accelerating their isolation and deterioration, a response as callous as it is unnecessary.

The purposes of an economy are by no means limited to increasing the real income of its members, important as that objective is. A properly functioning economy must aim to provide productive jobs for all who want to work because it recognizes that it is unconscionable for a progressive society to ignore the shortfall in jobs which condemns many workers to idleness and loss of income through no fault of their own; that denies young people the one opportunity they need to trade dependence for independence; that treats married women as if they were second class citizens, appendages of their husbands; that is insensitive to the support that the physically handicapped can derive from the stimulation of work and the companionship of the work place; that speeds the deterioration of its older citizens; and that remains insensitive to the unrequited desires of many of its citizens for equal opportunity in the world of work.

The purpose of an economy is to serve the needs of all its members and, as we have indicated, it is at present falling far short of this goal. Once the American people appreciate the extent of this shortfall, once they determine not to be any longer intimidated by inflation to the extent of relinquishing control of their own destiny, and once they determine to make the economy meet the job performance test the battle will be half won.

The commission thanks the authors for their contributions that will help it to chart an employment strategy. These will be critical inputs as the commission moves ahead to formulate its recommendations to the President and Congress about the constituent elements of a national manpower policy. In the commission's view such a policy must be anchored in a foundation that provides every American with the opportunity to work and thereby to realize his personal goals and to contribute to the strengthening of the body politic.

Moses Abramovitz

1

In Pursuit of
Full Employment

Two Routes toward Full Employment

Some thirty years have now gone by since the passage of the Employment Act of 1946. That act expressed the country's desire to reach full employment and confidence, in some quarters, that it had found a road to that goal in the skillful use of fiscal and monetary policy. In some ways, the hopes invested in the act have been realized. We escaped a major depression, and that alone is a fact of enormous consequence, perhaps outweighing all our failures. In other respects, however, our experience has fallen far short of our hopes. Average unemployment rates have been high compared with the record of other countries. They have been high for years at a stretch when measured by our own standards, and the overall record would look worse still if the years of strong demand during the wars in Korea and Vietnam were disregarded. Unemployment rates among blacks, unskilled workers generally, and young people continue scandalously high. Even so, mild inflation has been chronic and more rapid inflations have accompanied the two minor wars, culminating in the very serious inflation which began in the latter 1960s and which continues to the present time. Finally, our economic policies supporting employment required, or at least tolerated, a persistent balance of payments deficit, the ultimate consequence of which was a breakdown of the international monetary regime.

To expose the reasons for this very mixed record is no job for this author or this chapter. It is immensely hard to separate the consequences of monetary and fiscal policy from the new and changing circumstances

Moses Abramovitz is Coe Professor of Economic History, Stanford University and Distinguished Fellow, American Economic Association (1976). He was Economic Adviser to the Secretary General of OECD (1962–63).

in which the economy has worked since 1945. The postwar economy operated with new institutions which strengthened our financial system and provided built-in stabilizers for income and demand. Both the incomes and the productivity of our major foreign trading partners grew at an unprecedently rapid and steady pace. The political imperatives of hot and cold wars, on the other hand, seriously destabilized federal spending. In prewar times, free immigration permitted labor force growth to rise and fall with demand. Since the 1930s, a violently fluctuating birth rate has caused the subsequent growth of the labor force, and particularly that of young workers, to slow down and speed up without regard to the state of the labor market. Women became a much larger fraction of the work force. An extraordinarily rapid rise of farm productivity drove large numbers of people, especially blacks, into urban occupations at a time when technology, industrial organization, and final output were apparently shifting the demand for labor away from unskilled jobs. Without disentangling the effects of these and other circumstances, one cannot adequately appraise the contributions of economic policy.

The aims of the chapter are more limited. They are, first, to consider the difficulties which, in practice, hindered and confused the conduct of aggregate demand policy, our chosen first route toward full employment. An understanding of these practical difficulties and the ways they were faced in successive administrations is a necessary basis for an improved strategy of demand management.

Secondly, I will sketch the background of the government's increasing concern with the so-called "structural" aspects of unemployment. These reveal themselves most dramatically in the high unemployment rates for blacks, youth, and women, but they are not confined to these groups. Here we face the problems of bringing satisfactory workers into touch with satisfactory jobs and employers. In general terms, the problems are, in part, questions of information, guidance, mobility, and the reduction of barriers to entering occupations and employment. In part, they are questions of improving the qualities and characteristics of both workers and jobs to make the former more productive and the latter more desirable. And, in part, they are questions of reforming our systems of unemployment insurance and welfare so that they do not encourage irregularity in production scheduling or extension of job-search unduly.[1] Aggregate demand can make some contribution to solving these problems, but it has long been clear that they cannot be solved by demand-management alone. A more comprehensive employment policy is needed and, especially since the early 1960s, government has tried to meet this need through a variety of manpower programs. Because these operate so largely on the side of labor supply rather than demand and with the conditions and difficulties of individual workers rather than with the aggregate state of national markets, we can think of them as a second route toward full employment. As with aggregate demand management, however, our manpower programs have so far failed to meet the hopes many people placed in them. A reassessment of experience and reordering of strategy is unavoidable.

Conflicts and Constraints
in the Practice of Demand Management

Viewed from the standpoint of macroeconomic policy, the problem of full employment is usually expressed in terms such as these: to support aggregate demand by fiscal and monetary intervention so as to stabilize employment at high levels while maintaining reasonable price stability and balance-of-payments equilibrium. It is useful to begin by asking how well, in fact, we did.

THE POSTWAR EMPLOYMENT AND PRICE RECORD

During the 29 years from 1957 through 1975, the average rate of unemployment in the civilian labor force was 4.9 percent. The highest average rates for any five-year periods were 6 percent (1958–1962) and 6.1 percent (1971–1975). This was an immense improvement over the 1930s when the average rate was about 17 percent for twelve years (1930–41). It was also a great deal better than the rate during the mid-1890s when the country suffered an earlier severe depression. Indeed, the clearest and perhaps most important fact about the postwar record is that we escaped the mass unemployment associated with the protracted severe depressions of the past. Needless to say, this profoundly significant nonevent was the product of many causes which made the postwar period different from earlier times. How much discretionary policy, even the potentiality of discretionary policy, contributed to the outcome is impossible to say. But the fact must not be forgotten when we stress the shortcomings of policy in other respects.

Avoiding great depressions is one thing; achieving full employment and full use of resources is another. And when we leave great depressions aside it becomes very hard to appraise the postwar record in the light of the past. The pre-1929 employment estimates are derived by methods sufficiently different from the better data we now have so that close comparison is barred.

Contemporary comparison with records of other industrialized countries is, perhaps, more appropriate. Here the figures suggest that, except for Canada, other countries maintained lower rates than we did, at least in the years since their own postwar recoveries became well established. Adjustments to make the data comparable to U.S. definitions would reduce the U.S. disadvantage relative to several countries, but the BLS appraisal of the data concludes that "differences in collection procedures and definitions are but a minor factor in accounting for the higher level of unemployment in the United States. . . ." [2]

TABLE 1. AVERAGE RATES OF UNEMPLOYMENT IN THE TOTAL LABOR FORCE (PERCENT)

Years	Japan	France	West Germany	Italy	U.K.	Sweden	Canada	U.S.A.
1954–59	1.6	1.2	3.3	7.0	1.2	n.a.*	4.9	4.9
1960–65	1.4	1.2	0.7	2.5	1.4	1.6	5.6	5.3
1966–71	1.2	1.8	0.9	3.6	2.0	2.0	4.8	4.1

Sources: 1954–59—OECD, *Manpower Statistics,* Paris, 1965.
1960–71—OECD, *Labour Force Statistics, 1960–71,* Paris, 1973.
* n.a. = not available.

The lower level of unemployment in Western Europe and Japan is clear enough. What is not clear, however, is the extent to which the favorable foreign record reflected demand pressure, generally thought to have been greater abroad, or other differences governing the incidence of unemployment. By comparison with most of these countries, the U.S. agricultural sector is smaller, although not when compared with the United Kingdom. In the same way, the extent of nonfarm self-employment is smaller in the U.S. than in Japan, Italy, and France, but not smaller than in other European countries. The BLS also suggests that higher incomes and more generous unemployment insurance give U.S. workers more leeway to remain out of a job and that foreign workers are more firmly attached to particular employers and better protected by law or custom against involuntary layoff.[3] A lesser degree of demand pressure may, therefore, have something to do with the higher U.S. unemployment rates, but we do not know how much.

In the absence of any clear standard of appraisal either in the past or in the record of other countries, we are constrained to judge our record by internal criteria. The proper standard would be a state of affairs in which vacancies were as numerous as jobless workers, but we lack vacancy data. We are forced, therefore, to begin with the conventional 4 percent standard. This was originally proposed because many economists thought it could be achieved without generating serious inflation.[4] That was, indeed, roughly true in the years 1955 through 1957 and—if we can trust the unemployment estimates—also for some years in the 1920s. There is, therefore, a certain *prima facie* case for comparing the actual record with 4 percent.

Judged by that rule, our 4.9 percent average rate for the whole postwar period was high. Moreover, the average is itself misleading. It combines the record of seven years of war (1951–53 and 1966–69), when the average rate was 3.4 percent, with twenty-two years of peace. Taking the latter alone, the average rate rises to 5.4 percent. Moreover, during the twenty-two peacetime years, only six had rates below 4.5 percent. Only two years were at 4 percent or less, and those, 1947 and 1948, were in the immediate aftermath of the great war itself when backlogged needs made demand so urgent. Still more, the high unemployment rates of the peacetime years reflect not only the impact of brief recessions, but also two protracted stretches of high unemployment: from 1958 through 1964, seven years, when the rate lay continually above 5 percent and averaged 5.8 percent; and 1970–75, six years, when the rate lay continually above 4.9 percent and averaged 5.9 percent. Finally, the conventional unemployment figures cited here take no account of involuntary part-time employment or of the unemployment hidden because, when attractive jobs are hard to find, there is a net withdrawal of workers from the labor force.

In 1965, when the conventional overall unemployment rate was 4.5 percent, the manhours lost by the unemployed and by persons working only part-time for lack of full-time jobs was 5.0 percent of the available labor-force hours. In addition, the "discouraged worker rate" was 0.9 percent of the civilian labor force. This may overstate the net withdrawals from the labor force due to lack of work because some family members may look for work when the primary wage-earner is laid off. Still, the two figures just considered suggest that the percentage loss of labor time in a fairly good year exceeds the measured loss by over 20 percent.[5] Some estimates would put the figure even higher.

The figures, on their face, may suggest that there have been two protracted periods when high unemployment was due to inadequate demand. This, however, is probably an incorrect inference as regards 1970–74. The composition of the labor force changed during the postwar years and, more especially, in the course of the later 1960s and 1970s, in ways which make the overall unemployment rate an unreliable guide to the amount of potential labor input lost or to the sufficiency of aggregate demand. The general trend of the changes was to make the overall rate progressively overstate the degree of labor-market slack.

One major change was the decline of the population engaged in farming and a consequent decline in the proportion of the labor force who were self-employed or working as unpaid family helpers. In their former occupations, these workers were often underemployed or idle, but they were rarely, if ever, recorded as unemployed. The shift of these workers to employment for wages or salaries, however, exposed them both to the normal employment risks of the rest of the population and to the same probability of being recorded among the unemployed. A second major change was the rise in the importance of women and of youth of both sexes in the labor force. The increase of women reflects their growing participation in paid employment. The increase of youth during the 1960s and 1970s reflects the baby boom of the late 1940s and 1950s. It is due for reversal in the 1980s. For a variety of reasons, women and youth have higher unemployment rates than adult men. They are more likely to be entering the labor market for the first time or reentering after a lengthy absence. Their information about jobs and their contacts with possible employers are, therefore, poor. Because of competing family responsibilities, women are likely to be more selective about a job's location, burdens, and hours of work. Young people, building their own stock of experience and contacts, change jobs more often.[6] The upshot is that as women and youth grow in importance any given overall unemployment rate must be regarded as indicating a progressively tighter labor market.

The rise of women and youth has another implication. Compared with men, they provide, on the average, less effective labor service per person. Women, much more frequently than men, are part-time workers. Both women and youth are less experienced than men and, therefore, less productive hour by hour. The same overall unemployment rate, therefore, represents a smaller relative loss of potential labor service, the greater the proportion of the unemployed who are youths and women.[7] This also means that a given increment of demand is likely to produce a smaller response in real output as the employment rate rises. So the difficulty of reducing the overall unemployment rate to some target level, say 4 percent, without generating inflation is aggravated.

Rough estimates suggest that the shift from self-employment to dependent employment since the war increased the proportion of the labor force exposed to unemployment from about 80 percent to about 90 percent, or by 12 percent. This means that the 5.9 percent overall unemployment rate of 1971 corresponded roughly only to a 6.6 percent rate for those wage workers actually exposed to unemployment. By contrast, the 5.9 percent overall rate of 1949 would have corresponded to a 7.4 percent rate in the then smaller exposed wage-work sector.[8]

The effect of the increasing proportion of women and youth is fairly well indicated by a comparison between the general unemployment rate in the civilian labor force and the rate for married men. Take as one's standard the level of each rate in 1956, when the general rate was 4.1 percent and the rate of married men 2.6 percent. By either measure we suffered a protracted period of high unemployment from 1958 to 1964. The general rate in that period was 40 percent higher than in 1956; for married men, it was 50 percent higher. In 1970–74, however, when the general rate was 30 percent higher than in 1956, that for married men was only 5 percent higher. (In 1975, of course, all indexes of unemployment are elevated.)

A variety of other measures speak to the same effect.[9] Their broad implication is that, if 4 percent was an appropriate noninflationary target rate for demand management in the late 1940s and early 1950s, when it was first proposed, then by a comparable standard, we suffered a protracted period of unemployment associated with inadequate demand once in the postwar period, that is, from 1958 to 1963 or 1964. So far as the 1970s are concerned, however, our high unemployment rate, at least before 1975, may well have had more to do with a "worsening" of labor-force structure and of the so-called trade-off between unemployment and inflation than with any pronounced deficiency of demand.[10] That the 1970s have also been years of inflation is a fact consistent with this view, but, of course, is by itself hardly probative. Although I think the weight of the evidence supports this interpretation, readers should be aware that age and sex composition and distribution between wage work and self-employment do not exhaust the relevant structural aspects of the labor force, and I have not checked the possibility that occupational, regional, and educational compositions have changed in an off-setting way.

There is also another and more speculative area. The evolving attitude toward women's work, the accompanying decline in marriage and birth rates and the more flexible relations between work and school are changing not only the size and composition of the actual labor force but also those of the potential labor force. Attention so far has been concentrated on their effects on the actual labor force. We have become aware that an actual labor force expanded by the entry of women and by large cohorts of youth is likely to be a labor force in which labor turnover is more frequent and job search extended. But the new attitudes and circumstances may also be enlarging the number of women and youth, and that of old people too, who are not now in the measured labor force but who would join and look for work if reasonable jobs were available. Because people in these groups tend to work less regularly than others, their actual presence in the measured labor force makes the labor market look less tight than it is. But the potential workers from these same groups are a hidden labor reserve, and insofar as they exist, they make the labor market more slack than it looks. We know little about such changes in the hidden labor reserve now, but the unmeasured potentialities of our population for work when jobs beckon and when some guidance, training, and career possibilities are available should not be forgotten.

The mixed record with respect to unemployment was matched by an equally mixed record with respect to the coordinate goal of price stability. Judging by the consumer price index, there was a positive rate of inflation throughout the postwar years except for very brief periods during the business recessions of 1949 and 1954. For much of the postwar period the rate of price increase was low. But there was a distinct inverse relation between levels of unemployment and rates of price rise, and the periods of really tight labor markets were accompanied by rapid inflation. That was true during the Korean War and again during the Vietnam War. The inverse relation between unemployment and inflation does not mean that there was a stable trade-off between the two. The aggravated price increases which began during the Vietnam years accelerated and culminated in the double-digit and near double-digit inflations of 1973–75. Even if one allows for the fact that labor markets in recent years were tighter than the ordinary unemployment rates suggest, it remains true that inflation since 1970 ran at a pace which exceeds anything that would, in the past, have been associated with the existing degree of labor-market tightness.

Our mixed postwar record, including as it does protracted periods of excessive unemployment and excessive inflation, sharply poses the question: why was discretionary demand management inadequate? The answer, I suggest, lies in limitations on the employment of fiscal and monetary policy which were not clearly foreseen in the theory of "functional finance" from which the hopes originally placed in discretionary demand management were derived. I see three classes of conflicts and constraints from which the limitations arise. For the remainder of this section I will describe the nature of these troubles and then go on to show how they combined to permit, if not to produce, the stagnant labor market of the late 1950s and early 1960s and then the acceleration of inflation which followed.

CYCLE STABILIZATION VERSUS FULL-EMPLOYMENT GROWTH

In the background of the Employment Act's sponsors and in the minds of the economists of the 1940s, the dominant experience was the long decade of the Great Depression. For them, the disease to be managed was gross, unmistakable, and durable. The fiscal and monetary prescription was obvious. Deep and persistent depression, however, is not the target of macroeconomic therapy in more normal times. The usual malady is much less severe, sometimes hard to recognize. The prospects for relatively rapid recovery with little intervention are often favorable, and there is danger of overdosage if fiscal or monetary stimuli are applied too vigorously or too late.

The usual problem includes, but is not limited to the usual business cycle. It is in the nature of our economy to generate growth of output and employment at an unsteady rate. It is, moreover, part of the mechanism of business cycles to generate a faster pace of output growth during expansion phases than can be sustained later when excess machine capacity and underemployed manpower have been brought back into employment. At the same time, the rapid pace of growth during recovery both induces, and is supported by, higher levels and faster growth rates of investment in inventories and other capital than can be maintained when the economy inevitably slows down in it its approach to capacity limits.

The cyclical nature of growth means that economic policy cannot be directed simply at redressing a gap between the actual level of demand and the level required to support full use of resources. Its aim is rather to moderate recession and speed recovery by policies whose strength and timing will make the eventual peak as high as possible and at the same time permit it to be sustained as long as possible. This imposes contradictory requirements on policy. The aim of increasing jobs rapidly when unemployment is still high calls for accelerating the pace of recovery, with attendant high levels of inventory investment and other capital spending. The more rapid the expansion, however, the more severe the eventual retardation as capacity limits and full employment are approached. The impact of retardation, especially on inventory investment, is therefore, more severe and the chance of sustaining a high level of employment smaller. Rapid expansion, moreover, tends to produce a certain degree of inflation in the prices of goods and securities with accompanying speculation in both real and financial assets, incautious financial practices and heightened vulnerability to financial shocks. On the other hand, a slow recovery means a more protracted period of high unemployment without necessarily guaranteeing an eventual longer period of full employment.

This policy dilemma can be resolved in principle by stimulating business during contraction and switching to measures of restraint as an expansion gets under way. Such "fine tuning," however, is difficult to bring off. Success is limited because the effects of a change in policy are normally felt only months after it is applied. Moreover, decisions to alter policy can often be taken only after weeks or months of bureaucratic debate. In the case of tax or expenditure decisions needing congressional action, the delay is longer still. Important changes of policy, therefore. must be based on forecasts which look forward a year or even more. On the other hand, economists' ability to forecast cyclical developments so far ahead is sadly inadequate. It has, therefore, happened that measures designed to restrain expansion have come into force in time to aggravate contraction. On the other hand, there were at least two occasions when inappropriate tax reductions adopted, during periods of expansion or boom for reasons extraneous to employment management, fortuitously came into effect during cyclical downturns.

These difficulties were realized early in the postwar period. They led to several proposals designed to entrust cyclical stabilization entirely to the care of the built-in stabilizers provided by progressive taxation and the structure of income transfers, and to that of steady growth rates of federal expenditure and money stock. No administration, however, ever accepted such proposals as a deliberate constraint on their actions. Yet the need to adjust policy to the cyclical instability of business in the face of the difficulties of forecasting and of the long lags between diagnosis, policy-adoption, and effect was among the forces inhibiting the use and limiting the success of fiscal policy and, to a lesser degree, of monetary measures.

All administrations had to bow in some degree to the complications which cyclical instability imposes on demand management. Yet concern with business cycles itself fails to take account of substantial variations in the strength of demand which sometimes occur in ways not clearly connected with business cycles. Variations reflecting demographic developments or the exhaustion of war-generated backlogs of private demand are examples; so are the fluctuations of military expenditure. At the same time, the growth of the economy itself poses problems which transcend business cycles. The gradual increase of the labor force and of the capacity of the capital stock means that recovery of output to the level of an earlier cyclical peak is never enough to ensure full use of resources; output must go well beyond previous peak levels. The growth of private demand is usually enough to permit this, but sometimes not. Moreover, the growth of income at full enmployment produces "fiscal drag." It raises the revenue yield of stable tax rates and, in the absence of a comparable rise of expenditure, cuts the government's net contribution to demand. If there is a conjuncture in which the private propensity to spend and the government's net contribution both decline, demand management calls for measures looking beyond cycle stabilization. As argued later, it was the occurrance of just such a conjuncture, combined with a reluctance to take the special offsetting measures needed, which produced the failure of employment policy during the second Eisenhower Administration. And since the conflicts and constraints inhibiting the use of fiscal and monetary stimuli persisted through three years of the Kennedy Administration, the average unemployment rate remained above 5 percent continuously from November 1957 through June 1964, that is, for six years and eight months.[11]

INFLATION AND THE BALANCE OF PAYMENTS

The twin goals of price stability and high employment acted as mutual constraints on policy during the postwar period. For much of the time, fear of inducing or aggravating inflation inhibited governments seeking to support demand at levels consistent with full employment. But it was also true that the desire to keep unemployment low made governments accept some inflation throughout these years. And when the pace of inflation accelerated and stayed high for a protracted period in the latter 1960s and early 1970s, fears of triggering or aggravating recession or of retarding recovery seriously, limited policy to fight inflation.

This, of course, is a statement about policy and its result. It says that policy has been guided by the view that, at least in a rough way, there is a choice to be made between the level of employment we can seek and the pace of inflation we must tolerate. It does not mean that the rates of inflation we have actually suffered were, in fact, a necessary condition for maintaining the employment rates we did achieve.

The view that the postwar U.S. economy and, indeed, that of the whole world, was the victim of a chronic disposition toward inflation took hold early in the postwar period. And, indeed, prices have risen almost continuously, though at dramatically different rates, since 1945. This secular "trend," however, reflected causes which were partly episodic and only partly systematic.

The episodic causes were chiefly the wars and their sequelae. The compound annual rate of rise in the consumer price index was 7 percent from 1940 to 1948, representing World War II and its aftermath; 5 percent per year during the Korean War in 1950–52; and 5.5 percent from the beginning of the Vietnam escalation in 1965 to the end of 1974. But the rate was much lower in the two periods of peace: zero from 1948 to 1950 and 1.3 percent from 1952 to 1965. Manifestly, it was the political difficulty of imposing noninflationary war finance which was the immediate source of much of the postwar trend of prices.

The inflationary expectations which these developments generated were bolstered because our built-in stabilizers and other new forces acted to make recessions short and mild. In these circumstances, it was argued that business firms and labor unions enjoying positions of market power were in a better position to resist price and wage cuts during recessions while pushing for increases when markets were strong. And, indeed, prices fell but little in the recession of 1949 and not at all in those of 1954 and 1958. By the second half of the 1950s, this pattern was being adduced as proof of a new inflationary process—"cost-push inflation." It added to the hesitation which the controllers of fiscal and monetary policy felt in stimulating business during contractions and still more during expansions.

Behind these active forces, however, the national and international monetary systems acted as necessary permissive conditions. At the national level the Federal Reserve System had the technical capacity to monetize the federal deficit and more generally to create the money supply needed to support rising levels of nominal income consistent with rising prices and acceptable employment rates. At the international level, our very large initial gold reserves and the establishment of an international dollar exchange standard permitted the country to sustain the accumulating deficit on foreign account which our own inflation generated—having regard, of course, to the productivity trends in other industrialized countries, and to our own desire to export capital, aid poor countries, and support an active foreign policy by military expenditure.

In the absence of national and international monetary flexibility, the reaction to our Korean and Vietnam inflations might well have been postwar depressions. The fact that such flexibility permitted us to avoid serious contractions in the aftermath of the wars was an important contribution of the postwar international monetary regimes and of monetary-fiscal management. The result, however, was that inflation and foreign account deficits continued and gave rise to later efforts to contain them. The stagnant conditions and relatively high unemployment rates from 1958 to 1964 and since 1974, if not earlier, were in good part the cost of that effort.

The force of these considerations is now somewhat confused by the current debate over the existence of a trade-off between inflation and unemployment. Opinion has now swung strongly toward the view that a higher rate of unemployment is not a necessary *long-term* condition of slower rates of price increase steadily maintained. Yet few economists seriously doubt that when inflationary expectations have become established or when there are other causes of lags in the responsiveness of prices and wages to declines in money demand, a slowdown of money and nominal income growth will raise the unemployment rate for a time. Moreover, the lags in the responsiveness of prices and therefore, the unemployment accompanying an attempt to restrain demand, appear to have become greater as the strength of inflationary expectations have risen. So the attempt to oppose inflation under Eisenhower and, in some degree, in the early Kennedy period, did limit our capacity to maintain high employment rates. And the opposition to the still more intense inflationary spurt since 1969 has required still more unemployment without assured success as yet in breaking the price-wage spiral.

THE COMPETING FUNCTIONS OF FISCAL AND MONETARY INSTRUMENTS

We have been concerned so far with the conflicts of macroeconomic goals and the tactical complexities of using fiscal and monetary instruments. It is a serious complication, however, particularly in our system of government, that fiscal and monetary instruments serve, and are seen to serve, purposes other than the management of aggregate demand. Indeed, so far as taxation and expenditure goes, demand management is still a new function and hardly the primary concern of federal budget policy. Governments are not free to alter the level of expenditures to suit employment goals because expenditures define the scope of government, and people are concerned over the scale of government activity quite apart from the contributions of expenditures to demand. Moreover, it is not possible to persuade Congress to alter the level of expenditures without obtaining its agreement to the purposes to be served by the extra spending or to the categories of activities to be cut. It has, therefore, proven to be very difficult to use the expenditure side of the budget to influence demand significantly.

Similarly, it has been difficult to use the tax instrument. Congress and the President are always reluctant to increase tax rates; and while they have a disposition to cut taxes, both the executive and the Congress are usually divided in many ways over the form which a tax cut should take [12] and about the length of time for which it should apply. Moreover, although most politicians and much of the public now understand that demand management requires deficits during periods of recession, many are unwilling to see government give up the discipline which the need to balance the budget imposes on the size of government and on careless administrative practices.

Monetary policy can be deployed more readily than fiscal policy, and, in fact, played a significant part in moderating some of the recessions of the postwar period, particularly in 1953–54 and 1957–58. Yet the operation of monetary policy to support employment has its own elements of inflexibility. Like fiscal policy, it meets the conflicting demands of price stability and the balance of payments. Lags-in-effect are long and have produced perverse results.[13] In addition, however, monetary policy must serve purposes other than aggregate demand management even if they are not wholly unrelated. The Federal Reserve System's influence on interest rates imposes on it a serious concern for the prosperity of the building industry and the availability of housing. It must also be sensitive to its effect on the cost of government borrowing and the value of the government debt. Concern for the latter tied the system's hands during the attempts to control inflation before 1952. Similar concerns doubtless led the system to monetize the government's deficits in the latter 1960s resulting in a faster rate of monetary growth than it might otherwise have desired.

DEMAND MANAGEMENT THROUGH SIX ADMINISTRATIONS

It is time now to see how these difficulties actually worked. As already suggested, the problem of stimulating demand to support employment emerged in intense form only in the second postwar decade. The private demands released after World War II and then by the Korean War put the economy under strain. To moderate inflation, the Truman Administration did indeed try to limit aggregate demands by controlling government expenditures, by delaying the reduction of World War II tax rates, and by raising tax rates during the Korean War. Congressional opposition and the mood of the country, however, ensured that these efforts would be insufficient. For its part, the Federal Reserve, operating under its commitment to support the price of government bonds, was not free to restrict the growth of the money supply before 1952. Inflation, therefore, was rapid from 1945 to 1948 and again in 1950 and 1951. Moreover, although the condition of strain was twice interrupted by the recessions of 1949 and 1954, these interruptions proved brief and mild. The underlying strength of demand, the built-in stabilizers, tax reductions which came into force quite fortuitously, and the easier money conditions provided by the Fed soon turned business upward. It was a noteworthy feature of both recessions, therefore, that though they were preceded by bursts of inflation, they entailed only small or insubstantial price declines. The view that, in the postwar economy, business cycle expansions would see prices rising, while recessions would bring no comparable price decline, was strengthened. It was a vision of secular inflation destined to become widespread and to complicate policy in the years that followed.

The post-Korean recession was followed by a strong investment boom in 1955 and 1956, but this spurt apparently drained the last of the backlogged pool of demand with which the postwar era had opened. In the sequel, the economy suffered a long period of underutilized manpower and capital. From mid-1957 to mid-1964, the annual unemployment rates were always above 5 percent; the average was 5.8 percent. These seven years were the first serious postwar test of our capacity to support the demand for labor, and the protracted stagnation of these years is a clear reflection of the practical obstacles to mobilizing macroeconomic employment policy.

The broad features of the problem in the second Eisenhower Administration can be summarized briefly. Private sector demand had weakened because the country's capital stock had expanded rapidly. The capacity utilization rate in manufacturing had fallen from 93 percent in 1948 to 84 percent in 1957.[14] At the same time, fiscal support for demand was shrinking. Federal purchases fell from $70 billion (in 1958 prices) in 1953 to $50 billion in 1956.[15] Although taxes had been cut in 1954, the growth of the economy was raising revenues. The 1953 deficit of $6.5 billion had become a surplus of $4 billion in 1956.[16] The "full-employment surplus" was $5 billion in 1956, over 1 percent of the GNP.[17] On both private and public counts, therefore, the fiscal posture should have become more expansionary. The administration and its economic advisors, however, remained firmly opposed to fiscal stimulation even after the sharp but brief recession of 1958 had given way to the disappointing recovery of 1959–1960.

There were several reasons.[18] The first and perhaps the most basic was the Republican desire to reduce the scope of government by cutting expenditures. Although spending had been sharply reduced from Korean War levels, it was still twice as high in 1957 as it had been in 1950. True, a tax cut would have been welcomed, but the 1958 recession, by cutting revenues, itself produced a deficit of $12.9 billion, which was 14 percent of outlays in fiscal 1959. The administration had no stomach for anything bigger. To tolerate deficits was to prejudice the long-term aim or reduce spending. Tax reduction would have to await the appearance of a surplus.

The rationale for maintaining fiscal restraint in the face of unemployment, however, went beyond these longer-term objectives of public policy. It included concerns about inflation and about weakness in the balance of payments. Although prices had remained stable during 1954 and 1955, they began to rise again in 1956 and 1957. The recession of 1958 brought another pause, but with the return of cyclical expansion in 1959, prices again took up their slow advance. It was a "creeping" inflation, but it was seen as an extension of the price history of the 1940s and of the Korean War period. Arthur Burns and many others had noticed the tendency of prices to rise during business expansions but not to fall back in recessions. To many economists, the idea occurred that our institutions were supporting a new kind of secular inflation, whose origins were on the side of costs, pushed up when markets were strong but prevented from falling by unions and concentrated industries when markets were weak.[19] Those who were directing economic policy at the time were eager to check this tendency even at the expense of some unemployment. They feared the impact of inflation on income distribution and on the strength of financial markets. They feared even a slow inflation in part because of its cumulative consequences and still more because it might well accelerate.

The anxiety about inflation was aggravated by a new worry over the balance of payments. It is worth understanding the bases for this new concern which continued to influence monetary and fiscal policy into the Kennedy years and beyond.[20] The U.S. had been running an overall balance of payments deficit since 1950, but its size unexpectedly ballooned in 1958 and remained large in subsequent years. It was suddenly brought home to us that the very strong international position with which the country entered the postwar era had now weakened decisively. The European countries and Japan had recovered their productive capacity. Favored by very rapid growth of productivity, their exports were expanding rapidly and their needs for imports were less urgent. Our large overseas transfers for aid and military purposes could no longer be regarded as transient. The U.S. deficits which in earlier years had been tolerated and even encouraged as a means of redistributing our excessively large holdings of gold and liquid claims on other countries now lacked this *raison' d'etre*. The gold reserves and liquid dollar assets of both Europe and Japan had been rebuilt. The reserve position of this country on the contrary had been sharply depleted. In 1948, our gold and foreign exchange reserves had exceeded our liquid liabilities to foreign countries by over $18 billion. By 1959, however, this cover had fallen to $1.8 billion, just one-tenth as large. Perhaps in recognition of this fact, the form in which foreigners were taking payment for their surpluses was changing. From 1953 to 1956, they took only 18 percent in gold and other monetary reserve assets, leaving the remainder as short-term loans, but from 1958 to 1962, they took 48 percent in gold.

Prompted by this cumulation of views and circumstances, the Eisenhower Administration sought a budgetary surplus.[21] There was, indeed, a slight easing of the budget in 1958, a year of recession, but once it appeared that a cyclical recovery was underway, the drive for a surplus began again. The estimated full employment surplus was 0.7 percent of GNP in 1958, but it rose to 2.5 percent in 1960.[22] The Federal Reserve followed a similar policy. It too was intent on checking inflation and on protecting the balance of payments.[23] Therefore, while the growth of money supply was permitted to accelerate moderately in 1958, money growth was sharply reduced when it seemed that a cyclical recovery had begun. The upshot was the disappointing expansion of 1959–60 which left the unemployment rate at 5.2 percent at its low point; it quickly rose again to reach 7 percent in the first months of the Kennedy regime.

Eisenhower economics, though costly, simplified the task of the Kennedy Administration in two ways. By eschewing stimulation in the face of weak private demand, it created a large gap between actual and potential output, and by restraining inflation, it created an expectation of stable prices. Expansionary medicine could, therefore, be administered with less reserve than usual, and the Kennedy economists were prepared to prescribe it. If lower unemployment rates meant a somewhat faster rate of inflation, the price ought to be paid. They would try to minimize any inflationary tendencies by productivity guidelines, but they foresaw no danger of serious inflation before the output short-fall had been substantially reduced.[24] They appreciated the prospective impact of expansionary finance on the balance of payments, but they were concerned not to overstate its dangers. They saw the competitive position of Europe and Japan on current account weakening as these countries reached the limit of their labor supplies.[25] On capital account, they expected to restrain short-term outflows by giving interest rates a "twist." At bottom, moreover, they did not regard a continuing deficit as a serious danger to the dollar or to the international monetary system linked to the dollar. Since the dollar was now the world's transaction currency, larger short-term balances were needed and willingly held as the international economy grew. And insofar as dollar balances were unwillingly held, as they were to some degree by central banks, the latter had no practical alternative. A run on the U.S. gold window would force it to close, and then what would gold be worth? Foreigners, therefore, both wanted to and had to finance our deficits, and consequently we could treat the balance of payments with "benign neglect."

So we had the times for expansionary policy, and apparently we had the men for the times. And yet policy yielded only slowly to their persuasion. Demand management was not the sole concern of policy or of politics. A larger federal deficit—it was running at $3.8 billion in calendar year 1961 and 1962—was hardly consistent with the President's call for national sacrifice. Economic advisors might view an enlarged payments deficit with equanimity, but foreign policy advisors warned that a weakened dollar would constrict our ability to operate abroad. A larger budget deficit might be called for, but how to achieve it? Kennedy and many around him thought the country needed more spending to meet both social and military needs, but Congress was opposed. A tax cut, on the other hand, would prejudice the chance for bigger expenditures later. Kenndy, therefore, clung to the hope that business recovery without a tax cut would create the revenue base to support a larger budget.[26] And when he finally determined to support a cut, the sharing of the melon still had to be fought out in Congress.

Policy was not completely inactive in the face of these constraints. Money supply growth was permitted to accelerate a little. Investment was encouraged by liberalized depreciation guidelines and by an investment tax credit. The rise of military spending associated with the Berlin blockade was not offset by a tax increase. But the major tax cut, which was the decisive expansionary act, was not introduced until January 1963, and it was not signed into law until February 1964 (by President Johnson). The result was a moderately paced recovery which extended the period of high unemployment until mid-1965 when the rate finally fell below 4.5 percent.

In any event, there were certain fortunate, if unintended, consequences. The period of very slow price increase, which had started in 1958, was prolonged, and inflationary expectations were more thoroughly cooled. When taxes were cut, therefore, the stimulus made its impact on output more than on prices. Moreover, when President Johnson, rejecting his economists' call for a tax increase, translated the Vietnam War spending into a still larger fiscal stimulus, the economic expansion continued. Price increases accelerated visibly, but slowly, while output continued to rise, if at a retarded pace. It seems to be a fair judgment, therefore, that the interlude of very high employment rates from 1966 through 1969 owed much to the price expectations established during the preceding long period of stagnation and unemployment. And, by the same token, so did the unprecedented prolongation of uninterrupted output expansion from 1961 to 1969. At the same time, the continued expansion after 1965 was supported by the war in two ways: directly because it maintained a large and growing federal deficit which was monetized; indirectly, because in the absence of war the beginnings of significant and accelerating inflation might have been resisted by deflationary policy.

The very high employment rates of the Vietnam period, however, were only an interlude. As the Nixon Administration began its tortuous attempt to extract the country from Vietnam, so it began a hesitant and painful effort to restrain inflation without an excessive impact on employment.

The historical origins of the stagflation of the 1970s are now tolerably clear. Just as the long period of unemployment and associated price stability from 1958 to 1964 was part of the underpinning for the long expansion of 1961–69 and for the full employment of 1966–69, so the pernicious Vietnam War finance and accelerating inflation, which was the long expansion's other basis, was the source of our subsequent trouble.

Excess demand during the Vietnam period operated directly on the prices of our domestically produced goods. And by aggravating our balance of payments deficit, it also accelerated the growth of money supply and the pace of inflation throughout the world. After a time, we were reimporting our own inflation. The main point, however, is that with the end of the Vietnam War, the desire became strong to check an inflation already too rapid and accelerating. Unfortunately, the price expectations already established made the inflation resistant to the moderate levels of unemployment we were prepared to tolerate. If my interpretation of the data is correct, the unemployment record, though uneven, was not bad by normal standards from 1970 through 1973. On the other hand, inflation was not decisively checked. And when the dollar devaluations of 1973 combined with a world-wide boom and a poor year for agriculture to raise us into the world of double-digit inflation, and when these troubles were capped by the rise of oil prices, the oil shock combined with our renewed resistance to inflation to produce the most severe bout of unemployment since 1940.[27] So we have suffered the worst of both worlds—too much inflation to accept without checking the demand for goods and labor, but not yet enough unemployment for long enough to overcome the inflation we do not yet know how to live with.

AN INTERIM VERDICT

The lessons of this experience are not easy to draw. Our new national and international monetary institutions, the built-in stabilizers, and the promise and practice of fiscal and monetary policy have so far kept us free of major depression on the scale of past episodes. They have proved their worth under a variety of serious strains and shocks. But if we have escaped the worst, it is also true that full employment with reasonable price stability has escaped us. Even the "interim goal" of 4 percent has been hard to reach by demand management. With brief exceptions, we have, in fact, achieved it only under the pressures of war, or in its aftermath, and to the accompaniment of serious inflation. And the longest run effects of these inflations have complicated the problems of subsequent employment policy.

This outcome, we should now recognize, has not been accidental. Granted the existence of sticky wages and prices and of delayed response of expenditure to interest rate and price change, it is nevertheless hard to deploy the instruments of fiscal and monetary policy promptly and in adequate strength. Lags in effect, the cyclical dangers of overheating, the competing objectives of economic stabilization, the conflicts between fiscal policy for stability, and the broader objectives of government combine to inhibit vigorous stimulation of demand. With minor exceptions, it appears to have required the pressures of war to resolve these conflicts and release the constraints, with inflation as the result.

Behind these practical difficulties, moreover, lurks a basic problem: whether it is necessarily true that the power of demand stimuli, measured in money terms, weakens as they are used. There is still no settled answer. It is obvious that if inflation comes to be expected, a given money stimulus is less powerful, and larger stimuli and faster inflation are needed to produce the same support for employment. We do not yet know, however, just what circumstances generate price increases or inflationary expectations. As to the latter, how fast must prices rise and for how long and how steadily? Are there limits to a process of acceleration if it starts, and how soon would they be reached? How severe and protracted must an interruption to inflation be to break the expectations on which inflation feeds?

We shall not answer these questions quickly. Meanwhile it is clear enough that we shall not soon return to the price outlook of 1964 and that demand management will be more difficult for some indefinite time to come. This suggests two morals: we need to look again at the practical limits of macroeconomic policy and rethink the strategy of demand management, and we need to explore the possibilities of an attack on unemployment from the side of supply more vigorously. The next section of this chapter contains some historical notes bearing on the latter subject.

Struggling with Structure

PREWAR VIEWS ABOUT UNEMPLOYMENT

Before Keynes and before the Great Depression, the economists' maps divided all unemployment into three parts; frictional, seasonal, and cyclical, and all of it was "voluntary." Jobless workers, in one way or another, were regarded as holding out for real wages higher than the net revenues which their product would return to an employer. Any single unemployed worker could get some job somewhere by offering to work for lower wages. And, if workers generally would accept lower pay, more jobs would be available for all. Worker resistance to accepting lower real pay, therefore, was the basic cause of unemployment.

Cyclical unemployment was associated with a general decline in the marginal product of labor. It produced a general decline in the level of employment because it took time for jobless workers to accept the fact that they would have to work for less. Of course, something might happen to raise the real marginal product of labor again, but that something obviously could not be simply an increase in aggregate money demand, for that would not raise real productivity.

Frictional unemployment was that which would exist even if there were no general recession in the demand for labor and no change in the aggregate number of jobs offered at going wages. It reflected the difficulty workers find in adapting instantaneously to the ebb and flow of employment opportunities as the business fortunes of individual firms, industries and localities rise and fall in response to changes in the personal lives of businessmen, the shifts of products and tastes, the movement of population and the progress of technology. It also reflected the time spent by new entrants to the labor market in finding their first jobs and the time spent between jobs by the workers looking for better jobs or for employers who would find them satisfactory or for a locality congenial to themselves and their families. Workers could choose whether to look long for the job they liked or to take what was available at whatever pay offered. So, in a manner of speaking, their unemployment was again "voluntary;" but it was recognized that trade union and governmental barriers to wage flexibility and to entry into trades aggravated frictional unemployment. Seasonal unemployment was a particular source of frictional unemployment arising from intra-annual fluctuations in the business of particular industries or trades.

In the normal case, frictional problems were thought to impose only short spells of unemployment on individual workers, even though a considerable number of them might be out of work at any time. Massive changes, however, like the movement of the textile industry from North to South or the decline of machine tool manufacturing in New England would result in long-term unemployment because workers were slow to adjust to the obsolescence of skills or to follow the migration of jobs, and because firms were slow to move toward jobless workers. Such longer term maladjustments were sometimes called "structural," a term which has since been applied to unemployment in a variety of senses, all of them referring to joblessness which does not stem from deficiency of aggregate demand. Hence the title of this section.

With the sources of unemployment so identified, policy directed to reduction of unemployment looked to such matters as: (1) Improvement in labor market information and organization, as by labor exchanges; (2) The elimination of obstacles to wage adjustments, as by the repeal of minimum wage laws or the moderation of trade union power; (3) Schemes for evening out seasonal fluctuations in production; (4) Business-cycle stabilization—but how to achieve this was not clear, and one recurrent line of policy was to encourage wage reduction once a contraction in employment had occurred.

Keynes and the Great Depression changed the unemployment map in two important ways. Keynes argued that, at least for significantly long periods of time, there could be, and presumably was, such a thing as involuntary unemployment. By this he meant a situation marked by two elements. Workers were without jobs although willing to work for real, if not money, wages below the prevailing rates. Yet, as a group, they could not get jobs because the increment of aggregate real demand which their employment would create would be insufficient to absorb the goods which their work would produce. The policy for reducing involuntary unemployment, therefore, was not wage reduction or improved labor-market organization, but support for higher aggregate demand.

The Great Depression persuaded economists, many politicians, and much of the public that involuntary unemployment was by far the bulk of unemployment. The road to full employment, therefore, was mainly through demand management, and that became the view which underlay the Employment Act and dominated employment policy well into the 1960s. It is a view which had—and has—two great attractions: first, it contains a large element of truth, and secondly, it is administratively, if not politically, simple since it concerns itself with impersonal and aggregative matters, like money supply and the size of budgets, and not with the multiplicity of problems which beset people in their many kinds and conditions. Inadequate demand, however, does not contain the entire truth about unemployment—nobody ever thought it did—and attention has gradually turned back to questions which demand management alone cannot solve.

TOWARD A MORE COMPREHENSIVE EMPLOYMENT POLICY

Once one has left the confines of demand management, it is hard to find the limits of employment policy. It easily encompasses measures to strengthen the system of labor-market information and guidance and to encourage the mobility of workers and firms. It clearly includes the training of workers in specific skills and, more generally, in the routines of shop and office discipline. In an extended sense, however, it comprehends anything which raises and broadens the productive capabilities of people. Since they then have the potentiality for filling a wider range of jobs, the problems of matching workers with job requirements and of breaking skill bottlenecks to employment are correspondingly eased. In this extended sense, therefore, all the educational and health programs of government, though undertaken primarily for other reasons, are allied to employment policy. In this view, the country has been involved in employment policy from the side of labor supply since time immemorial. In the first decade after the war, the educational aspects of the G.I. Bill, the hospital building supported by the Hill-Burton Act, and the financial aid to universities afforded by government grants for research, all, in their ways, were important federal initiatives with employment implications, and this fact was recognized in successive economic reports of the President and Council of Economic Advisers. As Eli Ginzberg has said, however, such actions were manpower policy "by indirection." The beginnings of a more self-conscious and systematic attempt to stretch the scope of employment policy beyond demand management, however, appeared during the period of elevated unemployment rates of the late 1950s and early 1960s. From these beginnings, the strength of the movement grew through the rest of the latter decade, and it is useful to trace the forces from which the movement stems.

Perhaps the most important reason for the change is simply that we have so far avoided another protracted major depression with mass unemployment. When the unemployment rate is 9 or 10 percent, increasing demand to create jobs is clearly the paramount issue. But even in the less active postwar years, when the rate lies between 5 and 7 percent, demand may yet do a great deal, but fitting people to fill existing vacancies or simply matching people with such vacancies may do as much, conceivably more. In a sense, therefore, the new institutions, the circumstances of the time, and the potentialities of demand management all of which contributed to our escape from major depression, helped to turn attention to other aspects of a comprehensive attack on unemployment.

At the same time, our employment record as it stood *circa* 1960 was neither matching the apparent achievements in Western Europe and Japan nor showing signs of improvement. On the contrary, figures could be plausibly arranged to suggest a rising trend of unemployment rates since the end of the war.[28] One diagnosis of this disappointing record was, of course, that fiscal and monetary policy had not gone far enough to support aggregate demand, but the competing view was that our problems extended beyond the reach of demand. The country, it was contended, was experiencing a "structural transformation." [29] Automation was accelerating technical progress and the rate of worker displacement, and this alone meant that more people were necessarily in transition between jobs. More important perhaps, the labor being saved was relatively unskilled and semi-skilled blue-collar work. The jobs opening up were professional, technical, administrative, clerical and, more generally, jobs involving higher levels of education and a different kind of experience than the displaced workers possessed. Because workers with the education and training needed were limited in supply, expansion of jobs under pressure of demand would, it was feared, be blocked by labor-supply shortages before satisfactory employment levels were reached. Handling the new unemployment problem demanded education and retraining and a stronger system of employment exchanges, alongside demand pressure.

Still a third source of changing views about employment policy were the new bodies of data provided by the postwar surveys of the labor force. They furnished continuous records of the employment status of the population classified by age, sex, race, level of education, and other characteristics. Still other data provided information about unemployment by industry, occupation, locality, and region. The figures clearly disclosed that unemployment had a characteristic "structure." Unemployment rates were higher at all times among youth, women, nonwhites, the unskilled and less educated, so these groups accounted for greater proportions of the unemployed than of the labor force. Unemployment was also concentrated among blue-collar workers and in certain regions and localities.

The new figures were brought into prominence by the continued interest and successive investigations of the Joint Economic Committee of the Congress [30] and of the Clark Committee of the Senate. [31] Combined with subsidiary information about the gross turnover of people in both jobs and labor force, the new information gradually brought a number of problems into clearer focus: for example, the transition of youth from school to work; the high turnover rates of the young; the special problems of women stemming from their discontinuous experience in work and in the labor force itself; discrimination against blacks and women; the poor jobs to which school dropouts were confined; and their high turnover in these jobs.

Once revealed, the "structure" of unemployment persuaded many people that a more "active labor market policy"—a more comprehensive "manpower policy"—was needed. Strengthened employment exchanges would provide guidance and reduce transition time between jobs. Job training and retraining, longer schooling, and restraints on discrimination would help people in the vulnerable classes obtain jobs more quickly, find more satisfaction in them and hold on to them longer. Demand pressure might be necessary to create the vacancies for better workers to fill, but the availability of a more qualified and more mobile labor supply would permit demand management to press further without triggering serious inflation.

The new data were less persuasive, at least in the late 1950s and early 1960s, in establishing the proposition that the higher levels of unemployment following 1957 reflected aggravated problems of frictional or "structural" unemployment. The economists in and near the Kennedy Administration were concerned to rebut these views, and, on the whole, they were successful.[32] Their clear motive was to prevent theories about structural transformation or altered labor-force composition from distracting attention from the fiscal measures they thought needed to correct an existing failure of demand pressure. Yet, they were not opposed to a more comprehensive manpower program to help the more disadvantaged groups, as well as to establish a more favorable trade-off rate between unemployment and inflation. The Area Development Act and the first Manpower Development and Training Act were passed in 1961 and 1962. And once the tax cut of 1964 was successfully launched, the administration economists, now under Johnson, joined the President and the congressional forces in pressing for an enlarged and strengthened manpower program.

A final and decisive set of influences tilting the balance of employment policy from the demand to the supply side stemmed from questions bigger than the economics of employment. The 1960s were the decade of civil rights and of the war on poverty. A comprehensive manpower program became part of a much wider attack on poverty and discrimination in the interests of justice and social harmony.

The outcome of this conjuncture of forces was the proliferation of manpower training and related programs between 1962 and 1969, with some extensions in the following years. During this period, the actual return of unemployment rates to the 4 percent level under the pressure of Johnsonian war budgets (Vietnam, the War on Poverty) and the receptivity of Congress and the country to a more active labor market and educational policy caused employment sights to be lifted. In the Senate, the Clark Committee led off in 1964 with recommendations for training, wider opportunities for minorities, and a stronger Public Employment Service. The announced goal was a 3 percent unemployment rate by 1968.[33] R. A. Gordon's influential 1967 book [34] argued that a comprehensive manpower program, added to aggressive demand management, made feasible a 3 percent goal with reasonable price stability. He was less sanguine than the Clark Committee, however, that a manpower program, necessarily experimental in its early years, would yield its fruits quickly. By early 1970, the *Manpower Report of the President* [35] was able to list some twenty-four federally assisted manpower training and support programs. These were funded at about $2.5 billion for fiscal

1970 and enrolled almost two million persons, all in addition to expenditures for the Public Employment Service of about $500 million. Significantly, the 1970 *Manpower Report* [36] submitted by Secretary Shultz followed the Nixon Administration's first year of experience in administering manpower programs. The *Report* concluded its assessment on a hopeful note:

> Altogether, it is clear . . . that manpower programs have made, and will continue to make, important contributions to the solution of the Nation's social and economic problems. The experience with manpower efforts in the United States and other countries supports an optimistic assessment of what can be expected from these programs in the future.[37]

And, looking to help from improved worker quality and better labor market organization to slow down the inflation, the *Report* concluded:

> The very recognition that economic objectives can be effectively served by more than the traditional fiscal and monetary devices is one important step in the realization of the broad promise of manpower programs.[38]

BUT NOT SO FAST

The 1970 *Report,* however, marked the crest of the wave of effort that had started in 1961. Thereafter, there began a period of disillusionment and of increasing restraint, if not contraction. After a decade of rapid growth in the size of government, a central aim of the more conservative Republican Administration was to bring the federal budget under tighter control. The manpower programs, which had expanded so fast, were obvious candidates for reevaluation and trimming. The examination, though hardly conclusive, did, indeed, find plausible evidence that costs were very high, that net additions to employment and improvements in earning power in some programs were small. Defenders could urge in mitigation that large portions of budgets nominally attributable to training activity were in fact being used for what amounted to income-maintenance or emergency unemployment relief.[39] Yet this defense was itself vulnerable. The auxiliary uses of manpower funds for income maintenance, for community action, and for the support of cadres of minority-group administrators, were themselves distasteful to those anxious to reduce welfare burdens and sensitive to a certain recoil from civil rights and affirmative action. The desire to devolve responsibility to state and local authority was still another consideration urging the federal government to reduce its manpower activities.

WHERE WE ARE

The net result of these influences upon manpower programs is hard to put in capsule form. It is fair to say that the years since 1970 have seen the expansion of the training and other manpower activities stopped. In some directions, there has been contraction. More significant perhaps has been the growing realization that we have not yet managed to devise formulas, effective in American conditions and practical on a large scale, which can cope successfully with our more obstinate unemployment problems: the transition of youth from school to work; improvement in the skills and work habits of the poorly educated and poorly motivated; and improving the security and prospects of jobs open to disadvantaged people to a degree sufficient to reduce turnover and induce steady work. All this in addition to removing the barriers to employment interposed by arbitrary union rules, government licensing, and wage regulation and the encouragement to irregular employment which some aspects of our systems of unemployment insurance and welfare may afford.

One leading student and strategist of manpower policy has defined our situation in these terms:

> We get what we pay for. At a cost of one percent of the federal budget and 0.25 percent of the GNP, we have experimented with manpower programs. Some of them have proved sound; others have not. Critics notwithstanding, our option is not to discard manpower programming, but to strengthen and enlarge the existing structure. Certainly no advanced economy can afford to operate without effective manpower programs.[40]

That is true enough. But, as in the case of demand management itself, the "manpower" side of employment policy is also in a state in which the practicability and effectiveness of the programs originally devised are in doubt. We are faced with a need to redefine problems and to search for new strategies.

Notes

1. Martin Feldstein, "Temporary Layoffs in the Theory of Unemployment," Harvard Institute of Economic Research, Discussion Paper No. 419, June 1975 (mimeo); "The Importance of Temporary Layoffs: An Empirical Analysis," presented at the Brookings Panel of Economic Activity, December 4, 1975.

2. President's Commission to Appraise Employment and Unemployment Statistics, *Measuring Employment and Unemployment,* U.S.G.P.O., 1962, p. 257.

3. *Ibid.* Cf. Feldstein, *op. cit,* note 1

4. The Committee for Economic Development in its 1947 report, *Taxes and the Budget,* was among the first to propose the 4 percent rate as a feasible noninflationary target. See Herbert Stein, *The Fiscal Revolution in America* (Chicago: The University of Chicago Press, 1969), 220 *et seq.,* especially pp. 225-26. R. A. Gordon writes that when the Employment Act was debated, numbers suggested fell in the range of 3 to 5 percent of the civilian labor force and that the early reports of the Council of Economic Advisers sug-

gested a "moderate range around 4 percent." During the Eisenhower years, the Council resisted any numerical definition of a target rate, but the 4 percent rate became the announced "interim target" of the Kennedy Council. Gordon, *The Goal of Full Employment* (New York: Wiley, 1957), pp. 52-54.

5. The figures cited here, their definitions and sources can be found in the table under note 9 and the notes appended to the table.

6. U.S. Department of Labor, Bureau of Labor Statistics, "The Extent and Nature of Frictional Unemployment," Study Paper No. 6, *Study of Employment, Growth and Price Levels*, November 19, 1959. Prepared for the Joint Economic Committee of the U.S. Congress. See also Robert E. Hall, "Why is the Unemployment Rate So High at Full Employment," *Brookings Papers on Economic Activity*, 1970, No. 3 pp. 369-402, and George L. Perry, "Changing Labor Markets and Inflation," same journal, pp. 411-41.

7. Perry, *op. cit.* Also E. F. Denison, *Accounting for United States Economic Growth, 1929–1969* (Washington: The Brookings Institution, 1947), pp. 95-96.

8. These are crude indications obtained by dividing the standard unemployment rate for the civilian labor force by the ratio of full-time and part-time employees to total civilian employment including proprietors and unpaid family workers. These are figures based mostly on establishment data from Denison, *op. cit.*, Table C-4, for 1947–1969, extrapolated by the present writer to 1974 on the basis of the movement of the figures from 1965 to 1969. The apparent rise in the ratio from 1947 to 1969 would have been somewhat more pronounced had an alternative set of figures adjusted to the Current Population Survey been used. Cf. *op. cit.*, Table C-2.

9. The inference that continuing and serious general underutilization of capacity existed from 1958 to 1963 is borne out by Denison's estimates of the relation of actual to potential output. Denison's estimates, unlike the more familiar figures of the CEA, do not depend on the level of the general unemployment rate. See Denison, *op. cit.*, Ch. 7.

   The view that the general unemployment rate exaggerates the degree of slack in the economy in the 1970s is bolstered by a variety of figures provided by G. H. Moore who compares data for April 1973 with those for 1955 and 1965, two earlier years generally regarded as times of high employment. He has also compiled figures for December 1975, or fourth quarter 1975, to indicate the impact of the recession of 1974–75. Where possible I have substituted figures for the full year 1973 and 1975 by consulting later data in Moore's sources. [See the table on page 34.]

10. See also Perry, *op. cit.*, who presents an econometric analysis of the relation between unemployment, changing labor force structure, and inflation and reaches the same conclusion.

11. February 1960, when the rate fell to 4.8 percent was an exception.

	1955	1965	1973	1975
Unemployment rate, total (percent)	4.4	4.5	4.9	8.5
Labor time lost (percent)[a]	5.0[b]	5.0	5.2	9.1
Unemployment rate standardized by 1955 age and sex composition (percent)[c]	4.3	4.1	4.3 (Apr)	7.3 (Dec)
Unemployment rate, married males (percent)	2.8	2.4	2.3	5.1
Unemployment rate, household heads (percent)	—	2.7	2.9	5.8
Uemployment rate, experienced wage and salary workers (percent)	4.8	4.3	4.5	8.2
Unemployment rate, insured workers (percent)	3.5	3.0	2.7	2.9
Unemployment rate, job losers (percent)	—	1.6[d]	1.9 (Apr)	4.1 (Dec)
Discouraged worker rate[e] (percent)	—	0.9[d]	0.7 (Apr)[f]	1.0 (4th qtr)
Unemployment rate, 15 weeks and over (percent)	1.1	1.0	0.9	2.7
Average duration of unemployment (weeks)	13.0	11.8	10.0	14.1
Index of unemployment severity[g] (days)	2.9	2.7	2.45	6.0
Employed as percent of working-age population	55.1	55.0	56.9	55.3
Ratio, help-wanted ads to unemployed (1972 = 100)	62.5	75.4	81.9 (Apr)	54.0 (Nov)
Quit-rate, manufacturing (percent)	1.9	1.9	2.7	1.4 (Jan–Oct)
Overtime hours, manufacturing (hours/week)	3.2[h]	3.6	3.8	2.6
Average workweek, manufacturing (hours/week)	40.7	41.2	40.7	39.4[p]
Vendor performance, percent companies reporting slower deliveries	66	67	88	30

Source: From Geoffrey H. Moore, *How Full Is Full Employment?* (Washington, D.C.: American Enterprise Institute for Public Policy Research, 1973), Table 4.1. December 1975 rates supplied by Dr. Moore. Calendar year figures for 1973 and 1975 compiled by the present writer from the same source. Reprinted by permission of the publisher.

[a] Man-hours lost by the unemployed and by persons employed part time for economic reasons as percent of potentially available labor force hours.

[b] Average for May–December 1955. Data begin May 1955.

[c] See source, Table 4.2.

[d] Average for 1967, the initial year of the series.

12. Cf. Crauford D. Goodwin (ed.), *Exhortation and Controls, The Search for a Wage-Price Policy, 1945–71* (Washington, D.C.: The Brookings Institution, 1975). This fine study of the problems faced in controlling inflation provides extensive evidence of the barriers to using fiscal and monetary policy. One example (pp. 90-91):

> Early in Truman's first term . . . the apparatus of wartime controls was quickly dismantled or nullified, and the problem of rapid inflation had to be attacked almost with a clean slate. Moreover, it was quickly found that what could be written on this slate was disturbingly little. Monetary policy was severely constrained by the decision to maintain the value of government bonds. Requests to Congress were slow to be made and even slower to be granted. Fiscal policy as an anti-inflation device was readily comprehended and approved by Truman and recommended by his advisors. But it too was inhibited by a Congress anxious to lift the burden of wartime taxes and faced with inflexible expenditures for domestic programs and unexpected charges for foreign aid and cold war defense.

And this, by way of summary:

> One point at least should emerge clearly from these pages. Any attempt to portray the Truman years as a dark age in the attack on inflation, after which came blinding light in the 1950s, the 1960s or even 1970s is surely wrong. In fact, what may be the most depressing message is that since 1952 so little has changed.

13. See the discussion by H. C. Wallich and S. H. Axelrod, "The Postwar Record of Monetary Policy," in Neil H. Jacoby, ed., *United States Monetary Policy,* American Assembly, Columbia University, 1964, reprinted in Arthur H. Okun, *The Battle Against Unemployment* (New York: Norton, 1965), pp. 181-91.

14. This is the McGraw-Hill index. See the *Economic Report of the President,* February 1975, Table C-37.

15. *Ibid,* Table C-3.

16. *Ibid,* Table C-64.

17. A. M. Okun and Nancy H. Teeters, "The Full Employment Surplus Revisited," *Brookings Paper on Economic Activity,* 1970, No. 1, Table 2.

18. See Stein, *op. cit.,* Chs. 13 and 14.

19. See J. M. Clark, *The Wage-Price Problem,* American Bankers Association, 1960.

20. Walter S. Salant *et al., The United States Balance of Payments in 1968* (Washington, D.C.: The Brookings Institution, August 1963). This is the

---

e Persons not in labor force, who want a job now but are not looking because they think they cannot get a job as percentage of total civilian labor force.

f Data for I, 1973, not seasonally adjusted.

g Unemployment rate ÷ 100 × average duration of unemployment (in weeks) × 5 (to convert to days). See source, Table 3.1.

h January 1956, the initial figure for series. Annual average for 1956 is 2.8.

p Preliminary.

most penetrating and complete account of the development of our balance of payments troubles in the 1950s and early 1960s, pp. 9-12 provide a compact statement of the case.

21. Stein, *op. cit.*, Ch. 14.

22. Okun and Teeters, *op. cit.*, Table 2.

23. Wallich and Axelrod, *op. cit.*

24. Stein, *op. cit.*, Ch. 15 and Walter W. Heller, *New Dimensions of Political Economy* (New York: Norton, 1967); Ch. 1 tells the story of the Kennedy Administration's first encounter with employment policy.

25. I take the views of the Salant book, *op. cit.* to represent the general outlook among the Kennedy economists.

26. Stein, *op. cit.*, Chs. 15, 16; Heller *op. cit.*, Ch. 1.

27. W. Nordhaus and J. Shoven, "Inflation 1973: The Year of Infamy," *Challenge,* May/June 1974.

28. For example, Subcommittee on Economic Statistics of the Joint Economic Committee, Congress of the United States, 87th Congress, 1st Session, *Higher Unemployment Rate, 1957–60: Structural Transformation or Inadequate Demand,* Study Paper, November 29, 1961, pp. 4-5.

29. *Ibid.*, Ch. 2.

30. Hearings and Staff Report on *Employment, Growth and Price Levels,* Joint Economic Committee, Congress of the U.S., 86th Congress, 1st Session, 1959.

31. Successive Hearings and Reports of the Subcommittee on Employment and Manpower, Committee on Labor and Public Welfare, U.S. Senate, 1963 and 1964, esp. *Toward Full Employment: Proposals for a Comprehensive Employment and Manpower Policy for the United States,* April 1964. An important statement in the Hearings by C. C. Killingsworth is reprinted in A. M. Okun (ed.), *The Battle Against Unemployment* (New York: Norton), p. 53 *et seq.*

32. See *Economic Report of the President,* February 1962, Robert M. Solow, *The Nature and Sources of Unemployment in the United States,* Wicksell Lectures, 1964; R. A. Gordon, "Has Structural Unemployment Worsened?" *Industrial Relations,* vol. 3, no. 3 (May 1964), pp. 53-77.

33. *Toward Full Employment: Proposals for a Comprehensive Employment and Manpower Policy for the United States, op. cit.,* note 30, above.

34. *The Goal of Full Employment* (New York: Wiley, 1967), p. 181 *et seq.*

35. *Manpower Report of the President,* March 1970, App. A.

36. *Ibid.*, p. 19.

37. *Ibid.*

38. *Ibid.*

39. Eli Ginzberg, "Manpower Programs: Boon Not Boondoggle," *Challenge,* vol. 16, pp. 52-56 (September/October 1973).

40. *Ibid.*

Robert M. Solow

2

Macro-policy
and Full Employment

Introduction

If the government of the United States has a commitment to full employment, it is presumably embodied in the Employment Act of 1946. Here is the Preamble to that hotly-debated piece of legislation:

> The Congress declares that it is the continuing policy and responsibility of the Federal Government to use all practicable means consistent with its needs and obligations and other essential considerations of national policy with the assistance and cooperation of industry, agriculture, labor, and State and local governments to coordinate and utilize all its plans, functions, and re- sources, for the purpose of creating and maintaining, in a manner calculated to foster and promote free competitive enterprise and the general welfare, conditions under which there will be afforded useful employment opportuni- ties, including self-employment for those able, willing, and seeking to work, and to promote maximum employment, production, and purchasing power.

Language like that is a sure signal that we are in the presence of piety without policy. Since the act specifies no penalty for failure to carry out the "responsibility" it places on the federal government, it is not sur- prising that the record of achievement of "maximum employment, pro- duction, and purchasing power" is spotty, to say the least. And yet hardly anyone will be found who is willing to say a good word for unemploy- ment. There are lobbies for and against abortion, for and against nuclear power, for and against almost anything; but there is no lobby against jobs. So there is a question that calls for discussion: what does the man-

ROBERT M. SOLOW *is Institute Professor, Massachusetts Institute of Technology. In 1961–62 he was Senior Economist, Council of Economic Advisers. Dr. Solow is a member of the National Academy of Sciences.*

date of the Employment Act of 1946 mean? And what are the obstacles to its fulfillment?

One way to place this problem in context is to compare the performance of the U.S. economy and its government with that of other industrialized countries as regards unemployment rates actually experienced. Here a technical problem arises: different countries measure their unemployment rates in different ways and according to different definitions, so national statistics are not exactly comparable. In the U.S., for example, the unemployment statistics come from a monthly sample of the population; in many other countries, the unemployment statistics are a by-product of labor exchanges and unemployment-compensation payments. In one of the latter systems, you must be eligible for unemployment compensation to be counted as unemployed, but not so in the U.S. Attempts have been made, however, to adjust international unemployment statistics so that valid comparisons can be made across countries. The results can hardly be perfect, but they are unlikely to lead us astray.

Table 1 covers eight important industrial countries for the years 1960

TABLE 1. UNEMPLOYMENT RATES 1960–1974 (PERCENT)

Country	Highest	Lowest	Average
United States	6.7	3.5	4.9
Canada	7.1	3.9	5.4
Japan	1.7	1.1	1.3
France	3.0	1.6	2.3
West Germany	2.1	0.3	0.8
Italy	4.3	2.7	3.6
United Kingdom	5.3	1.2	3.2
Sweden	2.7	1.2	1.9

Source: Eva Christina Horowitz, "Unemployment Rates—An International Comparison," The Nordic Economic Outlook, mimeographed series B12 of the Federation of Swedish Industries, June 1975.

through 1974, and uses unemployment rates adjusted to the U.S. definition. The table gives, for each country, the highest and lowest annual unemployment rate experienced during the period 1960–1974, as well as the average of the fifteen annual rates. (If monthly data were available, the highest figure would be higher and the lowest figure lower in each country, but the average would be unaffected.)

It is clear to the naked eye that the United States and Canada experience far and away the highest unemployment rates in this group of countries. The lowest unemployment rate achieved in Canada during this period exceeds the average unemployment rate in every other country besides the U.S., and almost the same statement can be made with the U.S. and Canada interchanged. Indeed, the lowest annual unemployment rate achieved in the U.S.—3.5 percent in 1969 during the Vietnam War—is higher than the *highest* annual unemployment rate experienced by Japan, France, West Germany, and Sweden, at any time during the fifteen years. Those four countries clearly have very low unemployment rates, reaching levels unimaginable in the United States. In Japan, the unemployment rate hardly even changes: fourteen of the fifteen observations fall between 1.1 and 1.5 percent. Italy and the United Kingdom form a middle group presumably for quite different reasons.

No one who looks at Table 1 can doubt that there is a qualitative difference between the North American countries on one side, and the low-unemployment countries on the other. This fact at once suggests a very difficult sort of question: what is the source of the difference? In particular, one would like to ask if the United States has simply failed to carry out the responsibility laid down in the Employment Act of 1946, or if there is some deeper socioeconomic explanation of the difference in performance. Are American unemployment rates higher than European (and Japanese) unemployment rates mainly because we have managed our economy badly, whether through incompetence or inattention or political disarray? Or is there something special about the American labor market that makes it intrinsically more difficult to generate employment for an extra 2 or 3 percent of the labor force? On this side of the Atlantic (and the Pacific) does an unemployment rate of 3.5 percent (or 4 percent, or as some people suggest these days, 5 or 6 percent) represent "maximum employment" within the meaning of the act?

Related to this analytical question there is a matter of policy. In view of its legislative history, the Employment Act of 1946 stands as the charter for active macroeconomic policy on the part of the federal government. It is most often quoted in the context of fiscal and monetary policy, at budget time, when the issue is stabilizing the business cycle or managing the economy as a whole. But there is nothing in the language that excludes manpower policy or labor market policy from the set of "all practicable means." And, in fact, these and other microeconomic policies have, in recent years, played a larger and larger part in the work and deliberations of the Council of Economic Advisers and the Joint Economic Committee, the two bodies established by the Employment Act. To the extent that the poor unemployment performance of the American economy can be ascribed to bad management in the aggregative sense, better and more aggressive macroeconomic policy is called for. To the extent that high unemployment rates are ascribed to special characteristics of the American labor market (or of product markets), it is more natural to turn to manpower policies, or labor market policies, or policies that operate on other markets. This is a useful dichotomy, so long as it does not slide over into either/or. Macro and micro-policies are more likely to be complementary, to enhance each other, than to be rivals.

It is also important to try to understand the limits of both kinds of policies. One must be prepared, at least in principle, to find that there is only so much improvement in unemployment rates that can be achieved within our accustomed institutional framework. Beyond that, different people will view the alternatives in different ways. No purpose is served by ignoring the probable limits of conventional policies, and much is lost. One of the enemies of rational policy-making is the temptation to promise too much.

A Physical Barrier

What are the limits of macroeconomic policy? In a certain simple-minded sense, it is easy to get a partial answer to that question by looking at the recent past. In February 1969, at the height of the Vietnam War boom, the seasonally adjusted unemployment rate in the United States fell to 3.3 percent of the labor force. Unless something rather drastic happened to the working population of the country in the short span of six years, one must suppose that the unemployment rate *could* have been at least that low in February 1975, instead of the 8.2 percent figure that was actually recorded. That is to say, there was presumably no *physical* barrier to a macroeconomic policy that would have generated economic conditions like those ruling in 1969. There may have been political reasons why such a policy was not pursued. There may have been economic reasons—of a kind to be discussed later—why such a policy was not pursued. But unless we can identify some special bottlenecks that had narrowed significantly in the intervening six years, it would have been easy, so far as the economics goes, to find a peacetime macro-economic equivalent to the Vietnam War.

Had the composition of the labor force worsened in some sense between 1969 and 1975? Without asking why, without even inquiring whether the notion makes sense, let us suppose that the young and the female are to be classified as "hard to employ." Table 2 shows the proportion of the unemployed and the proportion of the civilian labor force that fell into those categories in February 1969 and February 1975.

Although youth and women were smaller proportions of the unemployed in 1975 than they had been in 1969, the same two groups did

TABLE 2.   AGE-SEX PROPORTIONS

	Percentage of All Unemployed Workers		Percentage of Civilian Labor Force	
	Feb. 1969	*Feb. 1975*	*Feb. 1969*	*Feb. 1975*
16–19 year olds	25	18	7.5	9
Women	47	41	37	40

Source: Compiled from information appearing in *Employment and Earnings and Monthly Report on the Labor Force,* March 1969 and March 1975, a publication of the Bureau of Labor Statistics, U.S. Department of Labor.

form slightly higher proportions of the labor force. If it is indeed the case, for whatever reasons, that mere expansion of the economy is less able to generate jobs for young and female workers than for others, then perhaps one could argue that what could be achieved by macroeconomic policy in early 1969 was no longer attainable in early 1975. But it is not much of an argument, because the effect is certainly trivially small.

Suppose we take the unemployment rates suffered by each age-sex–race group in 1969 and apply them, group by group, to a labor force with the age-sex composition that ruled in 1975. In that way we can construct an overall unemployment rate in which each group fares as well as it did in February 1969, but the economy experiences whatever excess unemployment its "worsened" demographic composition calls for. If we do that, we arrive at a hypothetical aggregate unemployment rate a trifle under 3.5 percent for February 1975. The difference between this figure and 3.3 percent measures the amount by which "deterioration" of the labor force limited the power of macroeconomic policy to reduce unemployment. So far as this kind of barrier to full employment is concerned, a macroeconomic policy as expansionary as that pursued in the Vietnam War could have reduced unemployment under 1975 conditions at least to 3.5 percent, and perhaps lower—because there is no evidence that the 3.3 percent of February 1969 was itself a rock-bottom minimum.

By the way, even in February 1969 there was a very wide range of unemployment rates for different demographic groups. Some did very much worse than the average: the unemployment rate for nonwhite females aged sixteen to nineteen was 24.9 percent, and that for nonwhite males aged sixteen to nineteen was 21.2 percent. (The corresponding figures for young whites were 10.7 percent and 11 percent respectively.) In contrast, white males aged thirty-five to forty-four experienced an unemployment rate of 1.6 percent. Whatever the source of that tremendous difference, it is not something for which macroeconomic expansion appears to be the sovereign remedy; although one is tempted to believe that prolonged high *general* employment is likely to be an indispensable part of any serious attempt to change the situation.

Naturally, the demographic composition of the labor force is only one possible "physical" barrier to the achievement of low unemployment rates, though it is perhaps the one most often mentioned. The availability of an adequate supply of skilled labor is presumably more important, and the demographic facts are used primarily as surrogates for training and experience. But it is surely implausible that the skills of the U.S. labor force had attenuated enough between 1969 and 1975 to force a perceptibly higher unemployment rate on the country.

The other important possibility is that the expansion of output and employment is limited by capacity bottlenecks, by general or specific shortages of plant and equipment. Measures of capacity and capacity utilization are not very good; but such as they are, they suggest rather strongly that there were no such capacity obstacles to the achievement of a low unemployment rate in 1975. One ballpark estimate is that there was room in early 1975 for at least a 25 percent increase in manufacturing output. But less than a 25 percent increase in GNP would have been needed to reduce unemployment to the 3.5 percent range. Manufacturing is not nearly all of GNP, but it is probably the part of aggregate output most subject to capacity limitations. So there was plenty of room for expansion. It is possible that capacity strains might have occurred in specific important industries, had such an expansion taken place; the primary processing industries have been suggested as a candidate for early bottleneck. Nevertheless, it is a reasonable working hypothesis that expansionary fiscal and monetary policy could have reached in 1975 and 1976, unemployment rates like those actually achieved in early 1969, so far as physical barriers are concerned.

In summary then, fiscal and monetary policy together generate employment by expanding the market for goods and services, directly or indirectly. As producers see new sales opportunities and increase production to take advantage of them, jobs are created and employment rises. It could conceivably happen that the limit to this process might be a shortage of qualified workers or of productive capacity. No such shortage appears to be the operative limit to the reduction of unemployment by macro-policy in the U.S.

The Inflation Barrier

In that the end of the story? Obviously not. I have dwelt on the possibility of physical limits to high employment only to get it out of the way. Although some public discussions of unemployment are made to sound as if they are about such physical barriers, that is not usually the heart of the matter. The real obstacle to a macroeconomic policy that would achieve low unemployment rates is something quite different. It is the belief and fear that such a policy would result in dangerously fast inflation.

Nor is the belief nonsensical on its face. The history seems to indicate that the expansion of markets pulls prices and wages up before anything like widespread bottlenecks appear. Back in 1964, when the unemployment rate averaged slightly higher than 5 percent, prices were rising at about 1.5 percent a year, and you could make a case that the price level was almost stable, given the biases of the price indexes. As unemployment fell toward its low point in early 1969, the rise in the price level accelerated. By early 1970, to allow for lags in causation, the rate of inflation was in the 5.5 to 6 percent range. All this happened, you will notice, long before oil and grain went through the roof. This notion, that a slack economy favors price stability and a tight, prosperous economy favors inflation, needs to be qualified; and some of the qualifications will be discussed soon. But *it* is what inhibits the all-out quest for "maximum employment, production, and purchasing power."

Two side remarks are in order here. First of all, the belief that reasonably tight prosperity produces unacceptable inflation, and the consequent tendency to go easy on expansionary monetary and fiscal policies, are not confined to the United States. The problem of "stagflation" has arisen all over the industrialized capitalist world, and the reaction to it has been broadly similar everywhere. The limits thus imposed are far from precise, and their location evidently differs enormously from country to country. So also does the revealed tolerance of different governments and their constituents for unemployment and inflation as alternative evils. But the underlying inhibition is world-wide.

Secondly, public discussion of this issue sometimes degenerates into a controversy about "who is to blame." One common line of analysis runs this way: prices are mainly cost-determined; low unemployment generates wages that outrun productivity increases, hence labor costs rise per unit of output, and thus the inflationary impulse is transmitted to prices. Once this happens, wages may react to rising consumer prices and a spiral begins that may take a long time to unwind. In some episodes, however, it may be the case that margins widen and prices rise before any substantial wage increase has occurred, and the interactive process starts from there. For obvious reasons much heat is expended over the question whether wages follow prices or prices follow wages; it is interpreted as being the same thing as the question whether trade unions or large corporations "cause" inflation. For the issues to be discussed here, it does not really matter and no position need be taken. In any case, no serious and responsible student of the relation between unemployment and inflation thinks that it can be resolved into some simple statement about unions and/or big business. There is much dispute about the precise nature of that relation; but whatever it is, it reflects many aspects of our economic system and its institutions.

The Phillips Curve

In the 1960s, the most widely held view accepted the existence of a fairly stable relation between the degree of prosperity of a given economy, as measured by its unemployment rate, say, and the corresponding rate of inflation of wages and prices. This relation was called the "Phillips Curve" after the economist who did the first systematic statistical study, using almost a century of English data. The basic idea itself is much older than that; but casual or anecdotal statement is one thing, and an apparently reliable statistical regularity is quite another. From the very beginning, economists understood that there were other determinants of the rate of inflation in addition to the unemployment rate, including perhaps the degree of capacity utilization in industry, the profitability of business, the cost of imports, raw materials, and farm products, and other indicators of economic conditions. There were also some economists who disbelieved in the Phillips Curve altogether.

The importance of the Phillips Curve view was not its precise character, but its stability or reliability. To the extent that the relationship between unemployment and inflation is stable and reliable, macroeconomic policy has to trade off one against the other. It is no use thundering about the immorality of fighting inflation by creating unemployment, unless one means that the proper target of macroeconomic policy is a low unemployment rate, no matter how fast the price level rises when it is achieved. It is no use thundering that inflation is Public Enemy Number One, unless one means that the proper target of macroeconomic policy is a low rate of inflation, no matter how much unemployment corresponds to that state of affairs. If there is a stable Phillips Curve, then macroeconomic policy can only choose the best *available* combination of unemployment and inflation from the limited menu offered it, and aim to achieve that combination. From a longer-run point of view one could try to *change* the Phillips Curve by adopting any number of different sorts of policies: busting unions, breaking up companies with market power, requiring public hearings for major price increases, legislating wage and price controls, issuing wage and price guidelines, expanding manpower training programs, strengthening the employment service, offering relocation allowances, encouraging domestic and international competition, lowering tariffs, and so on. All such institutional changes would certainly take some time to work, if they would work at all. In the meanwhile, macroeconomic policy would be limited by the existing trade-off relations.

This picture of the world held sway—despite the dissents already mentioned—because the evidence from the end of the Korean War until the mid-1960s seemed to support it. The facts of the U.S. economy did look as if there were a stable, though perhaps complex, relation between the tightness of the economy and price and wage behavior. In later years, however, those apparently reliable regularities failed. In particular, we have experienced simultaneous rates of inflation and unemployment both higher than would have been compatible, according to the old relationships. For example, the unemployment rate was 5 percent in 1970, 6 percent in 1971, and 5.6 percent in 1972, and the corresponding annual rates of inflation (in the price index for GNP) were 5.5 percent, 4.5 percent, and 3.4 percent. Notice that prices did definitely slow down during (in response to?) those years of moderately high unemployment. It is not as if the old regularities went completely haywire. But they did go wrong: a few years earlier, an unemployment rate above 5 percent would have been associated with considerably slower inflation.

There are several possible ways one might react to this story. (1) There never really was a Phillips Curve; it looked good for a while by accident, but now the truth is out. (2) There was a Phillips Curve, and there may now be another one, the trouble is that it is not very stable, but shifts from time to time in unpredictable ways. (3) Maybe those shifts are not unpredictable after all; careful study may let us include the deeper causal factors in our predictive relationship. (4) The Phillips Curve that people thought they saw is an inherently short-run thing; if you try to use it to play the trade-off game, it must eventually move against you. Society has much less control over its unemployment rate than one might think, unless you are prepared for ever-accelerating inflation, and maybe not even then.

My own guess is that the second of these alternatives is closest to the truth, though there is certainly something to the third and fourth too. The fourth interpretation is rather difficult and technical; I will come back to it soon in a different context, as a practical rather than a theoretical proposition.

If, as I have suggested, the fear of inflation is the important roadblock in the macroeconomic path to low unemployment, then the apparent breakup or adverse shift in the Phillips Curve would be expected to have an effect on the aspirations of macroeconomic policymakers. And so it has. Increasingly one hears that 5 or 5.5 or 6 percent is as low as the unemployment rate can safely go. At the beginning of 1975, with the unemployment rate above 8 percent and soon to reach 9 percent, a postwar high, the Ford Administration proposed a five-year target path for the economy that would bring unemployment down to 5 percent only toward the end of 1980. One year later, the new budget message confirmed this objective. Such remarks usually go with an obbligato to the effect that being without a job is not so painful as it used to be: the unemployed spouse of an employed spouse, or an unemployed youth living with parents, or a person returning to the job market after an absence from it and unable to find a job, or people seeking part-time work, or anyone who has only been unemployed for a few weeks—it is suggested that such a person is not "really" unemployed in the sense that anyone ought to worry about it. It is undoubtedly more comfortable to be unemployed if some other member of the family has a job than if not. It is only to be expected that most reentrants to the labor force will spend some time searching for a job. But it is hardly open to question that what underlies the downgrading of high employment as a social goal is the fear that nowadays inflation will set in even earlier than it used to, that the trade-off between unemployment and inflation is now more unfavorable, and riskier, than it used to be.

So we have come full circle to the important policy question. What is the appropriate target for macroeconomic policy? In the January 1962 *Economic Report* the Kennedy Council of Economic Advisers set a target in these words:

> The selection of a particular target for stabilization policy does not commit policy to an unchangeable definition of the rate of unemployment corresponding to full employment. Circumstances may alter the responsiveness of the unemployment rate and the price level to the volume of aggregate demand. Current experience must therefore be the guide.

In the existing economic circumstances, an unemployment rate of about 4 percent is a reasonable and prudent full employment target for stabilization policy. If we move firmly to reduce the impact of structural unemployment, we will be able to move the unemployment target steadily from 4 percent to successively lower rates.

The recent history of the U.S. economy contains no evidence that labor and commodity markets are in general excessively "tight" at 4 percent unemployment. Neither does it suggest that stabilization policy alone could press unemployment significantly below 4 percent without creating substantial upward pressure on prices.

In retrospect, 4 percent was the right choice, *given* the price-level constraint evidently felt and plainly expressed by the council. It has already been pointed out that the rate of inflation actually did begin to move up in the mid-1960s just about the time the unemployment rate reached and crossed the 4 percent mark. But "current experience must . . . be the guide." A casual reading of current experience suggests that the trade-off has worsened, and many voices seem all too ready to adjust the unemployment target upward. Why has the trade-off worsened? What accounts for the tendency of prices to rise even while unemployment is high and the economy depressed by any normal standards?

Why Has the Trade-off Worsened?

I want now to describe and evaluate the main explanations that have been given for this apparent state of affairs. Some of the arguments to be discussed are technical, subtle, and complicated. I apologize in advance that I will not be able to do them full justice in plain English. Nevertheless I think the effort is worth making. There is more than academic interest in these alternative theories of the inflation-proneness of the modern economy. Some of them suggest that the problem is inevitable and permanent, others that it is temporary, and—if we reject all the new explanations—we may even conclude that the problem is illusory. Without going that far, it is clearly important to know why the thing has happened if we would like to know how to make it go away.

THE DEMOGRAPHY OF THE LABOR FORCE AGAIN

One important view, espoused by George Perry, returns to the age-sex composition of the labor force, but in a slightly different context. Unemployment limits inflation because when many people are out of work, the employed (organized or unorganized) are less likely—other things equal—to press for large wage increases, and employers are less likely to offer them. Workers know that they can easily be replaced; and anyway business is bad. Employers know the same things. But perhaps it matters *who* is unemployed. It is not so plausible that each unemployed person should exert the same downward force on the level of wages as any other.

One natural possibility is to count not the number of unemployed people but the number of dollars worth of labor that are unemployed. The two differ because some people earn lower hourly wages than others; and some people normally work fewer hours than others. This view maintains that a worker who normally works forty hours a week at six dollars an hour represents more than twice as much unemployment as someone who normally works thirty hours a week at three dollars an hour—not in the sense that there is more than twice as much personal frustration or social damage, but simply in the sense that the unemployment of a high-wage full-time worker weighs more heavily on the tendency of wages to rise than the unemployment of someone who normally works part-time for a near-minimum wage.

In principle, one could actually count up the number of dollars worth of unemployed labor; but the available statistics only allow us to count by age-sex groups with allowance for the average wage in each such group, and the average number of hours worked. In his original article Perry computed such a "weighted unemployment rate" for the years 1956 to 1969. In 1956 the conventional aggregate unemployment rate was 3.9 percent, and in 1969 it was 3.5 percent. By the usual measure, unemployment was some 10 percent lower in 1969 than in 1956. Perry's weighted unemployment rate was almost 25 percent lower in 1969 than in 1956. That means, at the end of the period, women and youth accounted for a larger fraction of the labor force than at the beginning. Moreover, the relative unemployment experience of those groups was worse at the end of the period than at the beginning. In the mid-1950s, the unemployment rate for all women was 70 percent higher than that for males aged twenty-five to sixty-four; in 1969 that disadvantage had increased to 180 percent. In the mid-1950s, teenaged males had unemployment rates 3.7 times the prime-age males, in 1969, 6.8 times. For teenaged females the corresponding multiples were 2.7 and 8.0. As a result, much more of the unemployment in 1969 consisted of women and youth. Since those groups earn lower wages and work fewer hours on average than adult males, there was by the "dollars worth of labor" measure less effective unemployment in 1969 than the conventional measure suggests.

The implication that can be drawn from this analysis is that the inflation-unemployment trade-off has worsened. Perry estimates that a given (conventional) unemployment rate in 1970 would be associated with a rate of inflation 1.7 percent per year *faster* than the same unemployment rate would have signalled in the 1950s. That is not because workers behave differently or push harder for higher wages, but bceause the predominance of women and youth on the unemployment rolls means that any given conventional unemployment rate weighs less heavily on the wage level than it used to. The conventional unemployment rate understates the degree of tightness in the labor market.

One obvious weakness of this analysis was imposed on its author by the nature of the available data. There are other characteristics of workers equally or more relevant to their normal earnings than age and sex. Education, skill, experience, and location are obvious examples. An accurate measure of the underlying concept—dollars worth of labor unemployed—might not have moved at all like an estimate based only on age and sex. But Perry's argument is at least suggestive.

If the unemployment target that you set for macroeconomic policy is governed solely by the associated inflation rate, and *if* you despair of doing anything about the disadvantaged age-sex groups, and *if* you accept this analysis, then perhaps you might make a case for accepting a higher conventional unemployment rate than you might have done earlier.

Michael Wachter has attempted actually to estimate the "noninflationary unemployment rate" within this intellectual framework. His method, in essence, is to study the normal relation of the various age-sex-specific unemployment rates to the rate for prime-age males. Then, taking account of the changing demographic composition of the labor force, he can hope to estimate approximately the overall aggregate unemployment rate that would be compatible with a feasibly low unemployment rate for prime-age males.

The method is too speculative for me to reproduce the details here, but it is interesting to see the broad outline. Wachter's method suggests that the noninflationary unemployment rate was indeed near 4 percent throughout the 1950s, and into, say, 1962. Then, as the baby-boom of the 1940s began to add young workers to the labor force, and as the participation rate of women increased, the noninflationary unemployment rate, as estimated, began to rise. It reached 5 percent by 1968 and peaked at 5.5 percent in 1973–74. I say "peaked" because Wachter estimates that the predictable changing demography will push the noninflationary unemployment rate back down to 5 percent by 1981 and 4.5 percent by 1985. Needless to say, anything that depends so much on the age-structure of the population can never change very fast.

According to Wachter's estimates, the actual U.S. unemployment rate was well above the noninflationary level from the end of 1957 until early 1965, and then perceptibly below it from the end of 1965 until mid-1970. Thereafter the two curves intertwined in cyclical fashion until the sky-high 7, 8, and 9 percent unemployment rates of late 1974 and all of 1975 moved a whole 3.5 percent above Wachter's "noninflationary" rate.

Any such numerical discussion inevitably lends an air of spurious precision to the results, which are simplified, tentative, and inexact. But this survey does give the flavor of an important current of thought about the unaided capacity of macro-policy to reduce unemployment.

"VOLUNTARY" UNEMPLOYMENT

I turn now to several other lines of thought that lead in a different way to the suggestion that the feasible unemployment rate target for macro-policy might now be pretty high. These ideas have an important characteristic in common: they tend to regard much unemployment as *voluntary*. In principle, there is no reason why macro-policy could not and should not set itself the task of reducing voluntary unemployment as well as involuntary. That depends, as we shall see, on the reasons for voluntary unemployment. Nevertheless, the voluntary unemployment theories seem to end up by suggesting that the reduction of unemployment through general economic expansion is a less urgent task than it once seemed. This comes about in two ways. First, there is an implication that those who choose to be unemployed can hardly be in very dire straits. Second, there is the different sort of implication than an effort to tempt the voluntarily unemployed back into employed is very likely to require that wage increases be part of the temptation. These will spread to all wages and inflationary pressure will result. Another way to say the same thing is to remark that the voluntarily unemployed are not competing hard for jobs, and therefore not exerting much downward pressure on wages. The labor market is thus tighter than a mere count of the unemployed would suggest.

There are several strands to the voluntary unemployment theories. The first of them presumes that many of the unemployed are more or less productively engaged in *searching* for a better job than one they have left, or than one that they could have taken but have instead rejected. This search activity is productive even though it brings no current income; the payoff comes in the form of higher wages or better conditions in the job that will eventually be accepted.

This strand has two substrands. One of them holds that many searching workers are simply misinformed about labor market conditions. For example, suppose wages begin to rise abnormally rapidly, without any associated gain in productivity. Workers, who do not understand that prices will eventually have to catch up, will think that they have located extremely good jobs at high real wages. They will therefore cut short their average search time, and the volume of measured unemployment will be lower. The point of this story for search theorists is that it gives the appearance of a trade-off (lower unemployment accompanied by faster wage increase) but not the long-run reality. When experience teaches workers that the apparent real wage gains are doomed to be eroded by rising prices, their average search time will lengthen again; the unemployment rate will rise again. The extra inflation will still be with us, but the gain in employment will have been only transitory.

The second substrand does not require any misinformation on the part of searching unemployed workers. It rests on one or another genuine imperfection in the labor market that makes it sometimes more profitable and sometimes less profitable to search longer.

What are we to think of such theories? There must be something in them. Even in a relatively bad year like 1974, 15 percent of the unemployed had "left last job." Since 40 percent of the unemployed were new entrants or reentrants to the labor market, a quarter of all the unemployed who had just previously been employed were job-leavers rather than job-losers. Not all job-leavers fall into the voluntary-search category; however, one may leave a job for reasons of health, or because one's family moves. Nor is it clear that every job-leaver is searching in the sense that the theories require. Nor is it clear that active search for a better job necessitates leaving the old one. Nevertheless, one may grant that the search theories are not empty without believing that they are very important. Such indirect evidence as there is suggests that the "misinformed search" story has very little going for it. Even if it is sometimes true, it explains very little of the unemployment we actually have. There is very little evidence that bears on the other versions of the search story. A fair judgment might be that search unemployment would be worth thinking about in an economy with steadily low aggregate unemployment, but when the issue is whether policy can aim at 4 percent unemployment or must be content with 5.5 percent, the search theories will not help us.

A second strand to voluntary unemployment theory emphasizes that the *cost to the worker* of unemployment may be very low, so low that it becomes a reasonable part-time activity. The main protagonist of this view is Martin Feldstein, and the argument rests mainly on the characteristics of unemployment insurance. The key point is that wage earnings are subject to federal income tax, to a state income tax in many states, and to a (Social Security) payroll tax of almost 6 percent. Unemployment insurance benefits, on the other hand, are not taxable. A worker who suffers some weeks of unemployment in the course of the year loses only his or her after-tax earnings and receives the full UI benefit. The net loss can be quite small, especially if the worker in question is one earner in a two-earner family, so that the marginal tax rate on earnings is above the minimum. Feldstein produces an example of a worker with gross weekly earnings of $120, for whom the net cost of ten weeks of unemployment is not $1,200 but $227. Moreover, any saving of commuting costs, work clothing, or union dues must be subtracted from that.

A similar side effect of the unemployment insurance system must operate from the employer's side too. One can hardly doubt that seasonal work would be less attractive to workers were it not for the cushion provided by UI. Without UI, employers offering seasonal work would be forced to pay higher wages in normal times in order to attract workers of some given skill. UI is thus in part a subsidization of seasonal or casual employers by employers who offer regular work. The UI cushion relieves the pressure on employers to deseasonalize or decasualize the employment they offer.

Once again, it is hard to doubt the reality of the phenomenon. Nor is its existence automatically to be deplored. The *point* of unemployment insurance is to make unemployment less painful than it would otherwise be. It is very likely that there will then be some more unemployment. The important question is how much.

One fragmentary piece of evidence is to be found in a Labor Department survey of UI exhaustees (reported in the *Boston Globe,* February 29, 1976). Five hundred families were surveyed in each of four cities (Atlanta, Baltimore, Chicago, Seattle). The basic finding of fact was that one quarter of those surveyed had found jobs four months after the exhaustion of benefits. Another 14 percent had dropped out of the labor force, and the remainder—approximately 60 percent—were still unemployed. It would take detailed analysis of the complete data to extract meaningful conclusions, but this sliver of evidence does not suggest a large component of UI-induced voluntary unemployment. The figure of 25 percent is, of course, an upper limit to the number of voluntarily unemployed; presumably some UI recipients find jobs in the four months before their benefits are exhausted, and some of those in the sample who took jobs in the four months after exhaustion would have done so earlier had they been able to find work. No doubt further surveys and detailed statistical analysis will follow.

In the nature of the case, there can be no hard measurement of the size of this effect. A believer like Feldstein thinks that it may account for one percentage point on the unemployment rate, maybe more. Others estimate the probable effect to be more like half a point. In any case, the UI system was also there in the 1950s and early 1960s, when the noninflationary unemployment rate was no higher than 4 percent; of course, changing benefits and changing federal and state income tax rates must have affected the impact of the system since then. As a guess, I find it hard to believe that this factor can account for any very substantial recent *rise* in the noninflationary unemployment rate. Moreover, it bears repeating that even if Feldstein were right, it would not necessarily follow that the UI system ought to be changed drastically, any more than you would want to suppress a quick and painless cure for the broken leg on the grounds that it would encourage some people to ski carelessly.

A third strand to the voluntary unemployment argument has more to do with the *character of jobs* than the character of workers. It starts from the fact that a large part of the unemployment suffered by young workers—and also, to a lesser extent, by others—takes the form of many short spells of unemployment, and not a few long ones. Many of the separations are quits, not layoffs. The importance of this observation is that it suggests that many of the disadvantaged unemployed can find jobs, but the jobs are badly paid, unpleasant, and, above all, lead nowhere. Since such jobs are unattractive, and apparently easily available, it is no wonder that people whose opportunities are confined to those jobs frequently quit. Since the employer has made no investment in training the occupants of dead-end jobs, he does not hesitate to lay them off when business fluctuates. And so a lot of unemployment appears in this "secondary labor market" and the people attached to it.

Many explanations have been proposed for this state of affairs. It has been attributed to the youth culture, to the nature of the American educational system, to the minimum wage, to the long-time existence of an underclass who could be discriminatorily confined to the secondary labor market, and to the society's wish to preserve certain convenient services that can be provided cheaply by poorly paid, unskilled, casual labor. It is beyond the scope of this chapter, and certainly beyond my competence, to judge the weight of these various hypotheses. It is more to the point to ask if this situation has worsened sufficiently in the past fifteen years to account for any substantial rise in the noninflationary unemployment rate. We know that the proportion of youth (and women, and blacks) in the labor force has increased; to the extent that these groups populate the secondary labor market, the situation clearly has worsened. (But it would be important to study the facts on education and training as well.) One must avoid double-counting, however. Much, perhaps all, of any effect to be expected here is presumably captured in an exercise like George Perry's already described. This is merely a circumstantial account of one possible origin for the Perry shift in the Phillips Curve.

I do not think any of these stories is well established in a quantitative sense. It is well to remember that at best they represent reasons for pushing the noninflationary unemployment rate toward 5 percent. They are a story about inflation, not a story about unemployability.

INFLATIONARY EXPECTATIONS

There is another line of reasoning that has been used to urge that the noninflationary unemployment rate is now higher than it used to be. This argument has very little to do with the fine structure of the labor market, or of any other market. It is instead an argument that says the Phillips Curve was always less favorable than we thought. Pushed to the limit, it says there never was a Phillips Curve at all; society has really almost no power to choose its unemployment rate at all.

This story runs largely in terms of expectations, which means it is necessarily abstract. There is nothing observable to test it against. The story goes like this. Buyers and sellers of everything, from labor to lettuce, are aware that the value of money is changing. It is implausible to suppose that they fail to take account of their estimates of future inflation in making their decisions. They may well be wrong, but they can hardly neglect this factor. Thus it cannot be right to make a crude Phillips Curve statement like: a y percent annual rise in dollar wages goes along with an x percent unemployment rate. The significance of a y percent rise in dollar wages depends entirely on what the participants —workers and employers alike—expect to be happening to the general price level during the coming year. So one should say: a y percent annual rise in dollar wages goes along with an x percent unemployment rate provided the typical opinion is that prices will be rising at z percent a year.

Suppose it all comes true; but suppose that a wage increase of y percent is incompatible with z percent inflation, but actually pushes prices up faster than that. Then people will surely revise upward their expectations about inflation, perhaps quickly, perhaps slowly, but sooner or later. When they have done so, presumably the old x percent unemployment rate will go along with a wage increase bigger than y percent. So the *expectation* of faster inflation has worsened the trade-off. But there is worse to come. In the second year, since the wage increase will be bigger than y percent, the accompanying price increase will presumably be bigger than it was in the first year. So expectations will be revised upward again. If the unemployment rate hangs at x percent, the wage increase in the third year will be bigger than it was in the second, which was bigger than in the first. This process would go on until something happened which made everything dovetail: a combination of unemployment rate and expectations about inflation that give rise to a wage increase that is in fact compatible with the expectations.

At a minimum, this reasoning suggests that the Phillips Curve trade-off will be steeper in the long-run than in the short-run; a macro-policy that reduces the unemployment rate by one point, say, may generate only a slightly faster rate of inflation in the first year, but the inflation will worsen even if the new lower unemployment rate is held constant. At worst, it may be the case that the tail-chasing operation never ends: at unemployment rates that are too low, the inflation will keep accelerating. Presumably at unemployment rates that are too high, prices will fall faster and faster. (But this is so implausible that protagonists of the theory tend not to dwell on it.) In between there is an unemployment rate at which some sort of steady state is possible. This is usually called "the natural rate of unemployment" and, although it is hard to pin them down, believers in this theory seem to suggest something around 5.5 or 6 percent as a guess at the "natural rate" in the United States about now.

This theory can be made compatible with the apparently stable Phillips Curve of the 1950s and early 1960s if you are willing to accept a sort of "loss of virginity" amendment: if the rate of inflation is uniformly slow or slightly irregular, the expectations mechanism may be in limbo, but let the public once be sensitized to inflation, and the mechanism will come into operation. The presumption is that this kind of loss of virginity can be reversed only very slowly.

As already mentioned, a theory like this can hardly be tested directly because there is no body of fact to compare it with. I think it is fair to say that most close students of wage and price behavior accept the notion that the long-run trade-off is probably steeper than the short-run trade-off; there may be some argument about the timing and magnitude of the effect. The evidence for the existence of a "natural rate of unemployment" is very weak. Indeed, the weight of the evidence is probably against it, or postpones it to a very long run. This is a theory whose appeal is aesthetic rather than factual, and while that is a formidable advantage in a theory, it is no great advertisement for a guide to policy.

Concluding Remarks

1. It is almost certainly the case that the U.S. has had higher unemployment rates than most other industrial countries for *both* of the reasons mentioned earlier. We have pursued full employment more timidly and less assiduously than most of them. But our labor market has characteristics that make the base level of unemployment higher than elsewhere. There is more geographical and occupational mobility; scattered data suggest more voluntary turnover here than elsewhere. These characteristics are especially noticeable among the young. American youth move in and out of school, in and out of the labor market, more frequently than their contemporaries elsewhere. Much of this happens because the opportunities for steady work are pretty awful. But some of it happens for reasons of which we are rather proud in other contexts. In some countries youth unemployment rates are very low, apparently because most young people get out of school rather early, equipped and trained for only a narrow range of manual occupations, and reconciled to a correspondingly narrow set of life chances. No wonder they settle down quickly to steady jobs. It does not follow that we would wish to copy that pattern if we could. (Of course, neither should we ignore the many cases in which youth unemployment is not smilingly voluntary but rather represents a failure of labor market institutions to provide adequate employment opportunities for a segment of the labor force.) It is impossible to say how much of the excess unemployment in the U.S. arises from weak macro-policy and how much from other characteristics of the labor market. I would guess the two sources to be roughly equal contributors.

2. I have claimed that the effective barrier to high employment in the U.S. is the fear of inflation triggered by tight markets. It is possible to argue that the fear of inflation is somewhat overblown, in the sense that rising prices—within limits—do rather less damage than people fear. For present purposes, however, we must take the fear of inflation as a datum; it is what prevents us from pushing the unemployment rate at least to 3.5 percent by expansionary macro-policy.

3. If 4 percent was a reasonable target for noninflationary unemployment fifteen years ago, it is possible, perhaps likely, that a higher figure would be suitable now, *or else* we should face up to some genuine institutional changes. That says only a little; the important thing is the size of adverse change in the noninflationary unemployment rate.

4. I have tried to describe the various analytical reasons that have prompted economists and observers to believe in a worsening of the labor market situation. I do not believe it is possible to try them on for size, to evaluate the extent of the worsening—if any—to be attributed to each possible source. My pessimism does not rest primarily on the lack of diligence, intelligence, or imagination on the part of economists. We are talking about subtle effects. Not enough time has elapsed since their supposed occurrence to build up an adequate statistical record; and in any case much of the data we would need are simply not available.

5. It seems very likely to me that the magnitude of this problem has been exaggerated, and that this exaggeration is either the reality or the pretense behind economic policies that have maintained—and will maintain—high unemployment rates for a very long time. The exceptionally rapid inflation of 1973–75 drew little or no steam from the labor market. It was, in a nutshell, the response of an economy in which prices hardly ever fall to a series of very large price increases which were, so to speak, imposed on the industrial world from the "outside." The rapid increases in the prices of foods, imports in general, oil in particular, and many basic raw materials could hardly be offset by reductions in other prices. Instead they set off a series of cost-transmitted price and wage increases that could only stabilize, or even slow down, after a long time, when the new market realities will be finally reflected in relative prices. There is no reason to expect that episode to be repeated, barring another such set of major shocks to the price structure. But such episodes do have long-lasting effects, partly because they establish new patterns of expectations, and partly because it takes a long time for the cost-price interaction to work itself out in the real economy.

In 1976, our economy seemed to be "in neutral" with an annual inflation rate in the neighborhood of 6 percent. It would take a long, long time—or else maybe a 1930-style depression—to bring about a state of affairs in which the economy is adjusted to a 2 percent annual inflation, as may have been the case a decade or two ago. Even the Ford Administration proposals that will bring the unemployment rate down to 5 percent only at the end of 1980 do not seem to anticipate a rate of inflation any better than 4 to 4.5 percent a year. No adequate reasons have been given for the often-expressed belief that a faster approach to, say, 5 percent unemployment would move the rate of inflation above its 5 to 6 percent "free-wheeling" annual rate. If this belief is based on anything, it seems to rest on a probably illegitimate extrapolation to the future of the one-time events of 1973–75.

6. I cannot say if the "noninflationary unemployment rate" in 1976 is a 0.5 percent, 1 percent or 1.5 percent higher than it was in 1960. That seems to me to be about the limit of what the evidence will bear, and I do not think the evidence is very good. For those who regard unemployment, low incomes, and wasted output as a bad thing—which may not be everybody—a reasonable target for monetary and fiscal policy might

be a quick reduction in unemployment to about 5 percent followed by a cautious exploration of the territory beyond. One must be prepared to discover—though it is not a sure thing—that any more ambitious target is, for now, inflationary unless there are institutional changes.

7. What are the institutional changes one might realistically contemplate? One thought flows obviously from some of the things that have already been said: it would be a worthwhile effort to direct some of the effort of manpower policy away from trying to change workers and toward trying to change jobs. Maybe the decasualization of the docks could provide an example of what needs to be done. Deseasonalization in many trades would be a small but definite step ahead. If the social cost of fluctuating employment exceeds the private cost—if, for instance, stable business is subsidizing unstable business through the UI system or the tax system generally—then one might try to bring more pressure on businesses to stabilize employment, even if some lines of business could not survive at all. I go no further because I am out of my depth.

There seems to be an obvious case for paying more attention and devoting more resources to the transition from school to work.

There is ongoing debate about the merits of large-scale public employment to which I have only one remark to contribute. From the point of view of the inflation-barrier—which is not the only possible point of view—the effectiveness of public employment depends on the extent to which a worker so engaged "acts" like an unemployed worker in exerting downward pressure on wages and prices. If a worker engaged in public employment instead "acts" like a worker in private employment, nothing much is gained by public employment. Expansionary macro-policy could generate the same number of private jobs, with roughly the same effect on the rate of inflation and probably more effect on training and career development. One might still want public employment programs for other reasons, but not particularly for this one.

I have lost some of my enthusiasm for informal wage and price guidelines, but I think the circumstances now call for them. I do not know if they would do much good; but I cannot see that they could do any harm.

Formal wage and price controls are a more ticklish matter. Again from the narrowly economic point of view, the usual argument is that suppressed inflation is as bad as, or worse than, open inflation. The price system performs an allocative function that will not be performed if relative prices are controlled by a bureaucratic agency, even a better one than we are likely to get. Neither the flexibility nor the knowledge will be at hand to move prices in accordance with the real forces of supply and demand. One does not have to be a romantic about the normal functioning of the market economy to accept the basic truth of this argument. What it lacks is any kind of assessment of the cost of the inefficiency and misdirection of resources that would result, and a comparison of that cost with the losses the system suffers because it has to operate at high unemployment rates to avoid unacceptable inflation.

I would guess that the weight of professional opinion might accept the view that wage control would be less damaging to the efficiency of the market economy than price control, and might by itself be enough to cut the cost-transmission mechanism and reduce the inflation-proneness of the system. There are fewer basic wages to worry about than prices, and the labor market may be more segmented in the first place. The trouble with any such proposal is not merely that organized labor would oppose it. The trouble is that it would entail a genuine danger to equity. The object of the exercise is not to transfer income from workers to employers, or vice versa, but to find a way to reconcile high employment with stable prices or slow inflation. If one could be sure that, in a tight economy with wage controls but no price controls, the forces of competition among employers would be adequate to prevent a widening of profit margins at the expense of wages in general, then one might at least think about such a policy. No one can have that certainty. And if the only viable mandatory control system is a complete system of wage and price controls, it will be a last resort, in times of external crisis.

8. There are some suggestions for macroeconomic policy proper implicit in the modern view of the unemployment problem. As one would expect, they generally suggest making macro-policy a little less macro, a little more selective.

(a) For an economy that is persistently subject to stagnation, there is no substitute for generally expansionary fiscal and monetary policy. But once a reasonable balance is obtained, stabilization policy can be mostly concerned with the timing of private (and public) expenditures. The object, that is, should be to shift private spending away from boom periods into slack periods. Explicitly, temporary changes in indirect taxes and subsidies are especially well adapted to this purpose. When excess demand threatens, for example, a large temporary increase in an excise tax on consumer durables should have a strong effect in inducing consumers to postpone purchases, which is exactly the effect desired. In the same way, a temporary reduction in excise taxes should induce those who expect to buy fairly soon to buy now. Moreover, an excise tax reduction, while expansionary in its macroeconomic effect, has a downward impact effect on prices, so it is the ideal stimulus in a time of stagnation-with-inflation. The investment credit is exactly this kind of tax; it should be used aggressively.

(b) In the same vein, one might urge greater reliance on selective demand management to avoid bottlenecks which might trigger inflation prematurely. If there is slack in the construction industry, stimulate housing (presuming that more and better housing is felt to be a worthwhile social goal). When construction costs are outpacing other prices, cut back on housing and stimulate something else. I do not mean to single out housing for its own sake. If, as some fear, the next upswing should reveal tightness in a basic materials-processing capacity, then it should be possible to devise selective taxes and subsidies that would divert some of the demand pressure away from those industries, leaving enough to induce investment but not so much as to set off large price increases.

(c) Selective supply management to remove capacity bottlenecks would be a more drastic departure from run-of-the-mill policy, but it would be worth thinking about.

(d) On the borderline between macro-policy and conventional manpower policy, there might be experimentation with wage subsidies. If the unemployment problem is heavily concentrated on disadvantaged demographic groups or skill classes, then temporary subsidies could be offered to employers who make net additions to their work-forces by hiring these classes of workers. The subsidies could be accurately targeted by embodying them in "vouchers" distributed only to the intended groups, cashable by private or public employers. The device has two indirect advantages, apart from the direct advantage that it is aimed where the need is. First, the impact effect of a wage-subsidy is in the right direction. The higher costs of employing disadvantaged labor are offset by the subsidy, instead of being passed on in prices. Second, there is substantial recapture of revenues through the normal operation of the tax system. The wages of newly employed workers and the profits of their employers are subject to the usual taxation. Thus the aggregate demand–expansionary effect of selective wage subsidies need not be great, but the desired selectivity remains.

The single most important step toward full or fuller employment would be for most of the society to want it enough.

Arthur M. Okun

3

Conflicting National Goals

The goal of high employment is important in making national economic policy, but it often conflicts with other objectives and considerations. The first portion of this chapter is devoted to a review of the way the employment goal was conceptualized and implemented in relation to other national economic goals by the Kennedy and Johnson Administrations during the 1960s. I shall not attempt to interpret the goals of the Nixon and Ford Administrations, but I will draw upon the lessons of the 1970s as well as the 1960s in the second part of the chapter to discuss our current employment prospects and policies and their relationship to conflicting goals.

The Conflicts of the 1960s

The basic strategy of employment policies set forth by the Council of Economic Advisers at the start of the 1960s was followed consistently during the Kennedy and Johnson Administrations, although its implementation was initially deferred by political obstacles and subsequently distorted by the Vietnam War. The analytical framework, the basic empirical judgments, and the fundamental social values expressed in 1961 and 1962 held up extremely well during the decade.

When President Kennedy took office early in 1961, the economy was experiencing its third recession in seven years and the unemployment rate was approaching 7 percent. The Kennedy economists saw recession

ARTHUR M. OKUN, *Senior Fellow of Brookings Institution since 1969, was a member and Chairman of the Council of Economic Advisers (1964–68). The views expressed are his own and are not necessarily those of the officers, trustees, or other staff members of the Brookings Institution.*

and high unemployment as twin symptoms, in product and labor markets, of the traditional Keynesian disease of inadequate demand. While the Council's analyses stressed the human costs of unemployment as the greatest evil of a weak economy, they also emphasized the huge gap in production—proportionately three times the size of excess unemployment. The short-fall in average weekly hours of the employed, the presence of discouraged jobseekers who were not counted among the unemployed, and the depressed state of productivity in a slack economy all contributed to the size of the GNP gap.

Most of all, the Council sought to rally sentiment in favor of a strong and vigorous expansion, rather than for a mere turnaround from recession. It was in this context that a 4 percent target unemployment rate, which had been accepted at times under President Truman and not at all under President Eisenhower, was adopted by President Kennedy (without a specific target date of fulfillment) in 1961. As Heller reports, that goal was attacked from all sides.[1] In defending itself for not being more ambitious, the Council noted that "the experience of 1955–57 is . . . sobering . . ."[2] It did stress that the 4 percent goal should be achievable by stabilization policy alone and that other policy measures to improve the functioning of labor markets should "help to reduce the goal attainable in the future below the 4 percent figure."[3]

In implementing its employment strategy during the early 1960s, CEA had to overcome four principal obstacles: budget balancing objectives, price stability concerns, balance-of-payments worries, and the structural challenge.

THE GOAL OF BUDGET BALANCING

The most serious political opposition to the adoption of a vigorous fiscal policy in 1961 stemmed from orthodox budgetary principles through which balanced budgets were viewed as a virtue and deficits as a vice. Although such fiscal orthodoxy is generally linked to worries about the effects of budgetary deficits on inflation and the balance of payments, it transcends those specific concerns and is, in the minds of its exponents, a separate and indeed a prior goal.

After running a $12 billion antirecessionary deficit during fiscal 1959, President Eisenhower unfurled his 1960 balanced budget with the statement, "If we cannot live within our means during such a time of rising prosperity, the hope for fiscal integrity will fade."[4] The issue was integrity—not the price level or the gold stock. President Kennedy did not challenge such principles during the election campaign of 1960; indeed, in response to critics who implied that he would be fiscally irresponsible, he pledged himself to outperform his predecessor. And in 1961 he remained constrained by those campaign promises. However laudable that allegiance may have been on grounds of integrity, it set back the cause of economic rationality. The initial fiscal moves under Kennedy were very timid—calculated to be so small that the deficits of fiscal years 1961 and 1962 could be attributed to the unhappy heritage from Eisenhower rather than to any expansionary actions of the new administration.

Moreover, in January 1962 the President succumbed to the old orthodoxy, submitting a balanced budget even though the unemployment rate remained at 6 percent. It was only when the expansion faltered in the spring of 1962 that Kennedy reached a fork in the road of fiscal philosophy. Speaking at Yale University in June 1962, he "issued his own declaration of economic independence," as Heller has described it.[5] In that speech, the President labeled as a "myth" and an "old and automatic cliché" the proposition that deficits are dangerous and invariably create inflation. In August, Kennedy announced that he would propose a major tax cut in January 1963, which would obviously increase the deficit for the short run. From then until February 1964 "selling" the tax cut—making the case for that unprecedented stimulative measure—was the key assignment of CEA.

Heller and his colleagues had paved the way for the conversion of Kennedy by educating him and the public. One important educational device was the concept of the "full employment budget," which distinguished what the budget did to the economy from what the economy did to the budget.[6] The large surplus in that budget in 1960 and 1961 illustrated both analytical and doctrinal points. First, even though the actual budget was deeply in the red, the full-employment surplus showed that it was relatively restrictive. Second, the large size of the short-fall of tax revenues associated with a slack economy indicated that the best hope for balancing the budget lay in a return to full prosperity. That theme was intended to appeal to budget balancers; a fiscal stimulus would serve their objective, as well as the objectives of higher employment and output. Third, the new fiscal rhetoric implicitly accepted a revised, less dangerous form of fiscal mythology by promising to maintain some surplus in the *full-employment* budget even though Kennedy's economists did not believe that even full-employment deficits were necessarily inflationary under the circumstances.

As Heller reports, both Kennedy and Johnson "recognized that it was necessary to make concessions to popular economic ideology and precepts." In describing the strategy, Heller writes: "Acceptance of the huge tax cut was gained in part by claiming (a) that it was the surest way to achieve a balanced budget in a balanced economy, (b) that the debt would still drop as a proportion of GNP, and (c) that rigid frugality would be practiced in the federal budget." The economists had mixed feelings about "the homage thus paid to balanced budgets and the hostages thus given to the old deficit, debt and spending phobias. . . ." [7] Yet the whole strategy worked and the deficit taboo was basically shattered. In 1970–72 the Nixon Administration stressed full-employment budgeting as a justification for antirecessionary deficits, virtually reading the script that Heller and company had written a decade earlier.

THE INFLATION-UNEMPLOYMENT TRADE-OFF

Unlike fiscal orthodoxy, price stability was a major legitimate concern in the eyes of the Kennedy and Johnson economists. Indeed, it is generally recognized as the goal that conflicts most seriously with high employment.

The whole conception of the inflation-unemployment trade-off had changed in the 1940s and 1950s. The original Keynesian formulation of full employment did not pose an agonizing trade-off. It suggested that in a slack economy output would vary with no significant impact on the price level, because wages tended to be rigid. Beyond some point, however, extra doses of aggregate demand would strain the capacity of the economy and hence increase nominal GNP mainly through inflation with no significant further gains in output and employment. In such a world, "full employment" was well-defined. The assignment of fiscal-monetary policy was to locate and achieve the full-employment point—that level of demand that was high enough to maximize output and not so high as to cause inflation. And at that level of demand, unemployment was viewed as an irreducible minimum due to structural and frictional forces. The search for the precise balancing point was recognized as difficult, but not as a head-on confrontation between the objectives of employment and price stability.

The experience of the 1940s and 1950s made clear that such a model was unrealistic. As the unemployment rate plummeted during World War II, reaching an amazingly low 1.2 percent in 1944, it became evident that a sufficiently over-heated economy would melt frictional and structural unemployment. Clearly, if society would accept inflation—either open or else suppressed by controls—the vistas for job creation were boundless. On the other hand, the mid-1950s taught the lesson that inflationary problems could emerge at a time when demand in general was not pressing on capacity and the unemployment rate remained slightly above 4 percent. Inflation rates of 3 and 4 percent in 1956–57 seem mild by today's standards but were terribly disturbing at the time, in part because it was the first inflationary episode in two generations that was not attributable to a war. Moreover, it revealed a sharp political sensitivity to inflation, and that demonstration had a major impact on the attitudes of policy-makers.

That history was vivid in the minds of the Kennedy Administration economists as they formulated their strategy for the 1960s. The Council insisted in 1962: "There is a good reason to believe that upward pressures of this magnitude are not a permanent and systematic feature of our economy when it is operating in the neighborhood of 4 percent unemployment. The 1955–57 boom was concentrated in durable manufactured goods. . . . The uneven nature of the expansion undoubtedly accentuated the wage and price pressures. . . ." In making this argument, the Council was invoking Charles Schultze's "demand shift" explanation for the inflation of the mid-1950s.[8]

The design of the innovative guideposts policy also reflected the CEA diagnosis of that earlier experience, and their determination to prevent an encore. As Heller and his colleagues saw the problem: "Elements of major importance in the 1955–58 episode were thus the existence of relatively high demand, principally in one sector of the economy; the use of market power by management to maintain profit margins despite rising costs; the exercise of market power by labor unions in an effort to capture a substantial share of rising profits for their membership; and the transmission of these developments to other sectors of the economy." [9]

The wage-price guideposts were meant to deal with the second and third elements of that inflationary disease—the battle over income shares "where firms are large or employees well-organized, or both"; and where there is "considerable room for the exercise for private power and a parallel need for the assumption of private responsibility." [10] The guideposts were advanced as a guide to public understanding with the arguments that an informed public "can help to create an atmosphere in which the parties to such decisions will exercise their powers responsibly." [11] The guideposts themselves were a piece of arithmetic that spelled out sufficient conditions for price stability. If the rate of increase in wages (including fringes) in each industry equalled the trend of overall productivity increase for the entire economy, then labor costs per unit of output for the economy as a whole would be stable; if, moreover, prices moved in parallel with unit costs everywhere, then over-all prices would be stable, although some would rise and others decline.[12]

Just a few months after the guideposts had been promulgated, a sharp confrontation emerged between President Kennedy and the steel industry; it culminated in a roll-back of an announced price increase for steel and a victory for the administration.[13] From that point until the end of 1965, no further battles between business and the administration took place. The main deviation from guidepost performance on the part of corporations was a sin of omission—prices were not reduced in line with the guidepost criterion in some areas where productivity growth was especially rapid. Organized labor, on the other hand, consistently opposed the guidepost principle; indeed, it strongly resented the implicit acceptance of the existing distribution of income between employers and workers. Nevertheless, labor made no concerted "guidepost-busting" effort; the wage guidepost affected collective bargaining mainly by stiffening the backbone of business. It made productivity trend growth, a figure of roughly 3 percent, a wage limit that management could defend with patriotic fervor and made any price increases that would follow larger wage settlements harder to justify.

In fact, prices rose only slightly more than 1 percent per year from

1962 to 1965, and economy-wide wage increases averaged roughly 4 percent per year. To be sure, that was not guidepost perfection; indeed, by some standards, it remains puzzling that an economy with clear excess supplies (at least in 1962 and 1963) did not display a decelerating inflationary trend. Still the price performance was satisfactory and it dispelled the inflationary fears widely expressed at the outset of the decade. While it is impossible to know precisely how much the guideposts contributed to the good performance, there is substantial evidence that they did help some.[14]

The guidepost strategy was reinforced by other measures designed to reconcile the goals of high employment and price stability—that is, to shift the Phillips Curve in a more favorable direction. The planning for expansion sought a balanced advance of the various sectors of the economy—consumption, business investment, and housing—in an effort to avoid bottlenecks and pockets of excess demand. Within the administration the Kennedy and Johnson economists fought for a variety of microeconomic measures to improve the competitive functioning of markets, including liberal policy toward imports to insure their favorable price-competitive effects, reformed regulation of transportation and public utilities industries, the elimination of federal price "floors" on agricultural prices, resale price maintenance agreements, and various labor arrangements. Political obstacles to such structural reforms remained intense, and, outside the area of international free trade, the efforts were not very successful. As discussed below, manpower policies were also increasingly stressed as important tools for improving the trade-off.

With an expansion that operated within reasonable speed limits and with the aid of guideposts and other ancillary policies, the economy remained basically noninflationary as the unemployment rate moved down to 4.5 percent in mid-1965. Defense outlays for Vietnam first became a significant economic influence in July 1965, and they produced a major spurt in the economy during the second half of that year and into 1966. The war boom ended the era of price stability and initiated an era of inflation. Much of the inflation of the late 1960s is clearly attributable to the fiscal stimulus of the war and to the way the politics of limited war vetoed the recommendations of Johnson's economists to finance the war out of higher taxes. The balance of the expansion was disturbed by the big jump in demand for durable manufactures, and the reasonable speed limits were exceeded just as the economy neared the 4 percent unemployment target.[15]

If one abstracts from Vietnam—as I would love to do, for many reasons —it is nonetheless clear that the inflation problem would have intensified to some extent. By mid-1965, the absolute stability of wholesale prices that had marked the early years of the 1960s had given way to a modest upward trend. Some price pressures due to demand were beginning to appear. In my judgment, the 4.5 percent unemployment rate that had been reached by mid-1965 was on the outer edge of the danger zone. I would guess that even a moderately paced move downward to 4 percent unemployment through aggregate demand policies would have entailed a rising inflation rate—perhaps up to 3 percent. And I further suspect that such a rate would not have been acceptable to the nation. In short, I believe that the 4 percent unemployment target of aggregate demand policies adopted by the Council in 1961, though close to the mark, was probably a shade on the over-ambitious side.

When the economy became engulfed by excess demand during the Vietnam boom, the guideposts were badly battered. The first major outburst of inflation took place outside the province of big labor and big business—in food and services, and in wages of low-skilled workers. With nonunion wages accelerating and consumer prices rising 3 percent during 1966, it became patently unrealistic for the Johnson Administration to insist that collective bargaining settlements be limited to the 3 percent trend growth of productivity. The Council backed away from its numerical wage guideposts in 1967 and 1968, stressing the need for less than full escalation of wages, but offering no specific quantitative standard for a partial offset to increases in the cost-of-living. Jawboning efforts to curb price increases were stepped up, and informal campaigns were conducted to talk down wages in some specific settlements.[16]

The experience of 1969, when these efforts were disbanded by the Nixon Administration, indicated that the 1966–68 suasion had had some success.[17] But voluntary restraint had never been meant to hold back the tides of excess demand, and it did not. Some historical studies of the period imply that a more determined and better coordinated administration effort on specific wage settlements, like the airline mechanics in 1966, might have made the differences.[18] As I see it, with excess demand driving up prices and wages outside the big labor and big business sectors, the guidepost dike was fundamentally undermined. The particular wage negotiation that shattered the dike might have been altered; but its ultimate collapse was inevitable and could not have been prevented simply by better jawboning. With unemployment at 3.5 percent and industrial operating rates above 90 percent, demand was too strong to avoid inflation.

THE BALANCE OF PAYMENTS

Defending the dollar—or, more accurately, the convertibility of the dollar for gold at the stated price of $35 per ounce—was a major goal of policy in the 1960s, and it conflicted with the targets for domestic prosperity and high employment. The Bretton Woods system was predicated on the dollar's role as a reserve currency, which in turn was linked to its convertibility with gold. Maintenance of that role for the dollar was conceived as a part of U.S. world leadership and national security, and thus its perceived value to the United States transcended any objective economic calculation. After major U.S. payments deficits and gold losses

in the late 1950s, the commitment of the Kennedy Administration to
$35 gold convertibility was an issue of worldwide suspicion in 1961. To
restore confidence, President Kennedy made such convertibility an article
of faith and honor. President Johnson renewed those pledges with equal
vigor and vehemence when he took office. Thus, in order to help maintain
the exchange rate, our presidents gave hostages against any subsequent
devaluation. The presidential commitments delighted many Treasury
officials and most private bankers; but pained most economists—in and
out of government.

Attempting to reconcile the objective of international payments equilibrium at a fixed exchange rate with domestic full employment was a
challenging assignment for economic policy-makers. Clearly, higher
levels of domestic demand entailed higher demands for imports (and also
some discouragement to the supply of exports), which worsened the payments deficit. The Kennedy economists argued however that the U.S.
trade surplus would improve despite a return to full employment so long
as U.S. prices remained stable. That prediction was borne out during
the first half of the 1960s. Until the Vietnam inflation, the progress in
the U.S. trade account exceeded even the most optimistic estimates at the
beginning of the decade. In fact, relative prices improved as the United
States, unlike many of our major trading partners, maintained price
stability.

The reconciling strategy of the Kennedy economists also included other
elements. One was the role of supply capabilities in influencing the trade
account: "Advances in productivity and improvements in technology
will also enable U.S. goods to compete more effectively with foreign
products. . . ." [19] Competitiveness of foreign trade thus became a key
argument for the investment tax credit, as well as for accelerated depreciation and for a cut in corporate rates. Another element was "operation
twist," an effort to influence the structure of interest rates "so as to hold
down the cost of long-term funds for investment in new plant and equipment while raising short-term rates to minimize the outflows of volatile
funds to other countries." [20] Aid-tying, domestic procurement, and similar
measures were also used to save foreign exchange, but these policies often
pained the economists, who saw them as distorting allocation.

The Kennedy economists believed that, by providing more incentives
to invest at home, prosperity would curtail foreign investments, which
were a key outflow in the overall deficit.[21] That argument was logical
and plausible, and even had bipartisan support.[22] Nevertheless, it turned
out to be wrong—virtually alone among the many analytical principles
and predictions made by the original Kennedy Council. Domestic prosperity did indeed encourage investment at home, but not at the expense
of investment abroad; instead, it seemed to whet the appetite of the
business community for more capital spending everywhere. Early in
1965, the Johnson Administration launched a voluntary cooperation

program to hold down direct investment abroad by U.S. companies and foreign borrowings from U.S. banks. In 1968, these direct controls on capital outflows were made mandatory. Kennedy and Johnson economists had to grit their teeth repeatedly about these specific interferences with the international flow of capital; but they saw them as lesser evils than policies that would have destroyed jobs at home in order to attain payments balance. Flexible exchange rates (or devaluation) remained "unthinkable" alternatives throughout the 1960s, and CEA had to accept that fact of life. In retrospect, one can merely sigh with relief that the reconciling strategy kept us from doing even more foolish things than we did to "defend the dollar." It is more comic than tragic now that a valuation of the dollar, established at a time when Western Europe and Japan were in shambles, became a prime article of national prestige. It probably is no accident that it took a Republican administration to cut the link to gold (just as to forge a link to China!).

THE STRUCTURAL CHALLENGE

The final major obstacle to the implementation of the CEA strategy for full employment in the early 1960s was the alternative diagnosis of high unemployment as "structural" rather than macroeconomic. Emphasizing that even at the peak of expansion in 1960, the unemployment rate remained at 5 percent, and that unemployment was very uneven among demographic groups, occupations, industries, and regions, some insisted that the unusually high rate of unemployment in 1961 was far more than a cyclical phenomenon and that it lay beyond the reach of fiscal-monetary stimulation. They contended that the economy had experienced a structural deterioration in labor markets. Some linked this thesis to automation, for example, Robert Theobald predicted without qualification: "Unemployment rates must therefore be expected to rise in the sixties. . . . No conceivable rate of economic growth will avoid this result." [23]

It was an unfortunate historical accident that structural efforts to improve labor markets were presented to the government and the public largely as substitutes rather than complements for aggregate demand policies. To be sure, some eclectic economists thought that manpower programs deserved a greater emphasis right from the start and yet were prepared to support CEA's macroeconomic fiscal-monetary strategy. But the main emphasis on the structural side came from those who expounded a structural deterioration thesis that was inconsistent with demand stimulation. This group included some strange bedfellows. Its conservatives felt that structural deterioration made it necessary to do nothing and simply accept higher unemployment rates. A less conservative and less conventional splinter group advocated shorter work weeks, earlier retirement, and "make-work" projects of low productivity. Still another group advocated manpower training and labor market placement and information as ways to make the square pegs fit into the round holes of the labor market.[24]

At every step of its efforts to promote a more stimulative fiscal policy in 1961–63, the Council was challenged by the structural deterioration thesis. In the first major public presentation of its strategy in 1961, CEA offered a 13-page supplement that lined up the numbers to demonstrate that unemployment was not hardcore and that the "high overall rate of unemployment comes from higher unemployment rates group by group category by category, throughout the labor force." [25] The Council was supported by a JEC staff study later in 1961.[26] In promoting the tax cut in 1963, CEA was again battling the same enemy.[27] And as late as May 1965, I was involved in the old debate.[28] When the returns were in, it became clear that, as the CEA had predicted, the overall reduction in unemployment had strongly benefited those who had been at the back of the hiring line and viewed by the structuralists as "hardcore." Unemployment fell most among black adults, the less educated, the low-skilled and those in depressed regions.

Table 1 shows unemployment rates for various demographic, occupational, industrial, and educational groups for five years in the past generation: three prosperous ones in which the unemployment rate ran between four and five percent—1956, 1965, 1973—and two particularly bad years—1961 and 1975. By any reasonable standard, I believe the most significant message of the table is the stability of the structure of unemployment rates over time. If one adds roughly a quarter to each group's unemployment rate in 1961, a remarkably good estimate of its unemployment in 1975 is obtained (just as the overall rate rose by roughly one-fourth from 6.7 to 8.5).

There have been some detectable shifts over the period, nonetheless. Between 1956 and 1965, unemployment grew worse for teenagers, especially for nonwhite teenagers. Adult males, both white and nonwhite, have experienced a favorable shift over time, although a change in the unemployment questionnaire in 1967 was one contributor to this development. On the other hand, some particularly favored groups—white collar workers, government workers, and people with college diplomas —seem to have lost a bit of their sheltered position over time.

All in all, the one significant shift in the structure of unemployment has been the relative rise among teenagers. Their share of the labor force has increased enormously, reflecting the baby boom of the late 1940s and the 1950s, and their unemployment rates stayed high. I conceded that one point (and no more) to the structuralists back in 1965, but reiterated the importance of prosperity even for that group: "The stability and stubbornness of the teenage rate of recent years reflect a standoff between upward supply trends and downward demand pressures. . . . Their job gains tend to be especially small in periods of sluggish overall

TABLE 1. UNEMPLOYMENT RATES FOR SELECTED GROUPS, 1956, 1961, 1965, 1973
AND 1975 a

	1956 b	*1961* b	*1965*	*1973*	*1975*
TOTAL, ALL CIVILIAN WORKERS	4.1	6.7	4.5	4.9	8.5
BY DEMOGRAPHIC GROUP					
Nonwhites, 16 to 19	18.1	27.7	26.5	30.3	36.9
Whites, 16 to 19	10.1	15.3	13.4	12.6	17.9
Nonwhite males, 20 and over	7.4	11.7	6.0	5.7	11.7
Nonwhite females, 20 and over	7.8	10.6	7.5	8.2	11.5
White females, 20 and over	3.7	5.7	4.0	4.3	7.5
White males, 20 and over	3.0	5.1	2.9	2.9	6.2
BY OCCUPATION					
Blue-collar	n.a.	9.2	5.3	5.3	11.7
Service	n.a.	7.2	5.3	5.7	8.6
White-collar	n.a.	3.3	2.3	2.9	4.7
BY INDUSTRY c					
Manufacturing	4.7	7.8	4.0	4.3	10.9
Wholesale and retail trade	4.5	7.3	5.0	5.6	8.7
Finance and services	4.0	5.5	4.1	4.3	6.6
Government	1.7	2.5	1.9	2.7	4.0
BY DURATION OF EMPLOYMENT					
15 weeks and over	0.8	2.2	1.0	0.9	2.7
BY EDUCATIONAL ATTAINMENT d					
Less than 8 years e	7.1	8.8	6.8	5.6	12.4
8 years	4.7	7.2	5.0	6.7	11.3
12 years	3.0	5.1	4.1	4.6	9.1
13 to 15 years	2.9	3.7	3.3	4.0	6.9
16 years or more	0.7	1.4	1.4	2.1	2.9

Source: U.S. Department of Labor

a The subgroups within each group are ordered according to the rank, from high to low, of their 1961 unemployment rate.

b Unemployment rates by educational attainment are not available for 1956 and 1961. The rates shown are for 1957 and 1962.

c These data are for all wage and salary workers rather than all civilian workers.

d For 1957, 1962 and 1965, the data are for persons aged 18 and over. In 1973 and 1975, they are for persons aged 16 and over.

e This group includes persons reporting no school years completed.

increases of employment. . . . Teenagers are at the back of the hiring line. And it is, therefore, all the more important that the hiring line be shortened sufficiently to bring increasing job gains for them." [29]

CEA spokesmen had emphasized repeatedly that structural unemployment was a problem, although not worse than it had been in the 1950s. In March 1961, Heller and his colleagues had insisted: "It is no part of our intention to cry down structural unemployment or explain it away.

The problems of younger and older workers, of nonwhite members of the labor force, of the technologically displaced, and of the distressed need to be attacked at the source." [30]

The 1962 Report strongly endorsed employment services and training programs as ways of ultimately facilitating an even more ambitious unemployment target.[31] To the Council, success in training programs required an expansion of overall labor demands; thus Otto Eckstein warned against the danger of a "bitter harvest of trained and educated" jobseekers if labor markets were allowed to weaken as training was stepped up.

Consistent with that view, CEA enthusiasm for manpower policies increased during the latter 1960s when aggregate demand policies had accomplished (indeed, overaccomplished) their objectives. Gardner Ackley sounded a strong appeal for manpower activities in October 1966.[32] Both the 1967 and 1969 CEA Reports devoted substantial sections to ways in which frictional and structural unemployment might be reduced, including on the menu, relocation assistance, general education subsidies, programs to reduce seasonality, and direct training.[33] In the 1969 Report, the swansong of the Kennedy-Johnson era, the Council felt emboldened to express its concerns about "negative" manpower policies such as overly restrictive occupational licensing and excessively rapid rises in minimum wages.[34]

In retrospect, manpower programs had to compete with many other techniques by which Johnson's Great Society sought to advance social conditions at the same time that a war was being fought. Those programs experienced a major expansion, but, in my judgment, did not get as high a priority as they deserved. I suspect that the initial push for manpower policies by some of their advocates as substitutes rather than complements for macroeconomic policies harmed the cause of those programs throughout the debate.

In retrospect the basic Council strategy worked amazingly well and achieved full utilization of resources on a macroeconomic basis. While it lasted, full employment meant a great deal to the country. It restored confidence in the vigor and vitality of the American economy that had been seriously in question at the outset of the decade—when Khrushchev was threatening to bury us economically and Gunnar Myrdal was identifying the weakness of the American economy as the world's most serious economic problem. In combination with various new and expanded social programs, it helped to accomplish the remarkable 40 percent reduction in people under the poverty income-line during the 1960s, facilitated the mobility of workers that narrowed geographical income disparities, and widened employment opportunities for women and black men. It defused the political pressures for protectionism, make-work, and labor supply restrictions. Indeed, full employment did everything that could reason-

ably have been expected of it, and nearly everything CEA had predicted
—with the exceptions of foreign investment and teenage unemployment.
But the overfull employment of the Vietnam period did one thing that
was unexpected and unpredicted at the outset; it created a torrent of
inflation.

Challenge of the Late 1970s

The Johnson legacy to the Nixon Administration included the boon
of prosperity and the bane of inflation. From 1969 to 1976, prosperity
disappeared (except for a brief interval in 1972–73), but inflation was
preserved and seriously intensified (except during 1972). Apart from the
resort to comprehensive and stringent price and wage controls in 1971–72,
the primary instrument for fighting inflation since 1969 was fiscal-monetary restraint; and it lowered growth and raised unemployment. But, as
it turned out, high levels of unemployment have proved to be rather
ineffective curbs on inflation. Thus, the nation has had the worst of
both worlds. Macroeconomic strategies that required high unemployment were socially mitigated by extension of unemployment insurance,
a major growth in food stamps, and other palliatives that reduced the
human costs imposed on the victims of unemployment. While such
measures have made unemployment somewhat more tolerable and less
inhumane, it remains costly to its victims and to the nation.

The unemployment rates of virtually all groups in 1976 exceeded those
of fifteen years before at the outset of the Kennedy Administration. Un-
questionably, the medicine of macroeconomic stimulation—tax cuts,
increased federal spending, accommodative monetary policies—that generated the unemployment reductions of the early 1960s have the ability to
repeat the cure in the late 1970s. Again, the limitations arise from conflicting goals. But it is now a single conflict—not a fourfold set of obstacles.
Although budgetary orthodoxy has occasionally reared its irrational
head in the Ford Administration—as in the speeches of John Simon,
Secretary of the Treasury——it does not have much force. In that respect,
the 1960s accomplished a lasting improvement in fiscal policy-making.
The system (or nonsystem) of flexible exchange rates has clearly removed
the balance-of-payments constraint as a symbol of pride or prestige and
a do-or-die issue. The more valid parts and proposals of the structural
challenge have been gradually blended into a synthesis with macroeconomic policies. Three of the four major obstacles that stood in the
way of full employment policies in the early 1960s have been chopped
down if not fully rooted out. But the remaining obstacle—concern with
inflation—looms far larger today than it did then. We have dispelled
myths; we have changed institutions; but we have lost ground persistently
on the inflation-unemployment trade-off.

In this environment, the creation of jobs threatens the creation of inflation in the minds of the American public and their elected representatives in Washington. And that is why the prospects for employment during the remainder of the decade look so bleak.

The last bright spot in our economic annals was a period in 1972 when inflation was reduced to a 3 percent rate, while the economy gained momentum and unemployment declined. Although the abatement of inflation was enhanced by the price and wage controls in effect at the time, these controls clearly were not conflicting seriously with market forces during the course of 1972. The explosion of inflation that began early in 1973 is still hard to explain or comprehend in full. Labor markets were not tight, and wages did not accelerate for quite a while; the unemployment rate of 4.9 percent in 1973 was not accompanied by shortages of labor or indications that employment was overfull. Nor were industrial operating rates in the aggregate particularly high. The evidence does suggest, however, that excess demand became acute in certain world-traded commodities and in some key materials and materials-processing industries at home. Starting in the fall of 1971, the economy was spurred by highly stimulative fiscal-monetary policies, and it is clear in retrospect (but to me—and to nearly all economists—*only* in retrospect) that these policies should have been tightened sometime during 1972. Nonetheless, most of the explosion of consumer price inflation to a 9 percent rate during 1973 and a 12 percent rate by the end of 1974 cannot be attributed to fiscal and monetary policy by any stretch of the imagination. In my judgment, mismanagement of domestic food supplies added more to inflation in 1973 than did all the monetary and fiscal errors combined; from December 1972 to September 1973, the acceleration of food accounted for five-sixths of the total acceleration in prices. The devaluation engineered at the beginning of 1973 impaired price stability far more than had initially been recognized. By the end of the year, OPEC made fuel the key factor in the inflation that continued and intensified during 1974, even as the economy slumped into recession.

As a result of repeated decisions to use monetary and fiscal policy to fight the inflation rather than the recession, the economy experienced its most severe recession since the 1930s.[35] The decline in real GNP from late 1973 to early 1975 was twice the size of our deepest previous postwar recession. Unemployment averaged 8.5 percent during 1975, far above the previous postwar annual high of 6.8 percent for 1958. Inflation moderated roughly to a 6 percent rate early in 1975 but displayed little further deceleration during the course of the year.

Forecasts for 1976, including those of the Ford Administration, pointed to a continuation of 6 percent inflation. Indeed, the Administration predicted essentially the same figure for 1977.[36] In longer range projections that are carefully distinguished from best-estimate forecast, the Administration showed unemployment rates remaining high—6.9 percent in 1977, 6.4 percent in 1978, and 5.8 percent in 1979. This moderate but sustained recovery should ultimately, according to these projections, bring the inflation rate down to 4 percent at the end of the decade.[37] The assessment paints a bleak picture, both of our prospects for employment gains and of the effectiveness of high unemployment as a remedy for inflation. The pessimism on the latter count should be regarded as candid realism. Among the many statistical estimates made by economists, even the more optimistic ones suggest that about 2 extra points of unemployment for a year—a loss of roughly $100 billion in real GNP —are needed to yield a 1 point deceleration in the rate of wage (or price) increase.

THE SERIOUSNESS OF THE INFLATION CONFLICT

The Administration's strategy thus envisioned a large sacrifice of employment and output and only a modest further deceleration of inflation. Some who supported their aim of a moderate sustained recovery hope for greater gains on the inflation front. Those optimists argue that expectations of rapid inflation are a key influence on actual inflation, and that a sufficiently restrictive government policy can break the back of those expectations, producing a prompter and larger move to price stability for given cost in unemployment. On the other hand, one can be properly skeptical of even as much deceleration as the Administration projects. The experiences of 1933-37 and of 1959-63 call seriously into question the view that the inflation rate will keep decelerating during the recovery so long as the economy has a lot of slack. A decline in the inflation rate during the course of a recovery (with no controls) has never occurred in our modern history—although the high inflation rate that prevails at the start of this recovery is also unprecedented.

Obviously, the cost of the Administration's strategy is prolonged high unemployment. If, in the years after 1976, real GNP should grow at a rate of 8 percent rather than the 6 percent envisioned by the Administration, the unemployment rate would fall about twice as fast, reaching about 5.2 percent in 1978 rather than in 1980, as projected by the Administration. On a reasonable bet, I believe that the 8 percent growth path would probably not *accelerate* inflation during 1976–78; but I believe that it would foreclose any likely prospect for a deceleration below the 6 percent inflation rate. If unaccompanied by other policies, the rapid recovery scenario basically should be viewed as an acceptance of 6 percent inflation, a willingness to live with it, and a determination to stabilize it near the present rate.

Moreover, as I read the evidence, pushing the unemployment rate down below 5 percent through sole reliance on aggregate demand measures would make an *acceleration* of inflation likely. Indeed, allowing for the serious possibility that bottleneck factors creating excess demand inflation will again emerge from capacity limitations of specific industries (rather than from labor market tightness), unemployment rates below 5.5 percent must be viewed as getting into the danger zone. Obviously, economists will learn some more about the inflationary acceleration threshold of the economy as the recovery progresses. Conceivably, for once, we may be pleasantly surprised to find more elbow room for employment and production than we did in the disheartening experiences of the recent past. But if the nation insists on relying solely on aggregate demand policies and is committed to avoid a new acceleration of inflation, then I would reluctantly conclude that the lowest prudent, realistic target for the unemployment rate at the end of the decade is 5.5 percent.

Moreover, I do not believe that a mere levelling-off of the inflation rate at 6 percent was a credible or acceptable target under the circumstances. By the standards of any year prior to 1973–75, 6 percent is an extremely high inflation rate; it means that the purchasing power of money is cut in half in twelve years. As I see it, our economic institutions are not adapted to such intense inflation as a steady diet. If inflation does not decelerate, I would expect a drastic movement away from the current reliance on the dollar as a yardstick of measurement and a basis for calculating prices and costs.[38] The indexing of wages and salaries to the cost of living would become widespread, extending to areas where compensation has remained sticky (perhaps even including the pay of the Federal Judiciary). That could be a dramatic change since only 2 or 3 percent of all employees now have uncapped escalator clauses. The substantial fraction of private businesses that still do cost accounting on a FIFO inventory basis, that gear prices to original costs, and that accept fixed-price orders for future deliveries would be bound to alter those practices. Conventional limits to one price change per year in some industries would continue to disappear. The concept of replacement cost depreciation would be adopted into pricing practices to a much greater extent. Public utility and transport regulation would have to depart from the long established historical cost basis for price setting. Interest rates on thrift accounts could not remain at levels that give small savers negative real yields. Property tax assessments and specific excise taxes would be further reformed. Most of the adaptations in this process would tend to intensify inflation and thus to reduce the likelihood that the inflation rate could, in fact, be stabilized at 6 percent.

Against the background of history, I would expect that any acceptance of a 6 percent inflation rate in 1976 would lead to the acceptance of still higher inflation rates in the future, and I would expect most informed observers to reach the same conclusion and to behave accordingly. In the 1950s and most of the 1960s, 1 percent was regarded as the "normal" inflation rate of the United States, while 3 or 4 percent was viewed as the rate experienced in unusually inflationary years. By the early 1970s, 3 or 4 percent came to be regarded as the normal inflation rate, with 6 percent reserved for the really bad years. If, in the late 1970s, 6 percent is taken as the normal inflation rate, I do not believe that this will be the last turn of the ratchet. The inflation rate cannot be kept steady at 6 percent (or at zero or at any other rate); sometime in the future inflation will accelerate and society is again unlikely to take the steps necessary to lower it to its previous point; the ratchet will thus turn once more. In short, I am convinced that 6 percent inflation is not a credible target for policy.[39] It really reveals a willingness to accept any acceleration that comes along.

Any job-creating strategy that leads to accelerating inflation would, in my view, gain more employment now only at the expense of much less employment later. It would entail another recession whose job losses would swamp the job gains accomplished in the interim. Inflation breeds recession, not through any mechanistic economic process, but through the democratic political process. Because the public will not accept rising inflation, the policy-makers will respond to their wishes and attempt to stop it; and for that reason, they will resort to restrictive fiscal and monetary policies that will destroy jobs and spawn recession.

I believe that the public's antipathy to inflation is rational and sensible, not a figment of their imagination or a symptom of money illusion. But regardless of why the public hates inflation, the evidence that it does is incontrovertible. In October 1975, with unemployment at 8.5 percent and the inflation rate receding into the 6-7 percent range, 57 percent of respondents in a Gallup survey identified the nation's most important problem as inflation while 21 percent pointed to unemployment. A year earlier, with inflation at 12 percent and unemployment at 6 percent, Public Enemy No. 1 was inflation for 79 percent and unemployment for a mere 3 percent.[40] The fact that these attitudes are reflected in the political process offers testimony that democracy really works.

In that sense, if aggregate demand policies were the only available tools, the Administration strategy of slow growth and prolonged high unemployment would not be unreasonable. What is unreasonable is its narrow focus on aggregate demand policies alone.

THE POTENTIAL CONTRIBUTION OF OTHER POLICIES

There are important potentialities in a variety of measures that go beyond fiscal-monetary policies in ameliorating the bitter conflict between inflation and unemployment. The basic criterion for a successful policy of this type is not whether it creates jobs but whether it provides some elbow room for creating jobs without creating inflation. Even a humble economist can proclaim with confidence that we know how to create jobs; the problem is how we can put that knowledge to use without colliding with the goal of avoiding inflation. I shall discuss five types of policies, offering quite different verdicts on their promise and potential for the future. These include: (1) pinpointed job creation; (2) manpower training and related efforts; (3) policies to promote competition; (4) direct price-reducing measures; and (5) wage-price restraints.

Pinpointed job creation—Some efforts, like the current public service employment program, seek to fund certain job slots and establish eligibility requirements to ensure that they are filled by people who are unemployed or otherwise in need of a job. These programs do not purport to build careers or to train workers, and they are typically structured to be of a temporary character.

Such measures may be valuable, in my opinion, at a time of severe recession or early recovery in producing an employment gain more rapidly than tax cuts or transfer programs might accomplish, in redistributing the burden of unemployment somewhat less inequitably, and perhaps in permitting more of a job gain to be accomplished within the constraint of a maximum budget deficit. But I see no reason to believe that the programs presently in operation or even proposed offer any improvement in the inflation-unemployment trade-off. To the extent that they remove unemployed people from the ranks of applicants for private jobs, they must sacrifice downward pressure on the rate of wage inflation, just as any stimulative measure does. In principle, it would appear that some kinds of people in the ranks of the jobless may exert less of an antiinflationary effect on wages than do others, and if pinpointed job creation can fill slots with those people who make particularly small antiinflationary contributions by standing and waiting for jobs, the strategy could genuinely accomplish a greater reduction in unemployment for a given inflation performance than could general fiscal stimulation. On the basis of the evidence I know, however, the feasibility of such a refined selection from the ranks of the unemployed is virtually nonexistent. It is wrong to assume that unskilled workers represent such a group. Their wages are particularly responsive to labor market conditions; even though their unemployment rates are high, lowering those rates may reduce the antiinflationary pressure on labor markets as much as, or even more than, measures that put skilled people to work.

Much of the enthusiasm for pinpointed job creation rests on a much less sophisticated view that I have called the penicillin-in-the-throat fallacy.[41] Many political decision-makers, who trust their doctors' judgment that a penicillin shot administered in the rear will indeed cure laryngitis, do not trust the equally well-supported judgment of economists that fiscal and monetary injections into the spending stream will cure unemployment. Hence they prefer programs that directly and visibly create jobs without relying on the circulation of any medicines through the economic system.

Such naive views are even more blatantly apparent in proposals to deal with the unemployment problem by encouraging early retirement, shortening work weeks, and introducing greater protection against imports. By any reasonable standard, these are thoroughly counterproductive measures, representing the least efficient way to bring down the unemployment rate. They have to mean less production and more inflation than macroeconomic alternatives. Even if a shorter work week, for example, is not offset by higher hourly pay, it would lower unemployment merely by redistributing the existing amount of work with no extra production; and the resulting reduction in the unemployed standing in the lines of willing applicants must impose as much of a loss of anti-inflationary pressure as would a stimulative program that created the same number of added jobs with more production and more payrolls. The continuing popularity of such proposals reflects the basic misconception that it is difficult to create jobs, when, in fact, it is difficult only to create jobs without creating inflation. Such pinpointing offers no way to solve the problem of job creation without inflation creation.

Manpower training—In addition to their potential for equalizing employment opportunity, for augmenting human capital, and thus for raising the quality of jobs, manpower training efforts offer an opportunity to achieve lower unemployment rates for a given inflation rate. One way they can improve the trade-off is by reducing mismatches between the demands and supplies of various types of workers. To the extent that training can be channeled to expand the supply of workers for occupations or industries that have particularly strong demands, it can prevent bottlenecks in the labor market. Since pockets of excess demand for labor have greater inflationary effects on wages than the corresponding deflationary effects of excess-supply pockets of equal size, any improvement in the match is a bonus on the trade-off. In a sense, training is also a technique of pinpointing, but it aims at categories of jobs rather than of workers, and hence seems far more promising to me.

Another way in which training can provide such a bonus is by qualifying more people for the kinds of jobs that involve long-term attachments between employees and employers. Unskilled jobs typically have very high turnover rates—both quits and layoffs. As a result it takes a large pool of unemployed simply to balance the demands and supplies for such types of labor. On the other hand, in more skilled occupations, workers have a stake in their job and employers a stake in their workers. The turnover is thus much lower, and the required pool of unemployed needed to fill slots as they arise without creating inflationary pressures is much smaller.

In general, recent evidence about the workings of labor markets for teenagers and disadvantaged adults suggest that, in conditions of prosperity, their problems are primarily in finding good and lasting jobs rather than merely in finding jobs. The demographic and occupational groups that are most prone to unemployment have *fairly* short durations of unemployment in prosperity; they do find jobs, but they do not find jobs that are worth keeping nor employers who are interested in keeping them. The best promise for a major inroad on structural unemployment in periods of prosperity thus lies in the creation of good jobs and career jobs—with quality more important than quantity. In these efforts, proposals for government subsidies to employers and young workers who

stick together for some specified period seem intriguing as a way to reinforce the benefits of formal training programs.

In general, much needs to be done to evaluate alternative manpower
programs and to appraise their potential. It is not true that manpower
training has been tried and has failed: some options have not been
seriously tried, some have not been seriously evaluated, and some seem
to have had a fair measure of success. As Eli Ginzberg concluded in a
brief survey of these efforts: "Our option, the critics notwithstanding,
is not to discard manpower programming, but to strengthen and enlarge
the existing manpower structure." [42]

Promoting competition—In a variety of ways, government regulations
shelter various prices from competition and establish price floors without
price ceilings. Nearly all the economists participating in President Ford's
domestic "Summit" in the fall of 1974 signed a petition backing a program to slaughter these "sacred cows," whose existence has been popular-
ized by Hendrik Houthakker.[43] They listed many anticompetitive regulations, including acreage controls that remain on rice and a few other
farm products, milk marketing orders, shipping regulations that prevent
competition, resale price maintenance (since repealed), and federally endorsed union apprenticeship restrictions. A wide consensus within the
economics profession opposes such measures because they worsen the
inflationary bias of the economy. But there is extremely strong political
support for these measures; every sacred cow is the special pet of some
producer's interest group.

In contrast, there is no consensus among economists about the role of
monopoly and oligopoly in the inflationary process. The evidence is
compelling that prices in highly concentrated industries do not respond
promptly to excess supply pressures during recession and slack periods.
On the other hand, these prices also are sluggish upward in a period of
accelerating inflation, and it is not clear that they add significantly to
inflation on balance over an entire cycle. Much the same can be said of
collective bargaining arrangements, which appear to lag and display
inertia both on the upside and the downside. In my personal judgment,
specific reforms of anticompetitive practices in both product and labor
markets can help to improve the trade-off, but I do not see much potential gain from a general trust-busting or union-busting campaign.

Price-reducing measures—The government influences many prices and
costs directly through the tax system, stockpile programs, and international commodity and exchange-rate policies. Constructive and innovative use of these tools could provide a much more efficient and humane
way of cutting down the momentum effect of past high inflation rates
than that offered by the high-unemployment strategy. Particularly attractive are opportunities for restructuring taxes in recognition of the fact
that excise and payroll taxes are passed through into prices and costs
far more than are income taxes. If, for example, the $20 billion of tax

cuts enacted in 1975 had been used to reduce state and local general
sales taxes rather than federal income taxes, the increase in the cost of
living in 1975 would have been 2 percentage points lower than it was
in fact. In that event, wage prospects for 1976 would be more favorable,
reflecting the impact of past cost-of-living rises on wages through both
formal and informal arrangements.

On another front, much of the disastrous food price experience of
recent years can be attributed directly to federal policies of export promotion and to the absence of any public stocks of major farm commodities. A reassessment of these agricultural and commodity policies that
pays proper attention to their inflationary costs could brighten the prospects for the future. More generally, the current undervaluation of the
dollar in foreign exchange markets is benefiting our trade surplus, but
clearly harming our price performance. A higher exchange rate for the
dollar would, to be sure, cost some jobs in export industries, but could
well enhance the disciplinary effect of foreign competition on domestic
prices and thus provide the needed elbow room for pursuing more ambitious overall employment goals. Judging from the experience of 1973–74
when devaluation permitted U.S. firms to widen their profit margins because they had so much less to fear from foreign competitors, net exports
may be the most inflationary component of our GNP.

Wage-price restraints—Despite enormous slack in product and labor
markets, prices and wages are rising rapidly in 1976 because they have
been rising in the past. It is the heritage of past inflation that keeps inflation churning. Under these circumstances, both business and labor are on
a treadmill that they cannot get off through their own initiative. Every
group of workers must try to protect itself with larger wage increases,
and every business firm must act in self-defense and try to pass its cost
increases on to its customers. Yet, if there were some way by which all
workers and all firms could agree to raise all prices and wages, say, 3
percentage points less than they otherwise would, everybody would be
better off—with less inflation, more jobs, and more real income and output. This is a classical type of situation that cries out for cooperative
collective action. It is like the guntoting Western frontier town, where
no one could afford to disarm unilaterally, but where the collective political process provided a means to achieve personal security—a sacrifice
of the freedom to tote guns in return for the reduced risk of getting shot.
The inflationary firearms toted by American businessmen and workers
in recent years have caused a lot of accidental bloodshed, and bilateral
disarmament could serve their mutual interests.

Ideally, a government wage-price policy would achieve a parallel reduction in prices and wages below what they would otherwise be, thus
not distorting the structure of relative prices and wages or the basic
distribution of income. Obviously, such a perfectly "neutral" wage-price
policy is not feasible. The record of Phase III and Phase IV mandatory

controls in 1973 and early 1974 reduced the political acceptability of all types of wage-price measures. In retrospect, the Nixon controls were overly ambitious, overly rigid, and badly administered. But they do demonstrate the inherent difficulties of comprehensive price controls, which were fully recognized during the 1960s and which explained Ackley's and my opposition to controls even during the Vietnam War. The recent lessons underline the attractiveness of more informal and more flexible policies of government-business-labor cooperation, like the Kennedy-Johnson guideposts.

Under the circumstances which prevailed in 1976, a guidepost approach could be particularly effective. Suppose that after full consultation (although not necessarily full agreement) with business and labor, the President and the Congress established on a bipartisan basis a 6.5 percent guidepost for wage increases in 1976, along with a price guidepost that limited price increases to the pass-through of costs, with no margin widening. Even without any mandatory or statutory provisions behind these standards, the 6.5 percent wage guidepost would in my judgment, become an effective ceiling in the current labor market, just as a 5.5 percent standard under Phase II required virtually no enforcement in 1972.

In 1976 employers are raising wages rapidly mainly because other employers are also doing so; they feel obliged to treat their workers "equitably" to maintain morale and productivity and to hold down quit rates in the next period of prosperity. Once the government standard ensures that other employers will be limiting their wage increases, each individual employer is taken off the hook and happy to enforce the standard in a weak labor market. Moreover, every acceleration and deceleration in wages reliably shows up in a commensurate movement of prices after a very short lag. That statistical finding has stood up consistently through time in contrast with the reverse finding that what happens to prices is not reflected in wages on a one-for-one basis. Hence, if the standard forecast for 1976 of 8.5 percent for wage increases and 6 percent for price increases is correct, the hypothetical guidepost program could be expected to bring the inflation rate down to 4 percent by the end of 1976—not by the end of the decade after years of enormous slack, as the Ford Administration projects. Moreover, in the hypothetical world, if that program were successful during 1976, it could be repeated during 1977 with the targets lowered to perhaps 5 percent for wage increases and no more than 2.5 percent for inflation.

Clearly, the wage-guidepost side of this program would have more teeth through employer enforcement than would the price guidepost through any actions of the government. Understandably, political decision makers might be concerned that, despite the econometrician's conviction that labor costs show up one-for-one in prices, such a program might redistribute income away from workers and toward employers. I have previously suggested that such a concern could be appropriately met by contingent tax legislation that essentially provided "real wage insurance." [44] That legislation would provide that, if the consumer price index rises more than the target rate (say, 4 percent) during 1976, a tax credit on 1976 income payments would be activated for any worker with income under (say) $15,000, with the rate of tax credit set at the excess of any increases in the consumer price index above 4 percent. That tax credit would appear on tax returns for 1976 to be filed early in 1977; it would apply to the whole of wage and salary income up to the ceiling and not just to the part subjected to the income tax. For example, if the consumer price index rose 6 percent (rather than 4) during 1976, a $10,000 income worker would get back $200 through the tax credit.

With such a commitment from the government, workers could have confidence that the Executive Branch would do its utmost to meet the target, both to avoid the large drain on the Treasury that would accompany failure, and to pave the way for renewal of the program at an even lower inflation target for 1977. Meanwhile, the prospect of a significant deceleration in inflation would enable us to raise our sights on the vigor of the recovery and on manpower training and other routes to job creation.

Guideposts and real wage insurance are examples of the many items on the menu for a social compact to attain wage and price restraint equitably. As I see it, a happy ending to the stagflation story *must* involve some incomes-policy or social-compact arrangement. The experience of the last decade has demonstrated that our price and wage making institutions are prone to inflation, and our public is strongly adverse to it. The realistic alternative to wage-price restraint is prolonged high unemployment where long lines of applicants for jobs supply a costly and unreliable insurance policy against accelerating inflation. As I stated earlier in this paper, with no new arrangements to improve the price and wage performance of this economy, I would regard an unemployment target below 5.5 percent as unrealistic and imprudent. But if we can eliminate our inflationary bias and background, we can raise our sights. With the development of an effective wage-price policy, and with the support of measures to improve manpower training, promote competition, and take proper account of the direct price effects of a variety of public measures, I would be far more optimistic. I would personally bet that an unemployment target of 4 percent could be made feasible by 1980—although I would urge any public official not to commit himself to such an ambitious target until the policies are tested by experience.

Notes

1. Walter W. Heller, *New Dimensions of Political Economy* (Harvard University Press, 1966), p. 64.
2. *Economic Report of the President* together with the *Annual Report of the Council of Economic Advisers, January 1962*, p. 47. Hereafter these docu-

ments are referred to either as *Economic Report* or *CEA Annual Report* followed by the year.

3. *Ibid.,* p. 48.

4. *Public Papers of the President of the United States: Dwight D. Eisenhower, 1959* (1960), p. 12.

5. Heller, *New Dimensions,* p. 33.

6. *CEA Annual Report, 1962,* pp. 78-84.

7. Heller, *New Dimensions,* pp. 38-39.

8. See Charles L. Schultze, *Recent Inflation in the United States,* Study Paper No. 1 of materials prepared in connection with the Study of Employment, Growth, and Price Levels for consideration by the Joint Economic Committee, 86th Congress, 1st session (1969), pp. 44-77. The quote is from *CEA Annual Report, 1962,* p. 47.

9. *Ibid.,* p. 171.

10. *Ibid.,* p. 185.

11. *Ibid.*

12. *Ibid.,* p. 189.

13. See William J. Barber, "The Kennedy Years: Purposeful Pedagogy" in Craufurd D. Goodwin, ed., *Exhortation and Controls* (Brookings Institution, 1974), pp. 135-91.

14. See, for example, John Sheahan, *The Wage-Price Guideposts* (Brookings Institution, 1967), esp. pp. 79-95; George L. Perry, "Wages and the Guideposts," *American Economic Review,* vol. 57 (September 1967), pp. 897-904; comments by Paul S. Anderson, Michael L. Wachter, and Adrian W. Throop, and reply by Perry, *American Economic Review,* vol. 59 (June 1969), pp. 351-70; Otto Eckstein, "Money Wage Determination Revisited," *Review of Economic Studies,* vol. 35 (April 1968), 133-43; and Robert M. Solow, "The Wage-Price Issue and the Guideposts," in Frederick H. Harbison and Joseph D. Mooney, eds., *Critical Issues in Employment Policy,* A Report of the Princeton Manpower Symposium, May 12-13, 1966 (Princeton University, 1966), pp. 57-73.

15. See Arthur M. Okun, *The Political Economy of Prosperity* (Brookings Institution, 1970), pp. 62-99.

16. See James L. Cochrane, "The Johnson Administration: Moral Suasion Goes to War" in *Exhortation and Controls,* pp. 193-298.

17. See Arthur M. Okun, "Inflation: The Problems and Prospects Before Us," in Arthur M. Okun, Henry H. Fowler, and Milton Gilbert, *Inflation: The Problems It Creates and the Policies It Requires* (New York University Press, 1970), pp. 43-53.

18. W. W. Rostow, *The Diffusion of Power* (Macmillan, 1972), pp. 321-323.

19. *CEA Annual Report, 1962,* p. 162.

20. Heller, *New Dimensions,* p. 75.

21. Walter S. Salant and others, *The United States Balance of Payments in 1968*, materials presented by the Brookings Institution to the Joint Economic Committee for consideration in connection with its Study of the United States Balance of Payments, 88th Congress, 1st Session (1963), pp. 21-23.

22. See Paul W. McCracken, "The U.S. Balance of Payments Problem and Domestic Prosperity," in Paul W. McCracken and Emile Benoit, *The Balance of Payments and Domestic Prosperity*, Michigan International Business Studies, 1 (University of Michigan, 1963).

23. Robert Theobold, "Abundance: Threat or Promise?" *The Nation*, May 11, 1963, p. 394.

24. See Charles C. Killingsworth, "The Bottleneck in Labor Skills," in Arthur M. Okun, ed., *The Battle Against Unemployment* (Norton, 1965).

25. Council of Economic Advisers, "The American Economy in 1961: Problems and Policies," in *January 1961 Economic Report of the President and the Economic Situation and Outlook*, Hearings before the Joint Economic Committee, 87th Congress, 1st session (1961), Supplement B, p. 378.

26. Joint Economic Committee, Subcommittee on Economic Statistics, *Higher Unemployment Rates, 1957–60: Structural Transformation or Inadequate Demands*, 87th Congress, 1st session (1961).

27. *CEA Annual Report, 1964*, Appendix A.

28. Arthur M. Okun, "The Role of Aggregate Demand in Alleviating Unemployment," in William G. Bowen and Frederick H. Harbison, eds., *Unemployment in a Prosperous Economy*, A Report of the Princeton Manpower Symposium May 13-14, 1965 (Princeton University, 1965).

29. *Ibid.*, pp. 75-76.

30. Council of Economic Advisers, "American Economy in 1961," p. 382.

31. *CEA Annual Report, 1962*, pp. 92-95.

32. Gardner Ackley, "Vandeveer Memorial Lecture," delivered at Southern Illinois University, Carbondale, Illinois, October 26, 1966 (processed).

33. *CEA Annual Report, 1967*, pp. 100-13; and *1969*, pp. 98-106.

34. *CEA Annual Report, 1969*, pp. 102-3.

35. For a more detailed discussion of the 1973–74 period, see Arthur M. Okun, "What's Wrong with the U.S. Economy? Diagnosis and Prescription," *Quarterly Review of Economics and Business*, vol. 15 (Summer 1975), pp. 21-34 (Brookings General Series, Reprint 305).

36. *The Budget of the United States Government: Fiscal Year 1977*, p. 25.

37. *Ibid.*, p. 26.

38. See Arthur M. Okun, "Inflation: Its Mechanics and Welfare Costs," *Brookings Papers on Economic Activity*, 1975, no. 2, pp. 351-90.

39. For a fuller treatment of this issue, see the views expressed in Arthur M. Okun, "The Mirage of Steady Inflation," *Brookings Papers on Economic Activity*, 1971, no. 2, pp. 485-98, and other contributions to that symposium:

William Fellner, "Phillips-type Approach or Acceleration?" pp. 469-83; and Robert J. Gordon, "Steady Anticipated Inflation: Mirage or Oasis?" pp. 499-510.

40. *Gallup Opinion Index,* Report No. 125 (November-December 1975), p. 93.

41. Okun, "Role of Aggregate Demand," p. 80.

42. "Manpower Training: Boon, Not Boondoggle," *Challenge,* vol. 16 (September/October 1973), p. 56.

43. For a description of the proposed changes in government regulations, see Thomas G. Moore, "A Program to Ease Price Pressure," in "The Economists' Conference on Inflation: Report," vol. 1 (1974; processed), pp. 325-335. A listing of the economists who endorsed the proposals appears in *Ibid.,* pp. 11-13.

44. Arthur M. Okun, "Incomes Inflation and the Policy Alternatives," in *Ibid.,* pp. 369-70.

Lloyd Ulman

4

Manpower Policies
and Demand Management

The move to relegate the term manpower policy to the dustbin of
sexist nomenclature is accompanied by a tendency to broaden the jurisdiction involved and to include it in a more comprehensive collection of
policies to provide income support and direct job creation as well as
training and job search.[1] Minimum wages, public employment, unemployment compensation, and employment subsidies, together with manpower development and training, are included in this collection and,
therefore, in this discussion. These policies pursue certain common objectives, sometimes as competitors, sometimes as collaborators. Some of
the objectives of the various labor market policies are also goals of demand management; and this relationship has generated some of the
principal criteria by which labor market instruments have come to be
judged. Does the policy in question work at cross purposes with aggregate stabilization measures? If not, can it be a useful supplement to
demand management? And finally, can it serve as a necessary supplement,
enabling demand management to accomplish what it might not be able
to do on its own?

The Limitations of Traditional Demand Management

Some of the original labor market policies antedated the "Keynesian
revolution" and came to be regarded as institutional casualties of that

LLOYD ULMAN *is Professor of Economics and Director, Institute of Industrial
Relations, University of California, Berkeley. Dr. Ulman was Senior Labor
Economist, Council of Economic Advisers (1961–62) and in 1970–74 a member
of the National Manpower Advisory Committee. In 1966 he edited the American
Assembly's book* Challenges to Collective Bargaining.

revolution in economic thought and policy-making. To the extent that demand management could stabilize the economy at satisfactorily high levels of employment, there would be less need for labor market policies which were designed merely to alleviate the burden of current unemployment or to repair some of the ravages left in the wake of past unemployment.

Yet the Keynesian analysis also provided new justification for some of the major manpower policies, both in situations in which "Keynesian" policies would be efficient and in situations in which they would be inefficient in terms of the employment objective. In the first place, the Keynesians warned of the dangers of policies which aimed at achieving recovery through cutting money wages and prices: employers will expect wages to continue falling and thus will hold off rehiring workers; and workers, like all consumers, will expect prices to continue falling and thus will hold off spending more. The preferred alternative would be policies designed to raise demand in the various sectors of the economy; but policies which set floors under wages and prices—including minimum wage legislation—might at least help by stabilizing expectations in a situation which is already deteriorating. In the second place, Keynesians emphasized virtue as a stabilizer in some of the policies which had been put forward mainly as palliatives. Thus unemployment insurance was found to possess the properties of an "automatic stabilizer" because it tends to inject more spendable funds into the market economy than it withdraws when unemployment is high, while it withdraws in taxes more than it pays out in benefits when unemployment is low and inflation is the main threat. Moreover, in view of the considerable and persistent public distrust of deficit financing in the United States, a system which was consistent with the popular postwar objective of "balancing the budget over the course of the cycle" lent the Keynesian cause appreciable political appeal. The reverse was true of public works and other public employment measures; in this case, Keynes contributed considerably more, in the way of intellectual respectability, to the politicians than they returned in the form of contracyclical efficiency.

The appropriateness of a different set of labor market policies—measures designed to improve worker productivity—to conditions characterized by the coexistence of undesirably high rates of both unemployment and inflation can be found in a more generalized approach to the labor market, of which the standard Keynesian model is a special case. The sufficiency of expansionist monetary-fiscal policy can be inferred from the standard model because the latter explicitly assumes homogeneous and competitive labor markets in which employment and unemployment are measured in man-hours of equal economic productivity, or "labor units." Then successive equal increments of aggregate money demand fed out by the authorities could buy equal increments of employment at constant money wages until unemployment disappears, at which point any further increments in demand would go entirely into higher wages (and prices).

Under these conditions, labor market policies would not be needed to help the economy reach full employment without inflation; neither could they damp down any wage inflation which occurred after that point—which Keynes called "true inflation"—had been reached. This model served well enough to illustrate to Keynes' contemporaries how monetary-fiscal policy could reduce unemployment from the catastrophically high levels of the day; it also serves to show how money wages can rise while there are still unemployed labor units and, therefore, before the point of "true inflation" is reached. All one has to do is to relax the assumption that all job-seekers and job-holders are bundles containing the same number of homogeneous and identical labor units and assume instead (with later authors) that the unemployed bundles are queued up before the hiring gates of the economy in order of their skill and efficiency, with the most skilled and efficient at the head of the line. Now successive increments to effective demand will buy successively smaller increases in productivity and output and successively greater increases in unit costs and prices—assuming that all workers are not paid "in strict proportion to their efficiency." (Bringing progressively less efficient plant and equipment into production will produce the same sort of effect.) Moreover, the same results could be produced by lack of substitutability among different types of labor (and other resources), as a result of which bottlenecks would occur. (Now one might think of unemployed labor being arrayed in more than one queue, each specialized as to occupation or skill and with some shorter than others. Bottlenecks will occur after aggregate demand has increased sufficiently to eliminate the shorter queues of the [more skilled] unemployed, leaving the unemployed in the rest of the longer queues with no complementary labor to be paired off with.) Furthermore, hourly wage rates (as the numerator of the fraction unit labor costs) might rise as unions take advantage of the increased ability of employers to grant wage increases while their respective labor markets are still not tight enough to make them desirous of doing so in the absence of bargaining pressure.[2]

Finally, one must take into account not only such facts of life as labor—which is of varying quality and, in some cases, low substitutability—and collective bargaining, but also interactions among these factors, which are not independent of one another. (Moreover, apart from a reference to "the psychology of the workers," Keynes took no account of the potentially destabilizing effect of inflationary expectations of which so much has been made by some postwar neoclassical economists and which is evaluated in Solow's paper.) Evidently we must no longer assume that monetary-fiscal policy can suffice to bring about a noninflationary expansion up to the point of "full employment," beyond which lies "true inflation." Indeed, as Keynes put it,

> Up to this point the effect of monetary expansion is entirely a question of degree, and there is no previous point at which we can draw a definite line

and declare that conditions of inflation have set in. Every previous increase in the quantity of money is likely, in so far as it increases effective demand to spend itself partly in increasing the cost-unit and partly in increasing output.[3]

It would also appear that the road to full employment becomes progressively steeper as the summit is approached. At higher levels of employment more queues are exhausted and more bottlenecks may be likely to occur, and at higher levels of business activity union bargaining power becomes greater. Hence the Keynesian analysis seems to have foreshadowed the Phillips Curve which depicts an inverse relationship between the level of unemployment and the rate of increase in money wages and prices. Alternatively, it has been argued in effect that inflation can swallow up the whole of an increment to money demand short of full employment and that attempts to press beyond that point (the so-called natural rate of unemployment) will only result in ever-accelerating inflation, so that even if the summit is attained, it cannot be occupied for very long.

Solow argues strongly that, as an empirical matter, demand management can enable the American economy to approach much lower levels of unemployment without incurring unacceptable inflationary consequences than most policy-makers at either end of Pennsylvania Avenue believe. Nevertheless, the possibility of inflation occurring well short of full employment suggests that demand management might be made more efficient by complementary policies which are designed to make marginal costs and prices less steeply in response to increases in money income. Marginal costs may be approximated by unit costs, or resources prices (*e.g.*, hourly wage rates) divided by productivity; and so complementary policies are aimed either at holding down money costs or raising productivity, or both. Wage and price controls are an obvious example of the former variety; so is the reduction or elimination of minimum wages (which of course could involve decontrol); and even some public employment schemes have been urged for inclusion in this category. Raising worker productivity, on the other hand, is the major objective of the traditional set of manpower policies which are supposed to improve the efficiency, skill levels, or geographic mobility through the provision of information, training, and possibly subsidy.

Since both sets of policies could work to the same end and since some could be regarded as a competing alternative, while others work in a complementary fashion, it makes more than historic sense to place them all in the context of a national manpower policy for the purpose at hand. Unemployment insurance and public employment schemes should also be included, not because they potentially complement demand management in the ways described above but because they may be viewed either as ways of adapting to existing structural obstacles to noninflationary expansion or as special instruments of demand management.

But why stop there? If unemployment insurance and public employment fall within the purview of a national manpower policy in part because they can serve as instruments of demand management, why not include all of macroeconomic policy? Complementarity is a two-way street, although one of the lanes may be wider than the other. If the various labor market policies on our lengthened list are to be judged by the Keynesian criterion, among others, it is also important that macroeconomic policy be formed and formulated so as to bring out the best in the supporting labor market instruments. This would not necessarily constrain demand management; on the contrary it might require the authorities to take maximum advantage of whatever potentialities for expansion exist, including any which the labor market policies themselves might open up.

The bottleneck problem furnishes a case in point. One reason why more slowly paced, stretched-out recoveries might be less inflationary and peak at lower levels of unemployment (*e.g.*, 1961–65) than shorter booms is that they allow time for supplies of various categories of labor and plant capacity, which were relatively fully employed even at the trough of the cycle, to be increased in response to an increase in aggregate demand, so that the latter "may spend itself very little in raising prices and mainly in increasing employment." [4] To the extent, therefore, that publicly supported and/or conducted training can increase the flexibility and productivity of the labor force and hence the output potential of the economy in the short run, periods of recovery to acceptably high levels of employment can be shortened (after allowing for other special factors which Solow identifies as making a gradual approach desirable in the present context). But if the authorities fail to expand money incomes sufficiently to exploit the (now longer) stretch of constant costs which lies ahead of them, they could be perpetuating conditions for the potential emergence of more labor bottlenecks in the future and hence for the unpalatable alternatives of further stretch-out or future inflationary and quite probably abortive boom. This is so because high-level shortages of skills are created during periods when supplies are in excess of demand, so that firms reduce their training below long-term growth and even replacement requirements, while the skills of unemployed workers can become "rusty" or obsolescent.[5] *Thus prolonged stretches of high unemployment could adversely affect the unemployment-inflation trade-off.*

In summary, then, the extended Keynesian analysis yields two implications which are important for labor market policy. The first is that, while the problems of economic inefficiency to which some of the major policies of this type are directed can be generated at low levels of employment they tend to surface at higher levels of employment. The second is that one of these problems, the bottleneck problem, becomes greater in magnitude the more rapidly money income is increased, or, to put it in terms of the foregoing discussion, the larger the increment to the money supply injected at any point in time. If, therefore, manpower policy is not to be overburdened and if it is to be otherwise effective in making demand management more efficient, the latter must see to it that (a) the economy is in fact run at high levels of employment and (b) that demand management be packaged in such a way as to minimize the increment of money demand capable of yielding a given increment of employment within a given period of time.

Increasing Productivity: The Swedish Approach

The Swedes, who were the great innovators in what they termed active labor market policies, have probably come closer than any other country to meeting the conditions conducive to the effectiveness of these policies. Whereas the Keynesian analysis approaches the problems and their policy implications from the bottom up—as recoveries made in the course of an economic upswing—the Swedes have tended to view them primarily from the top as a means of maintaining (as well as regaining) full employment. This reflects a wholehearted, not to say singleminded, commitment to high-level employment; as Prime Minister Palme once expressed it, the only acceptable way to approach the inflation problem is first to realize the employment objective and then to seek to minimize inflation, employing only methods consistent with the satisfaction of that prior objective. In fact, the concept of active labor market policy was devised in the late 1940s as an alternative to a comprehensive set of controls, including price controls and a voluntary policy of wage restraint, which, with unemployment kept within a range of 1.5 percent to 2 percent, had proved ineffective in preventing inflation during the Korean War period and in keeping equilibrium on international account.[6] Thus the objective was to maintain full employment and regain sufficient wage and price stability at lower levels of money demand—in other words to lower the Phillips Curve.

To further this objective, Swedish active labor market policies have been propounded with the following attributes in mind.[7] (1) They are supposed to raise productivity growth, reduce unemployment and eliminate sectoral bottlenecks by facilitating the movement of labor from sectors of declining demand to sectors of increasing demand. Competitive theory relies on changes in wage differentials to induce such mobility, but the champions of Swedish labor market policy reject the wage mechanism. They regard wage differentials as weak and uncertain incentives to work mobility; they claim that attempts by employers to raise relative wages in sectors where labor demand has been increasing are often frustrated by matching efforts of unions in excess-supply sectors, with overall inflationary consequences; and they believe that wage differentials not fully based on differences in skill or other job attributes violate their egalitarian ethic and should be eliminated. (2) Moreover, maintenance of relative wages, in conjunction with relatively high levels of indirect taxation, may contribute to a general squeeze on profits and the prompt exodus of inefficient firms. (3) The squeeze on profits should also restrain the cost-push component of inflation. (4) Wage egalitarianism and profit squeeze have generated political support for active labor market policies; and the total Swedish effort is indeed one of considerable magnitude. (5) *Labor market policies and overall demand management should be integrated, and the latter must accommodate certain requirements of the former. (6) Demand management should, as far as possible, be implemented through selective measures targeted to particular problem sectors, which would allow an overall employment objective to be replaced by a number of sectoral subobjectives.* (7) Demand management must be prepared to accommodate (offset) the expansion or maintenance of effort by the manpower administration during upswings in economic activity or at satisfactorily high levels of activity; similarly, the manpower administration must be able to alter the proportions in which market adjustment and direct job-creating activities are combined. (8) An autonomous and centralized authority and subordinate decentralized administration are required to yield the degree of flexibility indicated by the need to apply different programs in different areas and to respond promptly to (imperfectly forecast) changes in demand. (9) Effective implementation of active labor market policies also requires active cooperation by private (union and management) groups with market power; and the more centralized these private interests are, the more flexibly the policies can be operated.

Increasing Productivity: The American Experience

The Americans have failed to practice much of what the Swedes have been preaching and some of what the Swedes have put into practice, like very high levels of employment. The Area Redevelopment Act, which was the first new operational labor market measure (and included a modest training component) since the end of World War II, was passed in 1961, a year of cyclical trough when unemployment averaged 6.7 percent. By the following year unemployment had recovered to a 5.5 percent average, but this was only half-way to the "interim" target of 4 percent proclaimed by the Council of Economic Advisers, which in turn was over two times as high as the unemployment levels which the Swedes would tolerate. Such earlier policy developments as the passage of the Smith-Hughes Vocational Education Act, the establishment of the United States Employment Service during World War I, and the funding of the Training Within Industry program during World War II had indeed occurred in a Swedish-type economic environment and were aimed at eliminating skill shortages. The postwar measures, on the other hand, were enacted against the Keynesian perspective—looking up from a deep recessionary trough. But these were conditions under which the homogeneity assumptions underlying the standard, or more restrictive, Keynesian model would presumably hold well enough to warrant the

expectations that increments to money demand would generate virtually
equal increases in output without turning up much in the way of bottlenecks until unemployment had been reduced by 25 to 30 percent. Moreover, the scarcity of specific job vacancies would deprive training
programs of training targets and thus reduce their potential effectiveness.
(Even the Swedish approach which would rely completely on selective
instruments to do the work of demand management would increase the
proportion of expenditures devoted to direct job-creating measures like
public works and grants to labor-surplus areas and decrease the proportion of expenditures devoted to training and mobility incentives during
their mild downswings.) Thus, while President Kennedy's Department
of Labor strongly supported passage of the Manpower Development and
Training Act, his Council of Economic Advisers wrote: "Unemployment
of 4 percent is a modest goal, but it must be emphasized that it is a goal
which should be achievable by stabilization policy alone." [8]

But the proponents of manpower policies doubted that stabilization
policy alone was up to the task. In their view much of the unemployment prevailing at the time was structural in nature and was due to
technological change, which was labeled "automation" to signify that
it differed in kind from all predecessors since it supposedly generated
widespread displacement of labor throughout the economy while glutting
the already affluent American consumer. Although they constructed their
hypothesis of an accelerated increase in productivity on dramatic examples of specific labor-saving innovations, they rested their conclusion
—that technological unemployment was on the rise—on two overall phe-
nomena. The first was "creeping unemployment"—the fact that unemployment was higher in each succeeding cyclical peak since the end of
the war (2.7 percent in 1953, 4.2 percent in 1957, 5.1 percent in 1960).
The second was the decline, or at least stagnation, in the employment of
blue-collar workers in manufacturing (from 14.1 million in 1955 to 13.2
million in 1957 to 12.6 million in 1960). Panel A in Table 1 makes the
same point in a slightly different way; it shows that the proportion of
production workers in durable goods manufacturing declined relative to
total employment (of production and white-collar nonproduction workers
combined) from 17 percent in 1954 to just under 15 percent in 1962.
(In both years overall unemployment averaged 5.5 percent.)

The Keynesian economists in the Kennedy Administration, supporting
the new manpower measures, sharply rejected the "structuralist" view
of contemporary unemployment. They argued that reductions in employment in particular economic sectors did not translate into increases
in overall unemployment if they were associated with greater than average increases in employment in other sectors. And they interpreted the
peak-to-peak increases in unemployment which did occur as due simply
to the Eisenhower Administration's failure to expand aggregate demand
enough to allow employment and output to grow as rapidly as increases
in the labor force and productivity would have permitted. They received

TABLE 1. PRODUCTION WORKERS AS PERCENT OF TOTAL PRIVATE EMPLOYMENT

PANEL A:

	1954	1959	1960	1962	1963	1972	1974	1974 Average Hourly Earnings	1974 Average Weekly Earnings
Mining	1.6	1.3	1.2	1.1	1.0	0.8	0.8	$5.20	$222.56
Construction	5.4	5.6	5.4	5.3	5.3	5.2	5.1	6.74	248.71
Durable Manufacturing	17.0	15.5	15.3	14.8	14.8	13.3	13.4	4.68	190.48
Services	n/a	n/a	n/a	n/a	n/a	18.6	19.1	3.74	127.16
Total Trade	22.4	22.3	22.5	22.3	22.2	23.5	23.5	3.47	118.33
Unemployment Rate	5.5	5.5	5.5	5.5	5.7	5.6	5.6		

PANEL B:

	1951	1968	1969	1974 Average Hourly Earnings	1974 Average Weekly Earnings
Mining	2.0	0.8	0.8	$3.61	$155.23
Construction	5.6	5.0	5.1	4.79	181.54
Durable Manufacturing	18.0	15.1	14.9	3.38	139.59
Services	n/a	17.4	17.6	2.61	90.57
Total Trade	21.9	22.3	22.5	2.55	90.78
Unemployment Rate	3.3	3.6	3.5		

Source: 1975 *Manpower Report of the President,* Tables A-18, C-1, C-2, C-3.

a fair amount of vindication on both counts. In the first place, the early manpower administrators were unable to uncover significant numbers of technologically unemployed workers whose skills had been displaced by automation. In the second place, the economy did go on to reach the council's interim target of 4 percent in 1965; moreover, it did so without departing from price stability. (The maintenance of price stability implied the absence of any serious skill bottleneck problems, although, as Abramovitz' interpretation of the 1958–64 period makes clear, it does not imply that the absence of bottlenecks is sufficient to insure price stability.)

However, it did take four years of expansion for unemployment to fall from 6.7 percent to 4 percent, and almost as soon as that interim goal was surpassed by a continued reduction in unemployment, prices began to rise again, and worse, continued to rise even after unemployment turned up once more and remained in the 5 to 6 percent range. Once again demand management received its share of the blame—in the first period because the stimulative tax cut advocated by the Council of Economic Advisers had not been enacted as promptly as they had wished; in the second, because taxes were not raised to counter the Vietnam War spending. But in addition the structuralist argument had resurfaced in a new form, this time directing attention to changes on the supply side of labor markets. Unemployment rates were highest, not among older, skilled, male workers (as the automation argument seemed to imply) but among women and youth—and particularly among nonwhite women, youth, and adult men as well. All of these high unemployment groups were increasing their respective relative representation in the nonagricultural labor force: the teenagers because of the postwar baby boom; the women because of the dramatic increase in their labor force participation; and the nonwhites in part because of the decline in agricultural employment. Individuals in these groups have traditionally been regarded by many employers as relatively poor substitutes for white middle-aged married men—whether because of lack of education, experience, or attachment to the labor force, or because of social prejudice —and, while their shares in total employment rose in the 1960s, so did their relative unemployment rates. Greater dispersion of unemployment rates has long been regarded as causing a more unfavorable trade-off between inflation and unemployment; and econometric and other evidence have been adduced to support this conclusion in the case of the U.S. economy.[9]

The Manpower Administration, after failing to sight its initial target among the ranks of family heads with work experience, began to concentrate its efforts on the groups where the incidence of unemployment was especially high. Its efforts were inspired and directed by the major pieces of social legislation that were the hallmark of the Johnson Administration: the Economic Opportunity Act and the Civil Rights Act (with its Title VII which forbids racial or sex discrimination in employment) in 1964; the Elementary and Secondary Education Act of 1965; the amendment of the Social Security Act (which established the Work Incentive Program) in 1967—in addition to the Vocational Rehabilitation Act, which had been passed in 1963. The new target groups included youth, old people, racial minorities, and welfare recipients. Unemployment remained for the most part a condition of eligibility for admission to the development programs, but the reduction of unemployment among the "disadvantaged" was regarded as meeting but part—although obviously an extremely important part—of the overall objective of ending poverty and economic and social inequality. At the same time, the older macroeconomic objective of improving the unemployment-inflation trade-off would be served as the different individual human bundles of labor were made more homogeneous and more equally accessible to the employing economy. In addition, the delineation of a larger number of target areas and the proliferation of programs which successive pieces of legislation brought in their wake were not incompatible with the Swedish model of multiple targets and multiple instruments. Thus accommodating the needs of the various subgroups in the disadvantaged population involved increasing and subsidizing on-the-job training as well as—and partly at the expense of—maintaining institutional training; it involved "screening in," instead of "screening out," applicants with the seemingly lowest economic potential; it involved subsidies to business enterprises (in the JOBS or Job Opportunities in the Business Sector) and to ghetto youth (in the Neighborhood Youth Corps Program); it involved running training programs in rural camps for youngsters from city slums (the Job Corps) and work relief programs for older men in rural areas (Operation Mainstream); it involved establishing Community Action Agencies in the inner cities which involved local organizations hopefully representative of minority client groups in the coordination and direction of all local antipoverty programs; it involved attempts to make welfare recipients employable (in the Community Work and Training, Work Experience and Training, and, especially, Work Incentive programs) and to employ unskilled and poorly educated persons in the performance of various routine operations performed by nurses and other professionals (the New Careers program).

But has the unemployment experienced in the 1960s and thereafter provided an appropriate set of targets for such measures; and, if so, have the latter been organized in a manner calculated to achieve a satisfactory overall impact on economic activity? Some economists, like Solow in this volume, argue that more expansionist demand management could have carried—and today could carry—the economy further in the direction of high-level employment than either converts to the new structuralism or the monetarists would allow. If so, structuralist measures could not have been expected to accomplish much in the aggregate, in an un-Swedish environment; but they might indeed be effective after general measures have driven the economy through the constant-cost terrain. But to others, including some who are more pessimistically impressed by the structure of contemporary unemployment, active labor market policies hold out virtually no promise.[10] They hold this view because, in their opinion, motivation, more than limited employability, underlies the high rates of unemployment experienced by the various demographic and racial groups to which we have referred. Their analyses differ but all are based on the position that unemployment among such groups— and especially among youth—tends to be caused by quits more than by layoffs, is of relatively short duration, and is indeed allegedly offset by job vacancies. In this sense, much of the unemployment has been voluntary. Nor, according to one school of thought, is it necessary to be deplored or reduced, for it represents purposeful investment by workers in search of better jobs and is thus conducive to higher productivity. The cost to the individual is loss of earnings during his period of search; the cost to the economy is measured in terms of job vacancies and their complementary unemployment. Some overall reduction in cost might be achieved if private investment were to be replaced in part by increased social investment in an improved Federal-State Employment Service, but duration is not a great problem in any event. Thus the search theory of unemployment affords little scope to manpower policy.

On the other hand, it is easy, as Solow points out, to exaggerate the importance of the search phenomenon (especially for economists armed with models of highly competitive markets and a neo-materialist interpretation of history). Studies have shown that only a minority of quits go into unemployment between jobs, and those who do find a better-paying job less frequently than those who remain on the old job.[11]

It would appear that on-the-job search is equally efficient and less costly, because direct applications to employers and tips from relatives and friends—traditionally the most popular methods of job seeking—are as readily available to an employed worker as to an unemployed worker. According to a recent study by the Department of Labor, the most popular and effective method of job seeking is direct application (without referral) to new employers, while job change on the basis of information supplied by friends and relatives yielded the greatest percentage increases in earnings (apart from Civil Service tests).

Nor does a divergent line of analysis point to manpower policy as a remedy. This is the so-called "dual labor market" theory; it holds that the economy suffers from a shortage of good jobs—characterized by high wages, "ladders" of promotional opportunity, and a high degree of income security—relative to the number of workers who would be qualified to hold them. They thus deny the existence of any shortage of workers with the educational background and native capacity satisfactorily to absorb the training offered by employers in these "internal labor markets." In fact, individuals who have completed high school and those who have completed up to three years of college have constituted dramatically increasing fractions of the civilian labor force in the postwar period—in the former case, from 27 percent to 39 percent between 1952 and 1974 and in the latter case from 8 percent to 15 percent. Moreover, these gains have been especially rapid among black and other nonwhite races where the proportion of high school graduates rose from 11 percent to 34 percent and the proportion of those with up to three years of college rose from 4 percent to 12 percent.[12]

Why the number of good jobs should be limited is not made clear. The best-known version of the dualist theory relates the existence of "internal labor markets" to technological characteristics which make it profitable for employers to provide specialized training and to protect their training investments by making conditions attractive enough to minimize quit rates; but the theory does not rely on technological change as a demand-limiting agent, as did the earlier automation arguments.[13]

On the other hand, there is no reason why there should be as many good jobs as there are qualified workers at every or any point in time. As a crude illustration—not a demonstration—of what might be involved, we might return to Table I and note that the relative declines in the employment of production workers since the beginning of the 1950s occurred in such high-wage sectors as mining and durable manufactures, while relative increases occurred in trade and services, where wages have been much lower. The latter indeed used to be called the "sponge sectors" of the economy; they absorbed workers who had been denied access to—not necessarily displaced from—the good-job sector. With lower wages and little in the way of good prospects for promotion, worker horizons are limited, and turnover tends to be high as people quit to job-hop or simply to leave the labor force once they have earned enough bread to tide them over for a while. Under these circumstances unemployment due to high quit rates is the product not of hope and search, but of frustration and apathy. But that scarcely cried out for alleviation through manpower policies which are primarily designed to cope with a shortage of good people, not with a shortage of good jobs.

Beyond the foregoing, it has been suggested by Rudolf Meidner that increasing productivity in the "goods" sector of the economy results in an increase in the demand for services as well as an increased supply of labor to the services sector; but, given the low productivity growth in services, their prices are raised to such levels that more and more of them become nationalized and incorporated into the growing public sectors of advanced economies.[14] Wages in the public sector, on the other hand, are high—and are maintained at high levels during general recessions—and this, according to Robert Hall,[15] has the effect of making laid-off workers in the private sector keep searching for good government jobs rather than underbid wages on good jobs in the private sector. Thus splicing these two lines of argument together, one returns to a variant of the old Demand Structuralism, whereby increasing productivity in the high wage, secondary (goods sector) generates growth and high turnover unemployment in the low-wage tertiary (services sector) and, indirectly, growth of the high-wage public sector which, in turn stimulates long-duration search unemployment in the goods sector in which the whole process started. And one might infer a rejoinder of sorts to the critics of the Demand Structuralists who held that reduction of employment opportunities in one or more sectors of the economy did not imply a rise in overall unemployment. The rejoinder is that limitations on demand—and wage rigidity—in certain high-wage, good-job sectors can induce supply reactions both in those sectors and in low-wage, bad-job sectors, which do add up to an increase in overall unemployment.

The argument that unemployment is high because unemployed workers walk around and search for job openings in the public sector can strike one as far fetched for any number of reasons. An objection made by Solow,[16] however, is particularly interesting from the viewpoint of labor market policy. This objection is that there is no reason to believe that unemployed production workers in the private sector possess the largely white-collar skills required in the public and (other nonprofit) sector. While Solow's point persuasively casts doubt on Hall's variant of search unemployment, those who nevertheless believe that such search is an important cause of cyclical unemployment might well advocate massive retraining programs to alleviate the problem. However, this assumes that there will be enough job openings to train for, and so we are returned to the objection of adherents of the dual labor market hypothesis—which is that there are not and that labor market policies are not capable of coping with the types of unemployment which result from shortages of good jobs. In fact, it is worth noting that, while in all noncommunist industrial countries the proportions of the work force in agriculture have declined and the proportions in the "tertiary" sector (largely services) have risen sharply in the postwar period, the proportions of the work force employed in the "secondary" sectors (manufacturing)—where the high-wage blue-collar jobs are mainly concentrated—began to decline in the U.S. while in Western Europe employment in these secondary sectors was still increasing.[17] Thus the task of manpower policy abroad was frequently to relocate people to and train them for employment at higher wages—especially in metal manufactures [18]—where the psychological pickings should have been relatively easy.

Yet the fact that there may be fewer good jobs than potential jobholders does not of itself foreclose a useful role for a well-designed set of labor market policies. Replacement needs exist on a considerable scale. Although quit rates are below average in high-wage industries, total separation rates are still high in absolute terms; thus in 1967, when unemployment averaged only 3.8 percent, the eight highest paying industries turned over three million production employees out of a work force of six million.[19] This afforded a not inconsiderable opportunity for civil rights policies to increase the proportion of minority workers in the high-wage labor markets; and these policies have included manpower programs targeted to the economically disadvantaged as well as affirmative action policies. The former might be regarded as complementary to the latter. If manpower services can equalize the economic potentialities of disadvantaged and more favored workers, affirmative action could dictate an employer choice on noneconomic grounds. (An analogy is presented by the following type of clause governing criteria for promotion in a collective bargaining agreement: "If ability, merit, and capacity are *equal,* seniority shall govern." This weighting of seniority is preferred by management to the union-written version: "If ability, merit, and capacity are *adequate,* seniority shall govern.") Manpower programs might help to equalize economic capability, partly because interracial differences in educational background, both quantitative and qualitative, still remain, but also because the higher levels of formal schooling now attained by members of racial minorities should make them better able to profit from supplementary occupational instruction. Finally, if affirmative action is effective in improving the quality of job openings for minorities, manpower programs should be more effective in remedying deficiencies in training and even in habits and attitudes which are often held to result from discriminatory foreclosure of opportunity. Thus when the goal is the redistribution and equalization of economic opportunity (and of unemployment), productivity-improving labor market policies would potentially be most useful when integrated with more directly restrictive policies like affirmative action in the U.S. or wage equalization in Sweden—just as when the goal is improvement in the inflation-unemployment trade-off they would be most useful when integrated with demand management.

But if policy targets do exist, are the instruments designed and operated efficiently enough to reach the targets? Tested against the Swedish criteria outlined in the last section, we do not score brilliantly. In developing a variety of programs, we have satisfied a necessary condition of effectiveness, but we have developed many of these programs independently of one another and in the absence of a set of well-defined and unifying overall objectives. This has resulted in duplication and overlapping of services at the local level, with each program often inefficiently small in scale, and competition among the chief administering agencies in the federal government. The Department of Labor favored on-the-job training for minorities and youth; the Department of Health, Education and Welfare supported the politically powerful state-controlled system of vocational education of the classroom variety; the Office of Economic Opportunity wanted community action in urban ghettoes to receive priority over the employment approach and feared that control by the state-controlled Employment Service would place the manpower programs out of the reach of the poor in the inner cities—and out of their political control. Meanwhile, as Stanley Ruttenberg wrote,

> In each major metropolitan area there were fifteen to thirty separate manpower programs administered by public and private agencies, all supported by federal funds. Prospective clients were badly confused, and serious gaps emerged when the programs, which should have been complementary, were developed separately.[20]

All this diffusion and confusion prompted efforts to coordinate the different programs and to allow the local community more autonomy in selecting and combining programs in accordance with its own needs and preferences. The prime Swedish requirement of flexibility was to be achieved through two types of activity—one, functional, known as "decategorization," and the other geographic, known as "decentralization." In 1967, a Cooperative Area Manpower Programs System (CAMPS) was established by Executive Order to coordinate the planning efforts of the various federal agencies in the field and to do so through regional, state, and local committees. However, budgetary control over the various programs remained at agency level and was not transferred to the states and local committees; moreover, jurisdiction was confined to MDTA programs in the Department of Labor.[21] Another experiment in coordination was the Concentrated Employment Program (CEP), which also began in 1967 and which was designed to pool some Manpower Development and Economic Opportunity Administration funds for use in areas of high unemployment, where a complete range of manpower policies would be offered under one contract with a single local "sponsor." This program has enjoyed some success, although both the Employment Services and the local vocational education systems have successfully resisted integration into a common program.[22]

However, decentralization and decategorization got their greatest boost from the revenue-sharing approach of the Nixon Administration, whose object it was to release funds to the states and local governments unconditionally (with the proviso that they be devoted to the provision of manpower services). After the failure of two legislative initiatives, the Comprehensive Employment and Training Act (CETA) of 1973 was enacted. Prior to the passage of this law, a number of pilot projects called Comprehensive Manpower Programs had been started, under which various governors and mayors received block grants which were used mainly to coordinate EOA and MDTA funded programs. This concept was greatly extended under the CETA legislation, which replaced MDTA and EOA by direct allocations to state and local prime sponsors. (The latter include any local government area with a population of at least 100,000 which makes application for prime sponsorship and also, at the discretion of the Secretary of Labor, smaller units as well.) Under CETA planning is done at state and local levels through manpower planning councils, which are appointed by the chief elected official (as distinct from unofficial neighborhood organizations which used to be eligible to contract for manpower funds) and on which representatives of management, unions, and manpower agencies as well as of client populations are represented.

It is still too early to determine how well this legislative authority will succeed where previous administrative initiatives failed. However, early returns do not furnish reassuring evidence in support of two assumptions on which, according to the National Commission for Manpower Policy, the CETA approach is based:

> The one common assumption is that these officials can get a better "fix" on manpower needs within their respective jurisdictions than national or regional authorities—and they will also have the necessary power, influence and incentive to deal responsibly with those needs in ways that maximize the coordinated use of limited resources.
>
> Secondly, CETA seems to assume that the target groups for manpower ser-

vices will be a source of political support for the local elected official who perceives their needs and does something about them.[23]

However, decentralization has its limitations as well as its obvious virtues. The commission notes that the jurisdictional boundaries of the prime sponsors need not coincide with the relevant local labor market areas. Moreover, the political assumption is invalidated: the local authorities do not have the power to achieve coordination of different programs or even to select or fashion those which they believe would be most helpful. The political power of such established agencies as the Employment Services, the vocational education and vocational rehabilitation authorities, and the Work Incentive Programs has not been diminished by CETA. Their activities were not incorporated under CETA, to begin with, and they have not coordinated their planning or delivery well with CETA officials at either federal, state, or local levels. The composition of the local prime sponsor planning councils is representative of the various community groups as required by law, but the latter thus far lack sufficient expertise—and possibly, in some cases, sufficient interest —to make an effective contribution. The Swedish requirement of active cooperation by labor and management in support of labor market policies is not fulfilled. Instead, the vacuum is filled by representatives of the Employment Service and the educational and vocational education establishments, secure in their separate statutory authority and with their political influence undiminished. The upshot is that "the elected official may decide that he has no real choice but to give the established agencies as well as certain community based organizations, a sizeable 'piece of the [CETA] action.' " [24] Thus coordination at the local level is severely limited by separate planning cycles for different programs and even lack of a standard terminology. Of particular importance is the unsatisfactory service provided—indeed, virtually forced on—local prime sponsors by the Employment Service, including insufficient and out-of-date labor market information.

The National Commission for Manpower Policy has made many sound suggestions to the federal and state agencies for improving coordination at and among all three levels of government, but the key recommendation is that

> Congress in its consideration of the renewal of the CETA authorization develops amendments to CETA *and the enabling legislation for the other enumerated programs* [emphasis added] to make clear that the mandate for coordination extends to those programs as well as to CETA.[25]

Clearly legislation is required to achieve coordination at the federal level, and clearly implementation of an extended mandate for coordination would require the existence of a manpower administration with broadened jurisdiction, whether interdepartmental or supradepartmental in structure. It might seem paradoxical that decategorization and geographic decentralization should entail more top-level centralization. However, decategorization and decentralization are ways of securing flexibility; and it will be recalled that the Swedes have always regarded a strong and autonomous central manpower agency as essential to securing flexibility in the selection and combination of labor market instruments— to say nothing of the mutual adaptation of those instruments and macroeconomic policy.

But the Swedes are not nearly as hung up over governmental direction as Americans tend to be. Undoubtedly it is easier to make central government more efficient in a small economy than in a continental economy, so that insistence on efficient performance can generate quite different attitudes and even ideologies concerning the role of government in the two cases. Be that as it may; the fact is that to many of the proponents of "manpower revenue sharing," diminution of the federal role has been a highly desirable end in itself. It now seems that, contrary to hope and expectation, we must face a trade-off between that objective and the goal of policy efficiency. Nevertheless, if it appears that the potential effectiveness of manpower policy—the excess of any economic and social benefits it might yield over the costs of resources which it consumes—is negligible under any circumstances, any foreseeable gain in effectiveness would not be worth what could be considered a cost in terms of centralization. If, on the other hand, our manpower programs have generated net benefits even when operated under conditions that are demonstrably not conducive to maximum efficiency, then any significant improvement in operating conditions might be expected to generate appreciable incremental social and economic gains.

In fact, the many administrative deficiencies and abuses which helped to enact the CETA legislation and which prompted calls for further reform have helped to give this dog a bad public name. Benefit-cost studies, which have attempted to go behind appearances and assess actual outcomes, have themselves been criticized for numerous methodological deficiencies. Some of these deficiencies—notably the virtual impossibility of pairing off program participants with otherwise identical control groups, measuring income differentials between participants and nonparticipants for only limited periods of time after completion of the program, failing to allow for the possibility that workers who completed programs might have merely displaced others from employment—have been held to bias the derived benefit-cost ratios upwards; others, like the inclusion among costs of income supplements to trainees who would otherwise have drawn direct income support, allegedly create a downward bias. But such defects have been detected in benefit-cost analyses in many other areas of inquiry where they have been accorded a degree of tolerance which is not infrequently enjoyed by the only game in town. In particular, the displacement by an ex-trainee of another worker who had been employed during the former's period of training does not imply overestimation of the program's effectiveness; it may simply signify that overall monetary demand had not been increased sufficiently to provide extra employment for a worker whose productivity had been increased by the manpower program. In fact, most of the studies of MDTA programs revealed high rates of return (measured in income differentials) over costs.

Studies have also shown that on-the-job training programs have been more cost-effective than institutional programs of the vocational education variety, and that individuals with the lowest pretraining earnings or education and who had experienced the most unemployment have benefited most. These results are consistent with a more recent analysis by Robert Flanagan of racial wage differentials, according to which black males would have benefited more from an extra year of training than from an extra year of either school, seniority, or labor force experience; moreover they would gain relatively more from more training than would whites, while their total years of training were lower than those enjoyed by whites. Flanagan notes that "to some extent the investment differences reflect employer decisions on the allocation of company training which could be compensated for by public manpower policies or reversed via the widespread enforcement of antidiscrimination measures such as Title VII of the Civil Rights Act." [26] The author goes on to demonstrate that if they received as much training as whites, large racial wage differences would remain; but it would nevertheless pay to give the blacks more training at least as long as their payoff is greater or, indeed, as long as it is positive.

Moreover, as we have suggested, as long as increased expenditures pay off for any one group, it increases aggregate employment and output potential; to the extent that productivity-enhancing labor market policies help to equalize the distribution of unemployment, they create a condition for improving the aggregate trade-off. So there is merit in Eli Ginzberg's argument, which Abramovitz quotes, that the obvious failure of manpower policy to prevent the apparent worsening of the inflation-unemployment trade-off in the U.S. after the mid-1960s can reflect, among other things, an insufficient effort—as well as, it might be added, inefficient deployment of the resources which were made available. One percent of the federal budget and 0.25 percent of the GNP of the United States can be contrasted with over 5.5 percent of the budget and 1.4 percent of the GNP which was taken up by labor market administration expenditures in Sweden in 1970. Yet it must be recorded that even the Swedes have not been too pleased with the results of their exemplary effort, for they too experienced an adverse movement in their Phillips trade-off. Lindbeck cites the

> disappointing lesson . . . that there is hardly any evidence that the energetic programmes for labour mobility and retraining the labour force have in fact reduced the inflationary propensity of the labour market (at a given level of unemployment) . . . possibly (partly at least) because other factors have tended to push the Phillips curve in the opposite direction.[27]

In part, the Swedes also feel that their own efforts, so ambitious by our standards, have not been pushed far enough. While it was indeed feasible to substitute selective manpower policies for traditional aggregate measures to increase demand during downswings, it was not politically feasible to restrain demand during upswings and then to rely on the selective policies to attack the islands of unemployment which surface after the level of overall demand has subsided. According to Meidner and Andersson, "In public opinion the employment goal is of prime importance. Restraint on expansion can in political debate be labeled as neglect of employment problems." [28] Political commitment to the realization of extremely ambitious employment goals is not likely to prove a barrier to the expansion of selective manpower policies in this country. Two additional obstacles reported by the Swedes are somewhat more familiar. One consists of instances of reluctance of the economically disadvantaged or dislocated labor, in smaller communities where employment has declined, to move to larger growth centers; this recalls the reluctance of congressional representatives from distressed areas to support relocation measures—as distinct from investment incentives—to create more jobs in their constituencies. The second (and somewhat related) obstacle is presented by a type of structural change in the economy allegedly resulting from intensification of international competition. The latter has resulted in reduced profit margins and an increase in the number of plant closures and firm mergers and hence a more rapid rate of structural change in the Swedish economy and of sectoral labor displacement. This is what the American Demand Structuralists of a decade back were complaining about (although they blamed the labor-displacing increase in productivity on accelerated technological change rather than on an accelerated pace of competition). This is why some of them rejected macroeconomic measures in favor of manpower retraining; however, Meidner and Andersson claim that "Rehn's model is basically a model for stability and growth, but structural factors obstruct the application of the model." [29] Why this should be so, is puzzling and disturbing, but Meidner and Andersson do cite a study which revealed that "a considerable number of those replaced have to accept lower wages and/or less advantageous conditions in their new places of work." [30] This recalls Table I, which shows the relative decline of high-paying production jobs in the U.S., and our previous observation that the European manpower programs were originally designed to move workers into, rather than out of, relatively high-paying jobs. To the Swedes this would doubtless constitute another argument in support of the solidaristic wage policy (which they have pursued as determinedly as they have sought to implement active labor market policy). We have referred to their opposition to relatively low wages in labor-surplus sectors on the grounds that they inhibit mobility by subsidizing labor demand by inefficient firms. Now they would doubtless oppose relatively low wages in growth sectors on the grounds that they act as a disincentive to mobility on the part of workers who would have to accept a wage cut.

Minimum Wage Cutting

In contrast to the dominant Swedish view, many American economists have preferred to grapple with the problem of cyclically increasing marginal costs by attacking the numerator of the fraction directly, rather than the denominator—by trying to hold down wage rates rather than by trying directly to raise productivity. Some attribute excessive market power to trade unions and also to firms in concentrated industries and advocate wage and price controls in order to prevent the type of "semi-inflation" which Keynes attributed to "the psychology of the workers and the policies of employers and trade unions." [31] Some, including those who disbelieve in the inflationary potential of trade unions nevertheless agree that semi-inflation can result "if the wage of a given grade of laborers is uniform irrespective of the efficiency of the individuals" and on that account would advocate the reduction (in real terms) of the national minimum wage or even the establishment of a lower minimum wage for youth among whom unemployment is so high.

The theoretical proposition that, other things being equal, a rise in a minimum wage will result in a fall in employment of the labor involved and a reduction in a minimum wage will result in an increase in such employment is elemental, but the empirical task of demonstrating that this is what has actually happened has proved to be rather tricky (as have some of the analytic and quantitative techniques employed). Two difficulties are relevant for our purposes. In the first place, it should be noted that, over the postwar period as a whole, the minimum wage, considered in relationship to average hourly earnings in manufacturing, has not increased; it has fluctuated narrowly about a 50 percent level. However, the proportion of aggregate employment covered by minimum wage legislation has been increased, and, of course, the proportions of young people and of women in the labor force—the groups particularly likely to be affected economically by the minimum wage—have risen greatly. (An increase in the supply of labor employable only at or under a given minimum wage can have the same effect on employment and unemployment as a certain increase in the wage affecting an unchanged number of workers.)

The second difficulty is the fact that much of the unemployment among youth is, as noted above, associated with high rates of turnover —including quits out of low-wage, deadend, temporary jobs—and allegedly with many job openings. How can a reduction in wages, which is supposed to generate more job openings, reduce unemployment which allegedly results from wages which are too low to induce people to accept the jobs that are being offered? One explanation is that minimum wages are in effect both too high and too low. They are not too high to make it unprofitable to employers to offer work to young, inexperienced, or discriminated-against labor; but they are too high to make it profitable for employers to offer good jobs—with training and promotional opportunities. And they are too high—or at least too rigid—for workers who might be willing to accept wages low enough to make it worthwhile for their employers to offer them training and opportunities for greater future returns, while they are too low to compensate the unskilled young workers for lack of economic promise.[32] Thus, even if lowering the minimum wage does not result in more job openings, it should, according to this line of argument, reduce unemployment from the supply side. It should increase the potentiality of economic expansion without rising unit costs because it would compensate workers further back in the efficiency queue with lower money wages to balance their lower productivity, but it would also tend to raise their productivity and to increase the proportion of good jobs, with "internal labor markets," to the total number of jobs in the economy. In this sense, a reduction in the minimum wage can be regarded as a productivity-enhancing labor market policy: it does not feature publicly offered training, but it does offer incentives to the expansion of privately offered training.

How effective it is likely to be can hardly be estimated. Since, according to this line of reasoning, the immediate result of reducing the minimum wage would be to increase quit rates and thus raise unemployment, this would have to be offset primarily by the ability of employers in various service industries (where so many youth are employed) to "internalize" and otherwise revamp their "secondary" labor markets. As noted above, human capital theory and dual labor market theory seem to agree in ascribing the high wages prevailing in internal labor markets to the desire of employers to protect their training investments. However, it could be argued (on the basis, I believe, of some good historic evidence) that in some important cases, the decision to pay relatively high wages—forced on employers by either the prospect or the presence of collective bargaining—came first and induced employers to introduce the modern battery of personnel policies and career employment in an attempt, as Sumner Slichter wrote, "to make their workers more efficient and more contented."[33] Thus, while the objective of good jobs might in principle be reached by the path of lower wages, that is not a trail which has been blazed by history.

There remains the possibility that lowering the minimum wage will reduce youth unemployment simply by making it profitable for employers to hire more young and inexperienced workers; and studies to indicate that youth employment (unemployment) responds in inverse (direct) fashion to changes in its relative wage. But how much of a given increase in youth employment and reduction in youth unemployment attributable to a reduction in the minimum wage would be reflected in a net increase in *total* employment and a net reduction in total unemployment, and how much would come at the expense of increased unemployment among older and more experienced members of the work force? Most observers would agree that the substitution effect should be minimized; in fact, some of the staunchest champions of lower minimum wages also insist that unemployment among youth and other groups (especially women) in the "secondary" work force is a much less serious social problem than unemployment of married men with families because the former have more economically valuable uses for nonworking time than the latter. How pronounced the substitution effect would be relative to the expansion effect would presumably depend, *inter alia,* on (a) the form of the minimum wage reduction and (b) the response of demand management. With respect to "(a)," if the reduction is made applicable only for certain age groups—the so-called "Youth Minimum Wage"—the substitution of youths for older workers, especially low-wage workers, would be more strongly encouraged than if the minimum wage reduction were extended uniformly to all covered groups. As far as "(b)" is concerned, the substitution effects of a reduction in a minimum wage would be minimized and the expansion effect maximized to the extent that the fiscal and monetary authorities would take advantage of the reduction in the wages of workers near the end of the productivity queues by further expansion of aggregate demand. If the authorities take up the slack paid out by a reduction in the minimum wage, then a reduction in disparities among sectoral unemployment rates would go hand in hand with a reduction in unemployment for all groups. If they fail to support this type of minimum wage policy, they will be relying on expansion solely through cost and price reduction, betting that the latter will prevail over the loss in real income suffered by wage earners already employed at, or in the neighborhood of, the minimum wage (which, studies indicate, would outweigh in most cases the increases in income enjoyed by those newly employed at the minimum wage).[34] An interesting analysis by Marvin Kosters and Finis Welch, which implies that a reduction in the minimum wage would increase the share of teenagers, in "normal" or trend unemployment and would reduce its share of "transitional" or cyclical unemployment, also implies that teenagers and also nonwhite adult males would suffer particularly from a slackened pace of economic activity.[35]

Public Job Creation and High Unemployment

Insofar as proposals to reduce minimum wages are aimed at developing both jobs and workers as joint products, they share, as we have noted, a prominent characteristic of American manpower programs. The latter have frequently combined job creation with worker development, partly because they were concentrated on supply targets among the economically disadvantaged whom they were supposed to provide

with "work experience" as well as skill training. The work experience
provided in the Work Incentive Program (WIN) and its predecessors
has been characterized by job creation in the public sector, rather than
in the private sector; but such new public jobs are supposed to be good
jobs—"either identical in pay and content to jobs in regular public
service or linked to them by, for example, apprenticeship positions."
Hence Michael Wiseman has distinguished jobs created in "antipoverty"
public employment programs from jobs created in "counter-recession"
programs, which "can be of any type and may be created in projects not
normally undertaken." [36]

Yet an antipoverty program may obviously serve as a counter-recession
public employment program, and, to the extent that it reduces unemployment that is structural in nature, it should be a particularly
valuable type of counter-recessionary program. In fact, it was recession-
related unemployment which generated the momentum behind the
passage of the Manpower Development and Training Act of 1962; and
the return of recession in the 1970s prompted the return of counter-
recessionary public employment programs for the first time since the
1930s. In 1971, a Public Employment Program (PEP) was established
under the Emergency Employment Act (EEA) of that year; and in 1973,
despite a decline in unemployment, the Comprehensive Employment
and Training Act provided for new public employment programs in
Titles I and II. Finally, in 1974, an Emergency Jobs and Assistance Act
was passed, which added a new Title VI to CETA.

Both the PEP and CETA programs were small-scale and both were
designed to accommodate Vietnam veterans and other nondisadvantaged
groups as well as groups heavily burdened by unemployment and/or
poverty. Nevertheless, such public service employment measures are held
to enjoy certain contracyclical advantages over both traditional public
works programs and the traditional methods of managing aggregate
demand. Public works programs have been criticized because of their
timing; they take too long to start up, and they frequently are not
completed until well after cyclical recovery has begun. Moreover, public
works projects are relatively costly in terms of equipment and materials
and also labor, which tends to be high-wage; thus, the number of jobs
directly created per dollar of expenditure is relatively small. New public
service jobs, on the other hand, can be created more rapidly, require
less equipment, and have entailed lower administrative and direct wage
costs.[37] Furthermore, the appropriate selective potential of public service
employment is greater than that of general macroeconomic policies and
certainly greater than that of public works measures, which frequently
are characterized by a high skill component. Since disadvantaged groups
with high unemployment rates to begin with typically suffer steeper
increases in unemployment in cyclical downswings, any general expansionary policy will tend to reduce unemployment among these groups
more than among others—simply by contributing to a cyclical upswing.

However, if the object is to reduce the relative unemployment rates of the high-unemployment groups at peak-level employment, general expansionary measures will not suffice. Selective measures, like public service employment, on the other hand, can make progress in reducing relative peak unemployment among the high-unemployment groups by enabling their members to jump the Keynesian queues instead of waiting their turn behind the more skilled workers, who normally tend to get reemployed first.[38]

But recent experience under our public service employment programs seems to reveal two and possibly three operating deficiencies. The first reflects limited effectiveness of these particular programs in increasing worker productiveness; the second affords a clue to one possible cause of that ineffectiveness; only the third might be taken as an inherent limitation of the method itself. The first relates to the problem of timing. While PSE programs can get started up rapidly in a recession, they can be hard to turn off after recovery has begun.[39] Political temptation to keep PSE going would appear to be related to the fact that many of the enrollees have not found new and better "permanent" jobs awaiting them, as they should have been able to do if the policy had reached its structural objective. In fact, while many PEP program agents did lower or suspend civil service hiring programs for participants, they did not provide much training, nor did they facilitate permanent upgrading by changing examination or credential standards in civil service systems. As a result, "this approach . . . established a special class of employees who were frequently locked into 'aide' and other entry-level positions outside the normal civil service progression." [40] At the same time, wages on EEA jobs were the same as those on regular low-skilled government jobs, while the latter, in turn, were typically above wages for comparable work in the private sector in major cities. This, in Wiseman's opinion, was partly responsible for "the failure of EEA employment to decline as the economy improved," [41] although, according to one study, those who did leave PEP were able to earn more in their new jobs.[42]

The second deficiency relates to the problem of "displacement," "substitution," or "maintenance of effort." While public employment legislation requires that the funds be used for new and additional government jobs, in fact there has been evidence of displacement, in the short run and increasing over time.[43] To the extent that substitution of federal funds avoids a rise or permits a reduction in state or local taxes, the expansionary impact on total employment is about the same as it would be if no substitution had occurred.[44] To the extent that regular, laid-off government workers are replaced by PSE participants, the structural objectives of public service employment are potentially served, although the more substitutable the newcomers are to begin with, the less disadvantaged they presumably are. Conversely, PSE workers are potentially "displaced" when PSE funds are used to employ laid-off regular employees, and this defeats the structural objectives of public service employment—just as hiring experienced unemployed workers from private industry under PSE programs would do. CETA tried to minimize displacement of the latter variety by reducing salary ceilings and requiring a minimum of 30 days' unemployment before hiring. But, under the impact of steeply rising unemployment, the minimum period was reduced to fifteen days in areas where unemployment exceeded 7 percent; and the career advancement and "transition" goals for PSE participants were made waivable. As Wiseman put it, "The real upshot of EJUA is that restrictions on entry have been relaxed to the point of inconsequence, and transition to regular public employment has been dropped as a matter of concern." [45] The subordination of antipoverty to counter-recessionary goals was of course a response to high and rising unemployment. If unemployment had not been sufficiently great, there would obviously not have been enough highly productive workers interested in crowding the less disadvantaged out of PSE programs intended originally to upgrade them. This simply illustrates both Solow's point that "room" still existed for more general expansionist measures and the Swedes' point that active labor market policies require—while contributing to—an environment of high-level employment.

Of course, the crowding and the political pressures reflect not only the magnitude of unemployment but that magnitude in relation to the scale of the public service employment programs; and an alternative way of making PSE large in relation to the volume of unemployment is to enlarge the PSE program to accommodate all applicants at any level of unemployment. This, however, raises our final problem, which has paraded—or slunk—under the soubriquet of "absorbability" by the public sector of the additional employment contemplated in PSE programs. There seems to be general agreement that the services performed by PSE participants were well received as responsive to public demand; and, since the public sector has been a rapidly growing one, it might be argued that there still exist unmet wants which could usefully be met by more public employment—which is what is contemplated as the end result of PSE "transitional" activities. On the other hand, the public sector is, in the aggregate, a low-productivity, services sector and, if the employment of labor in it runs ahead of demand, its productivity would be further depressed. It is nevertheless true that the economy's overall productivity would be increased if such an expansion were the only way by which the disadvantaged could be made more productive, acquire greater dignity, and best able to realize their own underdeveloped potential. Certainly this argues for the establishment of sheltered workshops and similar highly selective labor market institutions which have proved their economic worth in Sweden, The Netherlands, and other countries. The Swedes have also been leery of general public employment measures. They try to minimize them because of their adverse impact on productivity.[46] Opportunities being available, an expansion of good jobs in goods-producing high-productivity private sectors would be more effective than an expansion of good jobs in the low-productivity public sector in improving the inflation-unemployment trade-off.

Unemployment Compensation—Living with High Unemployment

While public service employment can be used most effectively as an antistructural measure when unemployment overall is relatively low, unemployment insurance (on a national scale) was devised during, and for, high unemployment. It was intended primarily as an alternative to means-rated "relief" for workers with histories of stable employment. The workers might draw income while unemployed as a matter of entitlement based on past contributions paid in on their account, and they might do so until (and only until) "suitable employment" became available to them or until their period of entitlement ran out, whichever occurred first. Following the successful example of workmen's compensation, most state plans made provision for "experience rating," whereby employer contributions were allowed to vary, within maximum and minimum limits, in accordance with the unemployment record of the employees in each firm. Experience rating was strongly supported by employers. It was opposed by unions, who regarded it as a way of reducing average contributions, and by most economists of the day, who doubted its ability to reduce unemployment in the aggregate and feared that, where effective as an employer incentive to regularize employment, its effect would be primarily to reduce new hires and to concentrate unemployment and instability elsewhere. Some economists, on the other hand, defended unemployment insurance because of its contracyclical impact on "purchasing power," an argument which was summarized in the title of a famous article written in 1931 by Sumner Slichter: "Pharaoh Dreams Again—Fat Years Must Take Care of the Lean." [47]

With the passage of time came a reversal of attitude, at least within the economics profession. The "search" value of the incentive afforded to the unemployed to hold out became regarded by some as outweighed by induced "malingering" (thereby increasing duration of unemployment), by higher rates of labor force participation (which would increase the frequency of recorded unemployment) and by holding a prop under wages (thus contributing to inflation). These incentives are powered by the level of unemployment compensation in conjunction with its tax exempt status; and it has been estimated that unemployment compensation replaces between one-half and two-thirds of the average recipient's after-tax income.[48] Martin Feldstein (whose own estimates of replacement rates were much higher and were criticized as atypical) has advocated taxation of benefits as a way to reduce these implicit marginal tax rates.[49]

The fact recently emphasized by the Council of Economic Advisers [50] and by Feldstein himself [51] that, on an average, 85 percent of layoffs were rehired since 1960, supports the view of Marston and others that this disincentive effect of unemployment compensation on the unemployed is of limited quantitative importance. On the other hand, it is regarded by the new critics as evidence of the need to remove the minimum and maximum limits on experience rating. They claim that, due to the relative ineffectiveness of experience rating, unemployment compensation in effect subsidizes employers who offer seasonal, highly cyclical or other types of unstable employment. In the absence of unemployment compensation, as Solow reports, they would be obliged to pay higher wages to attract enough labor and this, in turn, would furnish an inducement to them to regularize their employment. Higher contribution rates under unemployment insurance could offer the same incentive.

The objection of the original critics of experience rating—that firms which regularize employment (and thus add to inventories during periods of slack demand) would tend to reduce their permanent work forces—is in part conceded, but is asserted *a priori* that workers thus denied employment would find jobs elsewhere—provided that monetary policy is sufficiently supportive.[52] Assuming this to be the case, an old question arises again: what sort of jobs would these displaced persons get? Initially at least, experience-rated contributions would tend to rise within such sectors as mining, construction, and manufacturing, where unemployment among experienced wage and salaried workers has been relatively high since the end of the 1940s. These are also sectors in which collective bargaining is quite widespread (except nondurable manufacturing). Relative wages in such industries are not likely to fall once employment is regularized; on the contrary, union bargaining power is raised when unemployment among the membership is reduced, so that any subsequent reductions in unemployment compensation contributions resulting from increased regularization of employment would go, at least in part, into higher relative wages. This means that the incentive effect of the higher taxes on employers would be reduced. It could also mean that the jobs available to the displaced persons in low-unemployment sectors would be relatively worsened. Thus the good-job sectors would be made smaller while their jobs would be made better; the bad-job sectors would be expanded and the total volume of quit and similar "voluntary" unemployment could be increased therein. In any event, the consequences of a policy of raising relative labor costs in high-unemployment firms are far from obvious.

Finally, the old purchasing power argument came to be regarded as irrelevant as it became apparent that unemployment insurance possessed no inherent monopoly as a contracyclical stabilizer. This left the institution with no aggregate virtues to weigh in the balance against those presumably wage-and-unemployment enhancing features which potentially make for a more unfavorable trade-off than would otherwise occur. But even if the latter is true and even if nothing is or can be done to improve the system, unemployment compensation is entitled to support from advocates of restrictive demand management as the only effective way to fight inflation. It can claim support as an income-maintenance device and it can claim special support as a device to maintain (within a range) the *distribution* of labor incomes in a holding pattern—which indeed was its original *raison d'être*—until inflation can be wrung out of the economy. The fact that unemployment could reach 8.25 million or 8.9 percent of the labor force in May 1975 is hardly unrelated to the fact that 5.5 million people were beneficiaries of unemployment compensation programs and drew $19 billion in payments during that quarter. "Largely because of these [unemployment compensation and other income maintenance programs]," the Council of Economic Advisers reported, "per capita real disposable income did not decline in 1975 despite a decline in real output per capita. Because the number and size of counter-cyclical programs have increased over time, the extent to which consumer income was maintained was greater in this recession than in past ones." Then, referring to legislation which extended, in the form of Special Unemployment Assistance, benefits to state and local governmental employees, farm workers, and household employees during periods and in places of high (6 to 6.5 percent) unemployment, and which provided Federal Supplemental Benefits extending the maximum duration of benefits to sixty-five weeks, the Council noted, "Largely because of these programs a larger proportion of the unemployed received benefits in 1975 than in any prior recession." [53] Thus when, in the next chapter of its 1976 report, the Council duly recited the various disincentive aspects of unemployment compensation, it seemed almost as if it had decided not to let its right hand know what its other right hand had been doing. What the latter had been doing was to occupy a roost further down the presumably higher Phillips Curve, which the liberal congressional majorities had constructed in the distant and recent past, than it could have occupied on a lower Phillips Curve—*i.e.*, to manage demand more restrictively and possibly to restrain inflation more effectively, with more unemployment than would otherwise have been politically tolerable. (This is hardly the type of monetary environment, it might be noted, which is conducive to ambitious experimentation with experience rating.)

But the sixty-five-week maximum—which put an end to the insurance concept—and the $19 billion payout rate raised a more fundamental question: can we not do better than paying people for doing nothing? Thus the National Commission for Manpower Policy urges "a comprehensive study of how UI can be transformed in part into a manpower support program with particular emphasis on expanding training opportunities and mobility assistance." [54]

Subsidy: A Way to Reduce Stagflation?

In Europe, as in the United States, the inflationary recession which began in late 1973 or early 1974 prompted the extension of unemployment compensation benefit periods and coverage and the raising of benefit rates (relative to wages).[55] However, Charles Stewart noted "growing concern in Europe as to the disincentive effects of high wage-replacement benefits now [1975] prevailing." [56] Moreover, while coverage was extended to groups with lower employability—including older, younger, and handicapped workers—unemployment insurance was regarded as unresponsive to concerns over job security in countries where, as Stewart writes, "layoffs have ordinarily meant dismissal and a break in the employer-employee relationship." [57] This offers some contrast with the American criticism of unemployment compensation for subsidizing a continuing employer-employee relationship through periods of layoff; and European fears of job loss have led to a search for alternative policies designed directly to avoid layoffs.

Temporary public employment does not fill this bill (although public works and public service programs were expanded). On the other hand, one popular device has been the development of systems of "short-time benefits" in Canada, Japan, France, Germany, Italy, and the United Kingdom. In a country like Italy the alternative to short-time benefits equal to 90 percent of gross earnings is a minimal flat-rate unemployment compensation; hence employers have been under strong pressure not to lay off.[58]

Of particular interest has been the general extension of wage subsidies to employers, which had mainly been developed as structural measures, in connection with industrial development programs in declining regions with high unemployment, or to encourage the hiring of handicapped workers. Thus Japan instituted a program of subsidies to industries which would otherwise have to institute *temporary* layoffs only; [59] and Germany and Ireland instituted general programs of temporary subsidies with stated termination dates which would hopefully induce employers to increase the number of new hires more promptly in the expected upswing in activity. In the United Kingdom and France employer subsidy schemes have been targeted to particular groups—youth and, in the case of France, persons unemployed over six months. In Sweden, where (as in Norway) wage subsidies are extended for in-plant training as well as employment, they are targeted to particular industries (autos and steel) as well as to particular geographic regions.

In contrast, on the one hand, to the Keynesian problem, which consists of increasing employment without stirring up inflation (or avoiding "semi-inflation") and, on the other, to the Swedish problem, which has consisted of reducing inflation without increasing unemployment, the problem posed by "stagflation"—or (to adopt Lerner's term) inflationary recession—consists of reducing unemployment and inflation at the same time. Appropriately controlled monetary expansion has been put forth as a solution to this problem (as to virtually all others) and indeed it constitutes a necessary condition for solution; but it is not easy to control monetary expansion appropriately when unemployment is high and rising. Wage or employment subsidies to the private and nationalized market sectors have also been plugged as doing both jobs at once. They reduce marginal labor costs to employers while permitting fuller utilization of capital capacity, which furnishes an incentive to hire more workers, produce more output, and price more aggressively. They generate increased consumer demand, but the budgetary expenditures on subsidies are offset by budgetary savings in unemployment benefit payments and increased tax revenues contributed by workers employed under subsidy. Under an ideal system of subsidies, aggregate money demand would increase while declining in relation to output. In our original Keynesian terminology, an incremental increase in quantity of money and effective demand should yield a greater increase in employment and output and a smaller increase in costs and prices. Thus subsidy can be viewed as a politically effective means of achieving an appropriate monetary policy.

Concluding Comments

We might conclude by running the reel backwards, taking up in reverse order the manpower policies touched on in this chapter and relating each to various relevant properties of the wage/employment subsidy. Like employment compensation, employment subsidy provides income maintenance, but it also generates increased output and avoids the costs of incentives to idleness. Like public service employment (and public works), it generates increased output, but it does so in sectors where the favorable impacts on productivity and on prices are likely to be greater. Like a reduction in minimum wages, subsidy reduces hiring and raises layoff costs (operating like severance pay or experience rating in the latter respect); but, whereas reduction in minimum wages tends to facilitate the substitution of lower productivity for higher productivity labor or to threaten wage standards, a wage or employment subsidy program minimizes these effects by generating extra income and demand while reducing costs at going wage rates on the job. Finally, subsidy can enhance the effectiveness of manpower development and training by providing opportunity for on-the-job training at precisely those times when employers are most likely to contribute to future "full employment deficits" in trained manpower and when the crystal balls of the designers of institutional training programs are most likely to be clouded.

Yet it may surely be objected that we have been contrasting the virtues and beauty of an ideal with (in all cases save one) the vices and blemishes of assorted experiences, on which we have dwelled at some length. In fact, U.S. experiments with employer subsidies—in the WIN and JOBS programs—have not exactly drawn rave notices; and in fact the more ambitious German experiment was abandoned while unemployment was still rising.[60] The latter was marred by administrative difficulties which employers found oppressive and it also suffered because, with unemployment high, employers could exercise their preference for unsubsidized but more highly productive workers (whose unemployment experience had not been sufficiently adverse to qualify them under the program). This seems roughly to parallel the American experience, where the jobs offered under the JOBS program were frequently dead-end and low-paying jobs.[61] Moreover, seniority would work as a powerful counter to the hiring of economically marginal workers under a temporary counter-recessionary subsidy program in the United States.

Nevertheless, programs which are of longer duration, are targeted to particular disadvantaged groups, and both subsidize and require training as well as net additions to employment need not suffer from such disadvantages. Employers would be less reluctant to hire less productive workers if they were provided with the wherewithal to make them more efficient and if the subsidy period were long enough to cover the effective training period. Experienced employees and their unions would be less inclined to oppose subsidy programs given their protected seniority status, given that the subsidized employees would be paid the going rate of wages—which is indeed the case in Europe—and given the fact that the subsidy funds would help to generate the extra jobs which the recipients would occupy. We might thus end, if not on a high note, at least on an upbeat.

Notes

1. *Toward a National Manpower Policy* (Washington, D.C.: National Commission for Manpower Policy, 1975), p. 2.

2. M. Keynes, *The General Theory of Employment Interest and Money* (New York: Harcourt, Brace, 1935), pp. 41-42, 295-303.

3. *Ibid.*, p. 303.

4. *Ibid.*, p. 300.

5. See on the latter point, M. S. Gordon, *Retraining and Labor Market Adjustment in Western Europe*, Office of Manpower, Automation and Training, U.S. Department of Labor, Automation Research Monograph No. 4 (Washington, D.C.: U.S. Government Printing Office, 1965), pp. 25-26.

6. E. Brehmer and M. R. Bradford, "Incomes and Labor Market Policies in Sweden, 1945–70," *International Monetary Fund Staff Papers*, March 1974, pp. 102-6.

7. E. Brehmer and M. R. Bradford, "Incomes and Labor Market Policies in Sweden, 1945–70," *International Monetary Fund Staff Papers*, March 1974, pp. 102-106. G. Rehn and E. Lundberg, "Employment and Welfare: Some Swedish Issues," *Industrial Relations*, February 1963, p. 6. *Ibid.*, pp. 5-6; A. Lindbeck, *Swedish Economic Policy* (Berkeley and Los Angeles: University of California Press, 1974), p. 41. R. Meidner and R. Andersson. "The Impact of Labor Market Policy in Sweden," in L. Ulman, ed., *Manpower Programs in the Policy Mix* (Baltimore: The Johns Hopkins Press, 1973),

p. 129. Rehn and Lundberg, *op cit.*, p. 7. Meidner and Andersson, *op. cit.*, pp. 131-32; also Lindbeck, *op. cit.*, pp. 104-7. H. Håkanson, "Training Programs as an Employment Regulator," International Conference on Employment Fluctuations and Manpower Policy, 1969, Manpower and Social Affairs Directorate, OECD, mimeographed.

8. *Annual Report to the Council of Economic Advisers* (Washington, D.C.: U.S. Government Printing Office, 1962), p. 48.

9. See R. A. Gordon, *The Goal of Full Employment* (New York: Wiley, 1967) and "Macroeconomic Aspects of Manpower Policy," in L. Ulman, ed., *op. cit.*, pp. 16-33; G. L. Perry, "Changing Labor Markets and Inflation," *Brookings Papers on Economic Activity,* 1970, no. 3, pp. 411-441.

10. See, *e.g.,* R. E. Hall, "The Prospects for Shifting the Phillips Curve through Manpower Policy," *Brookings Papers on Economic Activity.*

11. Earlier reference to this was made in L. Ulman, "The Uses and Limits of Manpower Policy," *The Public Interest,* Winter 1974, pp. 101-2; and J. P. Mattila, *American Economic Review,* March 1974, pp. 235-39.

12. *Manpower Report of the President,* 1975, Table B-9, p. 264.

13. P. B. Doeringer and M. J. Piore, *Internal Labor Markets and Manpower Analysis* (Lexington, Mass.: D. S. Heath, 1971), Chs. 1-3, 8.

14. R. Meidner, *The Trade Union Movement and the Public Sector* (Stockholm: Public Services International, 1974), p. 12.

15. R. E. Hall, "The Rigidity of Wages and the Persistence of Unemployment," *Brookings Papers on Economic Activity:* 1975, no. 2, pp. 301-35.

16. *Ibid.*, p. 339.

17. Organization for Economic Co-Operation and Development, *Wages and Labour Mobility* (Paris, 1965), pp. 41-42.

18. See M. S. Gordon, *op. cit.*, pp. 63-65, Tables 10, 11, 12.

19. Ulman, *op. cit.*, pp. 102-3.

20. S. Ruttenberg and J. Gutchess, *Manpower Challenge to the 1970's: Institutions and Social Change* (Baltimore: The Johns Hopkins Press, 1970), p. 31.

21. *Ibid.*, pp. 7-8, 46-53; also S. A. Levitan, G. L. Mangum, R. Marshall, *Human Resources and Labor Markets,* Second Edition (New York: Harper & Row, 1976), p. 264.

22. Ruttenberg and Gutchess, *op. cit.*, pp. 65-71.

23. National Commission for Manpower Policy, *Manpower Program Coordination* (Washington, D.C., 1975), p. 33.

24. *Ibid.*

25. *Toward a National Manpower Policy, op. cit.*, p. 38.

26. R. J. Flanagan, "Labor Force Experience, Job Turnover, and Racial Wage Differentials," *The Review of Economics and Statistics,* November 1974, p. 526.

27. Lindbeck, *op. cit.*, p. 240.

28. *Op. cit.*, p. 151.

29. *Ibid.*, p. 152.

30. *Ibid.*, p. 154.

31. Keynes, *op. cit.*, p. 301.

32. M. Feldstein, "The Economics of the New Unemployment," *The Public Interest*, Fall 1973, pp. 14-17.

33. S. H. Slichter, "The Current Labor Policies of American Industries," *Quarterly Journal of Economics*, May 1929, reprinted in J. T. Dunlop, ed., *Potentials of the American Economy* (Cambridge, Mass.: Harvard University Press, 1961), p. 191.

34. See, for example, D. K. Adie, "Teen-age Unemployment and Real Federal Minimum Wages," *Journal of Political Economy*, March-April 1973, pp. 435-41.

35. M. Kosters and F. Welch, "The Effects of Minimum Wages on the Distribution of Changes in Aggregate Employment," *American Economic Review*, June 1972.

36. M. Wiseman, "On Giving a Job; The Implementation and Allocation of Public Service Employment," A Study prepared for the use of the Subcommittee on Economic Growth of the Joint Economic Committee, Congress of the United States (Washington, D.C.: Government Printing Office, 1975), p. 6.

37. Congressional Budget Office, *Temporary Measures to Simulate Employment: An Evaluation of Some Alternatives* (Washington, D.C.: Government Printing Office, 1975), pp. 35-36, 40.

38. On the latter point, see G. Pierson, "Union Strength and the U.S. Phillips Curve," *American Economic Review*, June 1968, pp. 456-457, as discussed in CBO, *op. cit.*, p. 37.

39. R. P. Nathan, "Public Service Employment—'Compared to What?'" in *Proceedings, op. cit.*, p. 116.

40. Manpower Report, *op. cit.*, pp. 47-48.

41. Wiseman, *op. cit.*, p. 12.

42. Levitan, *op. cit.*, p. 161.

43. A. Fechter, "Public Service Employment: Boon or Boondoggle?" in *Proceedings, op. cit.*, p. 137.

44. *Ibid.*, p. 126; also R. E. Hall, "The Role of Public Service Employment in Federal Unemployment Policy," in *Proceedings, op. cit.*, p. 93.

45. Wiseman, *op. cit.*, p. 130.

46. Rehn and Lundberg, *op. cit.*, p. 7.

47. *Atlantic Monthly*, August 1931, pp. 248-52.

48. S. T. Marston, "The Impact of Unemployment Insurance on Job Search," *Brookings Papers on Economic Activity*, 1975, no. 1, p. 17.

49. Feldstein, *op. cit.*, p. 39.

50. *Annual Report of the Council of Economic Advisers* (Washington, D.C., 1976), pp. 78, 111.

51. "The Importance of Temporary Layoffs: An Empirical Analysis" and "Temporary Layoffs in the Theory of Unemployment," in *Discussion Paper Series, Harvard Institute of Economic Research,* Nos. 447 (1975) and 419 (1975), respectively.

52. Feldstein, *Temporary Layoffs in the Theory of Unemployment, op. cit.,* pp. 31-32.

53. Council of Economic Advisers, *op. cit.,* pp. 81-82.

54. *Toward a National Manpower Policy, op. cit.,* p. 36.

55. A. Mittelstädt, "Unemployment Benefits and Related Payments in Seven Major Countries," *OECD Economic Outlook, Occasional Studies,* July 1975, pp. 4-22.

56. C. D. Stewart, *Recent European Manpower Policy Initiatives: A Special Report of the National Commission for Manpower Policy,* November 1975, Special Report #3 (Washington, D.C., 1975), p. 4.

57. *Ibid.,* p. 8.

58. *The Economist,* December 27, 1975, p. 44; also Mittelstädt, *op. cit.,* p. 5.

59. CBO, *op. cit.,* p. 25.

60. Stewart, *op. cit.,* p. 25.

61. Hall, "The Prospects for Shifting the Phillips Curve through Manpower Policy, " *op. cit.*

Barbara R. Bergmann

5

Reducing the Pervasiveness
of Discrimination

While everyone knows that white men have a substantially better
position in the American labor market than black men, white women,
black women, and other minority men and women, the explanations of
that fact differ markedly. Some observers place the major blame on currently occurring discriminatory acts by employers, while other observers
emphasize problems of education, motivation, and ability in the groups
that do poorly. Yet wherever one places the major responsibility, it is
clear that many of the leading problems of American society are in considerable measure attributable to the labor market situation of the disadvantaged groups.

Unemployment is the problem most frequently thought of under a
"manpower" heading, and at any point in the business cycle it is more
heavily concentrated among blacks and white women. Yet there are other
problems of our society not usually thought of as "manpower problems,"
which are quite obviously linked to the poor labor market position of
disadvantaged groups: poverty, welfare dependency among the able-
bodied, urban blight, and high crime incidence. With a better labor
market position—higher wages and less frequent unemployment—more
members of the groups now disadvantaged would be able to support
themselves and so stay out of poverty and off welfare. With better and
more regular jobs, these people would have a better chance to pay for
adequate housing, keep out of trouble with the law, and function as full
members of society. A substantial reform of the labor market would not
completely eliminate the need for programs to relieve poverty by transfer

BARBARA R. BERGMANN, *Professor of Economics at the University of Maryland,
was Senior Staff Economist, Council of Economic Advisers (1961–62) and President, Eastern Economic Association (1974).*

payments, to lessen welfare dependency by work incentives, to relieve urban blight by subsidies to builders, and to better control crime by setting up a more efficient justice system. Yet the need for some of these programs would probably be less acute and their scope and cost might be reduced if significant improvement in the labor market position of women and minority men were to take place.

In considering the ways and means to mount a program which will over the long run result in an improvement of the labor market position of disadvantaged groups, policies aimed at causing a reduction of the extent of discriminatory practices are bound to have a considerable role to play. The major questions at issue then are (1) whether a significant reduction in discrimination is feasible, given our other goals and our limited ability to engage in successful "social engineering"; (2) how much of a reduction in the relatively disadvantaged can be accomplished by a reduction in discrimination; (3) what other problems might be engendered or worsened by a reform of labor market practices which are discriminatory in their effect.

The Current Position of Minorities and Women in the Labor Market

More than a decade has passed since the enactment of the Civil Rights Act of 1964, which outlawed discrimination in employment by race and sex. Tables 1 to 3 present information on three indicators of labor market position by race-sex group for 1974. For purposes of comparison we have included data for 1966, which is the first year after the passage of the Civil Rights Act of 1964 for which comparable data are available.

Information on median incomes of full-time year-round workers by race and sex, which is the best proxy we have for wage rates, is presented in Table 1. The relative position of white women on the income scale changed hardly at all between 1966 and 1974; if anything their relative

TABLE 1. MEDIAN INCOME OF YEAR-ROUND FULL-TIME WORKERS BY RACE AND SEX

	1974		1966	
	Income	Ratio to White Male Income	Income	Ratio to White Male Income
White Male	$12,434	1.00	$7,164	1.00
Black Male	8,705	.70	4,528	.63
White Female	7,021	.56	4,152	.57
Black Female	6,371	.51	2,949	.41

Source: Current Population Reports, Series P-60

position worsened slightly on the average. Among blacks some change for the better was discernible, particularly for black women. Two-thirds of the difference in relative position between white and black women was erased between 1966 and 1974. For black men progress has apparently been much slower than for black women, although, contrary to some current impressions, black men continue to remain ahead of black women in terms of average wage rates. However, at the linear rate of increase in 1976, it would take about thirty-five years for the wage rate of black men to equal that of white men, by which time most black men in the labor force in 1970 would have retired.

The information in Table 1 may be summed up by saying that it has apparently been fairly easy for American industry to place a greater proportion of black women into the kinds of jobs hitherto reserved for white women, but that little progress has been made in placing a higher proportion of blacks and white women into jobs hitherto reserved for white men.

One important reason for the relatively low pay experienced by women and black men, on the average, has been their virtual exclusion from white collar occupations classified as managerial and administrative and from blue collar occupations classified as craft jobs. White men have had in the past almost a monopoly of access to these high paying occupations. Table 2 shows that the managerial and craft occupations continue to be

TABLE 2. SHARES IN EMPLOYMENT BY RACE AND SEX IN FIRMS WITH OVER 100 EMPLOYEES IN TWO OCCUPATIONAL GROUPS

	1974		1966	
	Managers & Officials (percent)	Craft Workers (percent)	Managers & Officials (percent)	Craft Workers (percent)
White Males	83.0	82.3	89.0	88.3
Black Males	2.1	6.0	0.6	3.2
White Females	11.9	6.2	9.1	5.6
Black Females	0.7	0.9	0.2	0.4
All Others	2.3	4.6	1.1	2.5
Total	100.0	100.0	100.0	100.0

Source: EEOC data tabulated in the Manpower Report of the President, April 1975.

overwhelmingly dominated by white men, although there seems to be a modest movement in the direction of greater participation in them by blacks and white women. The data in Table 2 derive from reports of firms to the Equal Employment Opportunity Commission, and it is possible that the figures in the table are for this reason not representative, since they come only from the larger firms, and among them from firms which are willing to cooperate at least minimally with the commission. In any case, the data seem to indicate that for reporting firms blacks and white women are still grossly underrepresented in the managerial ranks. White women represent about 33 percent of the labor force but have only 12 percent of the jobs classified as managerial and administrative, although their share has shown some growth. Blacks of both sexes are also seriously underrepresented in managerial jobs.

Black men in the reporting firms have 6 percent of the craft jobs, and thus appear to be within striking distance of achieving a share of total craft jobs commensurate with their 6.4 percent share of the labor force. Of course, if, contrary to the Civil Rights Act of 1964, one took the attitude that the craft jobs "belong" to men, then one would have to say that black men are seriously underrepresented in the crafts, since the share which black men have of these jobs is only about half as large as their share of the entire *male* labor force. It is an undoubted fact that black men have been and in some places continue to be excluded from craft jobs because of their race. It is also true that black and white women have been even more strictly excluded from craft jobs because of their sex, and that women are showing an interest in these jobs and want to enter them.

Unemployment rates by race and sex for 1974 and 1966 are presented in Table 3, which also presents data for 1964, a year in which the unem-

TABLE 3. UNEMPLOYMENT RATES BY RACE AND SEX

	1974		1966		1964	
	Unem-ployment Rate	*Ratio to White Male Rate*	*Unem-ployment Rate*	*Ratio to White Male Rate*	*Unem-ployment Rate*	*Ratio to White Male Rate*
White Male	4.3	1.0	2.8	1.0	4.1	1.0
Black Male	9.1	2.1	6.3	2.3	8.9	2.2
White Female	6.1	1.4	4.3	1.5	5.5	1.3
Black Female	10.7	2.5	8.6	3.1	9.2	2.2

Source: Labor Department data tabulated in *Manpower Report of the President,* April 1975.

ployment rate for white males was about the same as in 1974. It is apparent from the data that little or no progress has been made in erasing the differential between white male unemployment rates and the unemployment rates of disadvantaged groups, and it is possible that some deterioration may have occurred. White women continue to suffer unemployment rates 30 to 50 percent higher than white men, while black men and women have rates which are more than double those of white men.

Some observers of the labor market attribute the higher unemployment rates of white women and blacks to their higher turnover in employment and their more frequent departures from, and reentries to, the labor force. However, a case can be made that gross underrepresentation of blacks and white women in most upper echelon jobs (and many lower echelon jobs) in both the blue collar and white collar realms and their consequent concentration in relatively few occupations account for much of their unemployment problems, as it accounts for much of their wage problem.

Occupational segregation by race and sex divides the labor market into compartments, and the balance within compartments between the number of jobs and number of labor force members may differ from one compartment to another. Some of the compartments may be relatively crowded, because the occupational "turf" of a particular race-sex group —black males, for example—is small relative to the group's numbers, reflecting the group's inability to enter certain occupations. Overcrowding in a compartment may worsen when a race-sex group increases in its labor force representation relative to that of other groups, but is unable to conquer new occupational "turf." This has certainly been the case with white women. The number of white women in the labor force increased by 31 percent between 1966 and 1974 and a high percentage of these new women workers channeled themselves or were channeled into the already female-dominated clerical and service fields and increased the overcrowding there.

If wages were free to move, the already low wages in the more crowded compartments inhabited principally by women and minority men would fall still lower, possibly reducing labor supplied and increasing labor demanded so that unemployment rates across compartments would have a tendency to become equalized. However, minimum wage laws or business firms' job rating systems or labor union contracts may prevent this from occurring. In any case, a reduction in occupational segregation would probably improve the economic well-being of women, black, and other minority men more than would an increase in wage flexibility.

Alternative Views of Labor Market Disadvantages

Sociologists and anthropologists have long observed the tendency of human societies to form hierarchies with a person's rank in the hierarchy based on his or her race, sex, age, family connections, and religion. It goes without saying that these traits are not necessarily well correlated with those qualities which are most becoming to persons placed in the upper echelons of our social and economic structure—wisdom, magnanimity, competence at affairs, energy, and technical ability. When these social scientists looked at the labor market, and at the distribution of people among jobs, they viewed the results as an extension of the hierarchical nature of existing social relations rather than as the result of a continuing search on the part of employers for talent wherever it might be found. Accordingly, one could not expect equal life chances in the labor market for two individuals starting out with identical capabilities if they differed by race or sex. With this view of the social and economic system, an employer's actions with respect to hiring, promotion, and pay reflect the fact that he is a human being who has been socialized to accept and uphold a hierarchical system in which sex and race are major indicators of status. Such socialization makes it very unlikely that he would consider appointing a black man or a woman to a high status position, even if money could be made by doing so.

Many economists, on the other hand, have built their analysis on the premise that the basis for businessmen's actions is a virtually single-minded quest for monetary profits. These analysts have tended to treat businessmen's decisions on whom to hire for which job in the same framework as businessmen's decisions concerning all of the other inputs to the production process. When a businessman buys lumps of coal for his furnace, he may choose anthracite for some uses and bituminous for others, on the basis of their relative costs, their differences in burning qualities, and the technical characteristics of different situations in which each might be used. It all comes down to "productivity" per dollar of outlay, which gets translated into costs, which in turn affects profits. In considering how to fill the various jobs he has, a businessman can be pictured as making the same kind of calculations. In particular, when he hires a laborer, the productivity he may be looking for may reside in strength and application; when he hires a clerk, productivity may consist in literacy, attention to detail, and a compliant attitude, and when he hires a manager, productivity may consist, principally, in common sense and an air of command. An analyst of business behavior who emphasizes the businessman's search for profits and who observes that occupational segregation by race and sex within business organizations is in fact very widely practiced, reaches with alacrity the conclusion that the businessman finds differing qualities of labor in different race-sex groups. On this view, the businessman's disinclination to mix these groups in the same occupation or on the same rung of the ladder would be no more sinister than his disinclination to stoke a particular boiler with anthracite and bituminous at the same time.

Thus many economists have tended to occupy themselves by looking for factors which might explain the putative inferiority of women and black men in upper echelon jobs. As is usual in such searches, there has been no shortage of candidates. For black men, the factors which have been brought forward include low quantity and quality of education and an alleged lack of commitment to the work ethic. Allegations of inferior genetic endowment, which forty years ago provided an excuse for Nazi crimes against Jews and gypsies, have been recently dusted off for use in explaining the low scores of blacks on IQ tests and, inferentially, their poor position in the labor market. For white females, the factors adduced include "raging hormonal imbalances," and an alleged lack of serious interest in a career because of "their" family responsibilities. The latter is said to result in a lack of formal and on-the-job training because of an alleged disinterest in sacrificing current pay for future benefits and a propensity to leave the labor force for periods of homemaking. Black women presumably combine most of the disabilities of black men and most of those of white women, accounting for their position lowest on the totem pole.

There are thus two opposing views of the employer's role in the labor market treatment of women and black men. In one view the employer is the dispassionate purchasing agent, who is no respecter of persons, consigning each worker to that role in which he or she will be most productive, and paying according to productivity. In the other view, the employer is seen as society's gatekeeper, turning away from entry to high status roles in the workplace members of groups whom society has stigmatized as congenitally inferior.

Probably the most realistic explanation we can give of the position of blacks and women and other minorities in the labor market will extract elements of truth from both of these views and combine them. First of all, there has been a monetary incentive for an employer to duplicate the status hierarchy in society at large by arrangements within the workplace which put women and black men in low status positions. He may fear that to do otherwise—to allow women to supervise men or blacks to supervise whites, for example—creates a situation which is felt as anomalous, a situation in which the participants have not been socialized to feel comfortable, a situation which may very well lead to lack of cooperation or, in extreme cases, even to sabotage. Thus, it has been natural for an employer who does not want to see his profits drained by discord in the workplace to want to make the race-sex pattern in his workplace conform to the general social pattern of hierarchical relations. Other considerations such as wage costs or the antidiscrimination laws may put pressure on an employer to give individuals status within his workplace which differs from their status in society at large, but he may fear that if he does do so there may well be a shorter or longer period of costly difficulties.

One of the most graphic descriptions of the influence of societal status on employee relations within the workplace was given thirty years ago by W. F. Whyte in his analysis of the relationship among the workers in restaurants.[1] Whyte looked at the relationship among the customers, the waitresses, and the countermen who filled the orders they received from the waitresses. Whyte found that the relationship between the waitresses and the countermen was tension-filled and fraught with possibilities for service breakdown. This problem seemed to Whyte to derive from the fact that the waitresses, in bringing the orders to the countermen, "originate action" for them, something that women seldom do to men in other situations. Apparently, the countermen felt that the status advantage they got from their maleness was threatened and tended to react by asserting dominance over the waitresses in ways which might cause the service to customers to deteriorate. Whyte did not speculate as to why restaurant owners do not try to get people who wait on tables and counterpeople of the same sex, but his descriptions make it clear that the race and sex segregation of occupations and the assignment of particular occupations to particular race-sex groups is a phenomenon which grows up quite naturally in any society where race and sex make a difference in the respect accorded to individuals. Moreover, we must add that in most cases the employer himself is consciously or unconsciously committed to upholding the currently operating status system. In short, the employer's own socialization, his workers' and customers' socialization and the employer's desire for monetary profit all interact to affect the pattern of advantage and disadvantage in the labor market.

But what then of objective differences in productive abilities among the races and sexes? What part do they play and how important are they? The first thing to be said is that if such differences had never existed, we would still see occupational segregation by race and sex, with women and black men in a poorer labor market position than white men, for the reasons given above.

The second thing to be said is that some proportion of whatever differences in abilities by race and sex there are results from the effect of discrimination by employers on the development and expression of abilities in the individuals adversely affected. The restrictive hiring, pay and promotion practices which employers have applied to blacks and women have inevitably affected the education, training, attitudes, and labor force attachment of the people economically hobbled by such practices. The opportunities of individual black men and women to develop into economically productive individuals have been severely injured by the treatment blacks have received at the hands of employers. Millions of black girls and boys have been told by their guidance counselors to be "realistic" about their chances in this or that occupation, and have consequently reduced their aspirations, at a cost in bitterness which can only be guessed at. The ability to make education pay off in terms of economic benefits has been far less for blacks than for whites, with obvious effects on blacks' incentives. The ability of some black parents to educate their children and instill into them the habits of persistence and hard work has been undermined by the parents' own economic deprivation, the frustrations they have suffered, and the unfairness they have witnessed.

The practice of many employers of refusing to consider blacks for jobs with status or promotion possibilities has meant reduced incentive for blacks to compete vigorously in the economic race. While social stigmatization of blacks has led to inferior schooling and lack of access to information about good job vacancies, those blacks with good schooling and good information have in the past found most doors closed to them. All of this has combined to lower the potential productivity of many black people, setting up a vicious circle in which exclusion causes lowered potential, which in turn "justifies" exclusion.

The most injurious employer practice suffered by women has been the practice of barring them from jobs in which there is a significant opportunity to get on-the-job training, to learn by doing, and to gradually take on new responsibilities. Managerial jobs are of this type, and so are some of the crafts and technical jobs. Employers have rationalized this practice of exclusion partly by references to women's lower commitment to the labor force and a career, again creating a vicious circle, where poor career opportunities lead to lower commitment, which leads back to restrictive practices of employers.

The practices of employers in confining women to jobs with no future, little interest, and low pay have obviously influenced women's attachment to particular jobs and to the labor market. For the woman having a baby, the job opportunities open to her have influenced her decision as to whether to confine her absence from work to the three or so weeks it usually takes to recover from the physical trauma of birth, or to prolong her absence by months or years. A couple's willingness to accept offers to the husband of a better job in another city when this will mean the wife must leave her current job will depend on the nature of the wife's job. If the wife is a clerical worker with no promotion prospects, then migration of the couple from one city to another in pursuit of marginal improvements in the husband's career will be the rule. If the wife has a significant career of her own, less migration on behalf of the husband's career and more on behalf of the wife's is likely. The nature of a woman's job, the amount of pay she gets for it, and her prospects for promotion have also influenced the way she and her husband split up the work of running their household, which may affect her productivity on the job.

Not all of the problems which blacks, white women, and other minority people have in the labor market can be attributed to currently operating employer discrimination, or to the effect of past employer discrimination on the productive capacity of the disfavored groups. Some part of the problem is undoubtedly attributable to forces outside the labor market—to poor schools, to societal assumptions and attitudes wounding to self-confidence and self-esteem, and to the lack of out-of-the-home facilities for child care. Those who are not hopeful about the prospects of reducing the disadvantage in the labor market positions of women, black men, and other minority groups and those who are overtly or covertly hostile to reducing the primacy of white men tend to emphasize the importance of forces outside the labor market in explaining the absence of women and black men from certain jobs. The implication for those who hold such opinions is that actions on the part of government which would reduce discrimination would have a very small effect on the gap between the labor market position of the currently disadvantaged and the labor market position of white men. What does the evidence show on this point?

A great deal of research has been done by economists in attempts to gauge the importance of the part which discrimination has played in income differences among the race-sex groups. Although they have used a wide variety of data sources, and their methodologies have varied, the economists who have studied this matter are unanimous in declaring that discrimination is important in explaining the white-black earnings gap and the male-female earnings gap. Virtually all studies which have been done put the proportion of the sex differential and the race differential due to discrimination at greater than 50 percent.[2] A recent estimate by Alan S. Blinder is that "70 percent of the overall race differential and 100 percent of the overall sex differential are ultimately attributable to discrimination of various sorts." [3] Virtually all of the economic research on the factors accounting for sex and race differences in pay has been based on indirect statistical evidence, rather than on direct evidence derived from the hiring hall, the shop floor, the office, and the executive suite, where the crucial actions take place. Yet even making ample allowance for the limitations of the economic research on this issue, the direction of its findings is unmistakable. These findings lead to the working hypothesis that a reduction in the amount of discrimination in our labor markets would have an important effect in reducing the disadvantage of women and black men.

What near-term effects might we expect to see from a reduction in labor market discrimination? No one seriously claims that a reduction in discriminatory practices will cause the proportion of presidents and vice presidents of corporations or engineers who are black and/or female to approach 46 percent, which is the current share of blacks and females in the labor force. The integration of women and black men in good numbers into positions such as these will require a long lead time for the development of on-the-job experience and for the development of appropriate aptitudes and interests in young black and white girls and black boys preparing for their careers. Yet a cursory glance around the economy reveals the many large areas of white male exclusivity which could be integrated by race and sex with excellent effects on the position of the currently disadvantaged groups. Such areas include over-the-road trucking, police and fire fighting, some construction trades, municipal and long distance bus and truck driving, lower and middle level administrative positions in the federal, state, municipal, educational, health, and business bureaucracies. No lack of training or experience stands in the way of substantial near-term integration in such areas. What does stand in the way currently is the addiction to past practices which exclude women and black men, an addiction which employers are unlikely to try to break unless given incentives to break them.

A relatively enlightened employer may know that individual women workers or black workers could be as productive and as reliable as the average white man, yet he probably senses that even apart from problems he might have initially with his other employees or his customers, he would face additional risks and costs if he hires a black or a woman for a job usually restricted to white males. Even enlightened employers may not know how or where to find or identify the blacks or women who have been relatively unscarred by the system, and it would require some incentives not now in evidence to impel them to try to overcome their ignorance. The provisions of the antidiscrimination laws now in the books would seem to provide just such an incentive, if they could be enforced in an enlightened but vigorous manner.

Reducing Discrimination Through Law Enforcement

We may sum up the discussion up to this point by saying that the present labor market system in the United States includes as leading and intertwined elements both the profit motive and societal status differentiations. It has strong tendencies to persist in its ways, and the understandable reactions of the victims of the system to their treatment help to keep the system going and to reinforce the beliefs of employers in the soundness of their present personnel policies. Successful intervention to move such a system may well include some remedial work on the education, training, and habits of some members of the disadvantaged groups; this is the kind of intervention which has been traditionally viewed as the proper business of "manpower policy." However, it would be unrealistic to believe that remedial work on the victims will take us very far alone. Since discrimination figures at least as importantly among the factors which cause their lower status and pay as does their alleged personal shortcomings and habits, we must conclude that vigorous use of tools of traditional "manpower policy" must be accompanied by a strong effort by public and private policy-making bodies to change the employment and promotion practices of employers so as to reduce discrimination. If such a double-pronged effort could be effectively mounted, the disadvantaged position of women and black men might well be signficantly changed.

The prerequisites to effective government intervention to change labor market practices which affect disadvantaged women and black men are (1) public sentiment supporting social changes, (2) adequate legislation, and (3) an enforcement mechanism designed so as to work effectively.

Since the 1960s there has been considerable change in the views of many people concerning the proper place in American society for blacks, women, and other disadvantaged groups. This has been due largely to efforts by the disadvantaged groups themselves to protest the indignities and the denial of opportunities to which they have been subjected. A large majority of respondents to public opinion polls now say that they believe that black people should be treated the same as white people.

Equality of treatment in employment is endorsed by a high proportion of poll respondents, even by those who admit to wanting to limit integration in education or housing. While there is somewhat less unanimity in the desirability of allowing and encouraging women's access to the full range of labor market opportunities, support for an end to discrimination against them by employers has been growing, and now represents majority sentiment. Of course, a benign answer to a pollster by no means guarantees benign behavior by the respondent in the workplace. The person who declares herself or himself free of bias may find innumerable excuses to act in such a way as to disadvantage peers, subordinates, and supervisors in the workplace because of race or sex. Nevertheless, the trend is clearly going in the direction of more societal support for more equal treatment on the job.

These changes in public sentiment in the United States have resulted in the passage of legislation, most notably the Civil Rights Act of 1964, forbidding discrimination in employment by private employers on the basis of race or sex. Other legislation includes the Equal Pay Act, which mandates equal pay for equal work, and the Education Amendments which extend the prohibition against discrimination in employment to schools and colleges and prohibit differing treatment of male and female students. Furthermore, Executive Orders of the President require that firms and universities having government contracts not discriminate by race or sex on pain of cancellation of the contract.

Thus, the laws which are among the prerequisites to significant change in labor market practices in the United States would seem to be in place. The attitudes would seem to have changed in the right direction. The third prerequisite—administrative machinery for effective enforcement— has clearly not matured in a satisfactory way. The experience of the last ten years or so of operation under the machinery set up to administer the antidiscrimination laws and orders has been deeply disappointing to those who had hoped for early substantial progress. Symbolic of the failure to make headway against discrimination is the mountain of 98,000 unresolved complaints at the Equal Employment Opportunity Commission (EEOC), which administers the Civil Rights Act. There is also the failure of the Office of Federal Contract Compliance to cancel the government contracts of construction firms which continue to exclude black men from craft jobs, the deaf ear which has been turned by the Department of Health, Education and Welfare to the complaints of women academics against the universities, and the continued sparsity of black women and men and white women in the middle and higher ranks of the federal civil service. The effect of this administrative failure has been the growth of a belief on the part of both employers and members of the aggrieved groups that the probability of timely government action in any particular discrimination case, no matter how egregious, is close to zero. The everyday experience of most citizens could lead them to no conclusion other than that the habits of the ordinary employer in thinking about whom to hire and promote for which job has changed hardly at all.

A depressing illustration is a newspaper story in 1974 which revealed that the offices of at least some Congressmen, including some who had voted for the Civil Rights Act of 1964, were blatantly discriminating in hiring.[4] At least twenty U. S. Congressmen who had hired office personnel through the Congressional Office of Placement and Office Management had included in their written job orders such phrases as "no minorities," "white only," "no blacks," and "no Catholics."[5] According to the story, officials of the Congressional Placement Office said that in sending applicants to be interviewed the office attempted to conform as closely as possible to the criteria listed by the Congressmen. The form the placement office uses, in addition to giving ample room for "special requirements," such as racial restrictions, also encourages the prospective congressional employer to specify sex and a desired age range. In a follow-up to the story, an administrative assistant was quoted as protesting the allegations of discriminatory practices in his office: "I go over to the personnel office. I tell them *whether we want a girl or a man.* I've told them time and time again it doesn't matter on minorities or anything else." [emphasis added][6]

Why have the antidiscrimination laws been administered in a way which has so far seemingly had so little impact on employer habits? One answer which presents itself is that the antidiscrimination legislation was passed by the Congress and was signed by the President as a gesture to groups whose deprivations were regarded by men of affairs as regrettable, and a burden on our consciences, but not, in practice, as something on which to expend a great deal of capital. On this view, the low budgets allotted to the enforcement agencies and the administrative ineptitude and indecision these agencies have displayed are evidence and illustration of a lack of desire on the part of the body politic. In some cases political pressure seems to have prevented the imposition of sanctions on firms in clear violation of the law. Some federal antidiscrimination offices have left budgeted positions unfilled and have turned substantial funds which could have been used for enforcement activity back to the Treasury.

A reading of the critiques of the antidiscrimination efforts of federal agencies by the U. S. Commission on Civil Rights and the General Accounting Office,[7] which give myriad details on the flounderings and outright failures of these agencies might lend support to the hypothesis that a discrimination-free labor market has been very low in our national agenda, if it is really on the agenda at all. Of course, the importance that the leadership of the Executive Branch gives to antidiscrimination efforts is crucial. Unless the administration provides adequate funding and leadership to those agencies which are intended to help the disadvantaged, their effectiveness will be limited. It is possible that the past lack of administrative accomplishment on equal employment has been due, at least in part, to lack of a commitment to combat discrimination on the part of the administration. Future enforcement of the non-discrimination statutes will depend vitally on the commitment of those in future administrations.

Whatever one may believe concerning the past and future position of antidiscrimination enforcement on our national agenda, one thing has been made clear by our experiences: even with maximum goodwill devoted to the job, the task of changing the labor market in so fundamental a way as to remove occupational segregation by race and sex is far from easy or simple, and a slow and halting start was to be expected.

A major practical difficulty facing the agencies attempting to enforce equal opportunity in the job market is that when the law was passed it made a nearly universal condition into a legal offense. Robbery is a crime committed by a small minority and murder by an even smaller number, but employment discrimination is routinely committed by almost everyone who has the opportunity to do so. In enforcing the laws against murder and robbery (and most other criminal and civil offenses) the authorities have traditionally concentrated their resources on the investigation of complaints and the prosecution of cases arising from those complaints. The use of this strategy by the Equal Employment Opportunity Commission (EEOC) has proved to be a misallocation of its very limited resources. As might have been predicted, the volume of complaints has been enormous, and even with a much larger budget EEOC could not have been expected to cope with more than a small fraction of them. While the EEOC has been expending much of its energy on the cases of relatively few aggrieved individuals, many of them with little or no exemplary effect, large firms with thousands of workers have continued openly to maintain a pattern of occupational segregation by race and sex with hardly more than an admonition from the EEOC. The strategy of dealing with complaints in order of filing, regardless of the nature of the complaint, has left most of the people who have complained as well as millions of discriminated-against non-complainants without relief.

An alternative strategy, in which most of the resources of the EEOC would be devoted to systematic investigations of occupational segregation in the largest corporations, would clearly be more productive. There is ample precedent in the investigative activities of the Internal Revenue Service, in which the largest companies and highest income individual tax-payers come in for the most concentrated attention.

An efficient use of the EEOC resources would concentrate them on the elimination of discriminatory practices which are clear-cut and easy to demonstate, and the elimination of which would make a large impact. The institutionalized practices of large companies which separate the "ports of entry" of white males from those of everyone else are a case in point. An excellent example is provided by the case of the Liberty Mutual Insurance Company, which was sued under the Civil Rights

Act of 1964 by some of its employees. The situation in Liberty Mutual between 1965 and 1970 with respect to "technical" employees in the claims department is shown in Figure 1.[8] People were recruited from outside the company for the jobs of "claims adjuster" and "claims representative" and in both cases the only formal requirement was that the

Fig. 1. Liberty Mutual Insurance Company Claims Department—Technical Employees Lines of Responsibility and Promotion Prior to 1970.

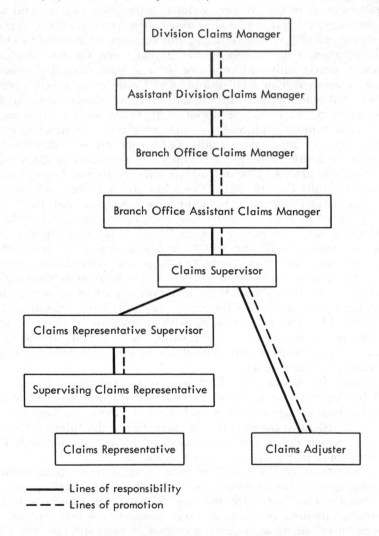

Source: Brief of the EEOC in Wetzel vs. Liberty Mutual Insurance Company (U.S. Court of Appeals for the Third Circuit.)

person be a college graduate. However, only men were permitted to become claims adjusters, while the claims representatives were almost exclusively women. During this period, the company hired over two thousand adjusters. Despite the fact that the company was not recruiting women as claims adjusters, it did receive applicants for the job from a substantial number of them, but it did not hire any. Starting claims adjusters were paid $2,500 more than claims representatives, and it was only from the adjuster's slot that it was possible to obtain promotion beyond a low level supervisory position.[9] The federal judge who saw these facts on the record, all of them derived from material put into the record by Liberty Mutual, entered a summary judgment on this aspect of the case. It is probably safe to say that if the EEOC were to concentrate substantial enforcement resources in large firms with practices similar to those of Liberty Mutual, the award of large settlements, including back pay to affected employees, might be expected to have a substantial demonstrable effect, at least in the large firms. There is some evidence that the case of the Bell Telephone System, where a settlement cost the company $22 million in back pay, has had an impact on other firms. A lessening of segregation by race and sex in "port of entry" positions would by no means end the problem of discrimination, especially for middle and upper level management positions, but might lead to accelerated progress.

In many cases the offense of discrimination consists largely in sins of omission. Recent survey research by sociologists has shown that most people get their jobs through being tipped off by a friend. People not tipped off never get to apply. Naturally, the friends tend to be of the same race, sex, and social class. This mode of filling jobs has been found to be more prevalent the more desirable the job is. Even a well intentioned management, if it takes no new steps to change its recruitment, hiring, and promotion practices (practices it may feel have achieved its goals), will continue to fill its upper level jobs with white males.

What is an appropriate instrument to change this situation? A firm may express a resolve to hire and promote in a nondiscriminatory way, but the EEOC could hardly accept the mere expression of such a resolve as fulfilling the law. The continuation of the same old personnel practices is too comfortable, too ego-satisfying, too familiar to those doing the hiring to be abandoned without *force majeur*. A firm needs to be held to a credible measure of progress in eliminating discriminatory practices, and no one has yet come up with anything which could substitute for the requirement that establishments set and adhere to numerical goals and timetables by occupation. With all their faults, numerical goals and timetables are indispensable, in the absence of some other valid yardstick for measuring progress.

Another indispensible component of a firm's affirmative action program is the setting up of an internal incentive system to see that the goals and timetables are met. This may be relatively easy, since the modern breed of business manager is used to managing "by the numbers." Executives are already accustomed to having their performance rated by the extent to which they have met or exceeded numerical goals in sales, costs, and production. Rating executives' performance in part on their success in meeting goals for hiring or promotion by race and sex is a natural extension. The firms which are claiming success at reducing occupational segregation (including components of the Bell System) have used this method to motivate changes in practices.

Discrimination and the Rate of Employment

The common wisdom is that periods of high unemployment provide a relatively unfriendly environment for making progress against discrimination. When employment is falling, the operations of the seniority system cause disproportionate layoffs of blacks and women. In the recovery phase of the cycle, while unemployment is still high, an employer who wants to fill a job vacancy of a type usually reserved for white males will find many well qualified white male candidates available during such periods, including his own laid-off workers. However, there is another side of the coin usually ignored in discussions of this issue. In periods of slack, an employer who tries the experiment of putting women and black men into jobs which are unconventional for them runs less risk of serious trouble from his experienced white male employees. There is more chance of the white males' cooperation with the newcomers and less chance of their quitting since even white males have reduced opportunity of finding another good job at such a time. By the time opportunities have improved, the white males may have found that they have reconciled themselves to the change.

Whatever we may conclude concerning the balance of forces during periods of slack labor markets, it is certainly far from clear that progress against discrimination is automatic in tight labor markets, or that the problems which discrimination causes would end if tight labor markets could be maintained consistently. The black unemployment rate does tend to go down two points for each point of decline in the white unemployment rate. However, even at times of low overall unemployment, the unemployment rate for blacks continues high—about twice the rate for whites. In other words, during periods when there is general public satisfaction with the state of the labor market, the unemployment rate for blacks remains at levels which are considered disastrous when they apply to whites. More fundamentally, in the absence of effective pressure from law enforcement agencies, little progress is made in dismantling occupational segregation by race and sex even in times of high prosperity, and what gains are made seem to melt rapidly in the recession which follows.

There were three continuous years of acute labor shortage during World War II. In a time of national danger from external enemies it seemed patriotic to put women and blacks into jobs usually reserved for white males, and in some firms it was done on a considerable scale. Very little if anything was said at the time about the lack of training of blacks, or their lack of good education or their poor work incentives. Nor were the alleged incapacities of women emphasized. Once they were on the job few complaints were heard about their lack of competence. In fact, the media portrayed these workers as performing amazingly well. In the postwar period, many blacks and female workers could claim a documented "track record" of competence and experience in jobs which had in the pre-war period been closed to them. Nevertheless although some gains were preserved most doors to good jobs slammed very tight against them in the postwar period, as the nature of the patriotic act changed to the hiring of returning veterans of the armed forces. To be more specific, almost all of the good jobs were reserved for white male veterans.

While even prolonged periods of high demand for labor do not necessarily spell rapid or permanent progress in breaking down occupational segregation, a period of decline in employment clearly destroys much of whatever progress had in fact been made in the period just preceding. The major factor responsible for this is the operation of seniority systems which mandate the rule "last hired, first fired." These seniority arrangements have their greatest impact on efforts to integrate the crafts and factory operative occupations, since these jobs tend to be subject to union-management agreements containing provisions for layoffs in reverse order of hiring.

In considering possible directions for public policy on this issue, it is worth considering briefly the benefits of seniority systems in our general labor relations setup. Seniority protects older workers, whose productivity may have declined, and who would have a hard time in getting an equivalent job (or indeed any job) from a new employer. A seniority system also removes discretion from the process of choosing those to be laid off. Since layoffs are independent of performance ratings, a worker is assured that minor incidents which displease his supervisor but are insufficient to cause his dismissal in good times will not be dredged up and used against him in bad times. The seniority system is thus an amnesty system for petty offenses. Both of these effects may tend to be more or less depressing of efficiency in the economy, but they undoubtedly contribute an important element of greater humaneness in relations between workers and their supervisors.

Could the seniority system be altered in such a way as to maintain these beneficial effects, while reducing its retarding effect on occupational integration by race and sex? One possibility might be a revision of the seniority system so that for a limited time—ten years, perhaps—seniority would be awarded to an individual woman or black man equal to the average seniority of people his or her age within the company. Such a modified system would preserve pretty much intact the benefits we have identified for the present system, while removing at least some of its consequences for integration by race and sex. To the extent that most of the women and black men hired through affirmative action programs are going to be relatively young, the revised system suggested here will only partially eliminate the disproportionate effects of layoffs on women and blacks, but at least within each age cohort the effect of the revision would be to reduce the excess risk of layoffs women and blacks now suffer because of past discrimination.

Will Attempts to Eliminate Discrimination Create New Problems?

If efforts to reduce discrimination in employment are successful, white males currently in the labor market will probably be only minimally affected, but the life chances of white males entering the labor market in the future will be reduced. White males in the future will have less probability of upward mobility, less chance at interesting jobs, less chance at high paying jobs, less chance at jobs which confer high status. More of these jobs would go to black men and to black and white women. A white man who wants his own sons to have all of the privileges he has and who does not care that this arrangement is at the expense of the labor market chances of his own daughters and the sons and daughters of black people will consider this a problem. However, it hardly has the status of a social problem.

The effect of this redistribution of life chances will be somewhat mitigated by the fact that if the pool of eligibles for presently good jobs increases there is likely to be a change in the nature of jobs themselves and in the wage differentials between them. Interesting jobs now tend also to be high paying. Allowing competition for the more interesting jobs among a larger group should lower the relative pay of these jobs, and raise that of the less interesting jobs. Since the present pool of applicants for less interesting jobs would tend to dry up, we might expect to find employers restructuring their less interesting jobs to make them more interesting. For example, fewer people would type full time; a larger proportion of people would do a modest amount of rough typing, and a computer-assisted typewriter would do final drafts. Possibly there might also be some decoupling of high status and high pay, although this is more doubtful. These effects would mean that the labor market "lottery" in the future would have more "prizes," each of a smaller average value than is now the case.

The notion that there ought to be some redistribution of life chances between white men and black men is not controversial to most people. What is controversial is the amount of redistribution which would be accomplished within the context of a system where people are allowed to compete fairly on the basis of ability. Some people believe that any enforcement system which in fact resulted in the hiring of more black men for the kinds of jobs currently monopolized by white men would of necessity be a system in which government coercion resulted in the hiring of incompetents.

It should be noted, however, that so far no documentation has been presented that this is the case, and until such documentation appears, the case must be considered unproved.

When we consider the redistribution of life chances in the labor market as between women and men, the issue of the forced hiring of incompetents also arises in some quarters, again without documentation. More serious, however, are anxieties concerning the issue of sex roles, and the effect of changes in sex roles on raising children and other domestic activities. If women are given a chance to compete with men in the labor market and want to take advantage of the opportunity, how will children be raised? The answers which have been put forth include fewer or no children for many couples and the establishment of more child care facilities outside the home. In Sweden, the government is trying to popularize the idea that both the father and the mother of young children should have a period of lesser labor force attachment subsidized by the state. People are bound to differ on how they view the prospect of a change in sex roles; what looks like a hopeful move to one person is viewed by another person with deep misgivings; in discussing these issues, there is not one of us who does not have a built-in conflict of interest.

Antidiscrimination Enforcement and Its Impact on Business

As we have seen, successful enforcement of the antidiscrimination laws would mean that the government would have to find ways to get businessmen to cease longstanding practices in employment, pay, and promotion which may be congenial to their social training and prejudices despite the fact that these practices may in the shorter run at least prevent frictions within the workplace. They would do so, of course, because through the political process the judgment has been made that discrimination is unfair and that the disabilities experienced by the people who have suffered discrimination should dwindle and eventually cease, even at some cost to business firms in the loss of convenience and temporary disharmony, and at some cost to white males in their share of the high status positions. The job of enforcement is made difficult by the fact that these practices are (unlike restaurant seating) usually done in private, and are virtually universal among business firms.

Like the antidiscrimination laws, the prohibiton of alcoholic beverages in the United States was an example of an attempt to make an offense out of something which was an almost universal practice. Here too, we may question whether the attempt to enforce prohibition was high on the agenda of people in powerful positions. What enforcement there was did not succeed in lowering by very much the amount of drinking, and side effects of the enforcement effort included corruption of the police, the taking over of a sizable industry by criminals, the criminalization of many, and the propagation of a widespread disrespect for law and law enforcement. Prohibition was eventually repealed, to the relief of most people, and the sardonic label "the noble experiment" was placed on its tombstone.

Of course, one major difference between prohibition and antidiscrimination legislation is that drinking is a victimless crime, at least in its initial impact, whereas discrimination is not. It is enlightening to see discrimination as one of a growing class of newly created civil offenses (none of them victimless) currently being committed by a substantial proportion of business enterprises; offenses which include violations of the newly stricter health and safety rules in the workplace, violations of the regulations governing pollution of the environment, violations of stricter regulations concerning proper labeling, safety, and efficacy of consumer products. Public enthusiasm for regulating all of these practices has grown over the last decade, and as has been the case with antidiscrimination legislation, enforcement has been slow to take hold. The establishment of effective methods of acting against pollution or on-the-job hazards is at this writing not much further along than the establishment of effective methods of acting against discrimination.

We are probably entering a new era of stricter and more detailed government overview of the behavior of individual businesses. Conservatives continue to sound the call for government to "get off the backs of businessmen," but most citizens want business to pollute less, endanger their workers less, and discriminate less. If we want a labor market free of segregation by race and sex, cleaner air and water, less noise, safer workplaces, and consumers better served by the products they buy, then a more vigorous and more burdensome oversight of business by the government is necessary, at least until the day when these offenses are as infrequent as theft and murder.

Notes

1. "The Social Structure of the Restaurant," *American Journal of Sociology,* January 1949.
2. For a review of studies on the sex differential in earnings, see Isabel V. Sawhill, "The Economics of Discrimination Against Women: Some New Findings," *Journal of Human Resources,* vol. III, no. 3, Summer 1973. For a bibliography on the race differential in earnings, see Stanley H. Masters, "The Effect of Educational Differences and Labor Market Discrimination on the Relative Earnings of Black Males," *Journal of Human Resources,* vol. IX, no. 3, Summer 1974.
3. "Wage Discrimination: Reduced Form and Structural Estimates," *Journal of Human Resources,* vol. VIII, no. 4, Fall 1973, pp. 436-466.
4. Story written by Francie Barnard of the *Fort Worth Star-Telegram* in August

1974, and published in the *Washington Post.* The Civil Rights Act of 1964 excludes from its coverage the employment practices of the Congress itself, but a Justice Department official indicated that prosecution under other statutes was possible. Needless to say, it has not occurred.

5. The job orders from one congressman's office included the phrase "no water signs," which meant to exclude from consideration persons born under the astrological signs of Scorpio, Pisces, and Cancer.

6. Associated Press story published in the *Washington Post.*

7. *The Federal Civil Rights Enforcement Effort—1974,* volume v "To Eliminate Employment Discrimination," a report of the United States Commission on Civil Rights, July 1975, and *The Equal Employment Opportunity Program for Federal Nonconstruction Contractors Can Be Improved*—a report for the use of the Joint Economic Committee by the General Accounting Office, May 5, 1975.

8. This diagram was drawn not by a social scientist, but by Beth Don, who was the EEOC attorney on the case, and it appears in the opinion of the trial judge.

9. It has been theorized by economists that jobs which have a significant proportion of on-the-job training (much as the claims adjuster's job at Liberty Mutual, which is the training ground for higher positions) should pay less than those which do not, and that the former would be shunned by women who would not want to make the sacrifice of current income. The lack of realism in this theory is amply illustrated by this example, which appears to be quite typical.

Andrew F. Brimmer

6

Economic Growth and Employment and Income Trends among Black Americans

Introduction

In this chapter, an assessment is made of the economic progress of blacks in the United States during the last decade and a half. This assessment is made against the background of the changing rate of economic growth in the economy as a whole. The focus is primarily on blacks' experience during the decade of the 1960s and during the five years 1969–1974. The impact of variations in economic activity on blacks' employment and incomes is examined in some detail.

The picture which emerges from the inquiry is a mosaic of progress and stagnation. In general, blacks are moving ahead on the economic front, but a number of divergent trends are evident. The implications of some of these developments for the future of blacks—and for other minority groups generally—are potentially serious.

The strong expansion in overall economic activity during the decade of the 1960s stands out clearly. Likewise, the relative stagnation since 1969—a period during which the economy was wracked by intense inflationary pressures and two recessions, the latter of which was the worst since the end of World War II—is also unmistakable. These developments have been particularly detrimental to blacks.

On the basis of the evidence, it is clear that the economic condition of blacks—as well as that of poor whites and members of other racial minority groups—is not likely to be eased very much through the rest of

ANDREW F. BRIMMER *is Thomas Henry Carroll Ford Foundation Visiting Professor at the Harvard Graduate School of Business Administration. He has been Assistant Secretary for Economic Affairs, U.S. Department of Commerce (1965–66) and a member of the Board of Governors of the Federal Reserve System (1966–74).*

this decade if national economic policy remains on the present course. For that reason, it is vital that the federal government pursue a more vigorous policy to promote economic expansion.

Contours of Economic Growth

The principal factor influencing the employment opportunities for blacks during the last decade and a half has been the behavior of the national economy. Partly because of the strong upsurge in economic activity during the 1960s, blacks improved their situation relative to the country as a whole. However, because of economic stagnation between 1969 and 1974—which, in turn, was due to two recessions and one of the worst bouts of inflation on record—blacks did worse than the rest of the nation during the last five years.

The principal trends in output, employment, and prices during the years 1959–1975 are shown in Table 1. The strong growth in economic activity is evident. Reflecting these real improvements, total employment rose rapidly, and until 1969 unemployment fell sharply. Between 1961 and 1969, the civilian labor force expanded at an annual average rate of 1.7 percent. However, new jobs were created at an even faster pace (2.1 percent per year), and the level of unemployment declined to an annual average rate of 3 percent.

The recession which began in late 1969 checked these improvements and ushered in a period of stagnation that is still with us. Gross National Product (measured in current dollars) rose at an annual average rate of 8.5 percent between 1969 and 1974. But most of this expansion was attributable to inflation since the GNP deflator rose by an annual average rate of 5.8 percent. Over the same years, real GNP recorded an annual average rate of increase of only 2.2 percent. Industrial production expanded at an average rate of 2.4 percent. Although total employment rose at an average rate of 2 percent, the labor force expanded even more rapidly—by 2.4 percent a year. Consequently, the level of unemployment climbed dramatically. By late 1973, a recession was definitely under way, and the downtrend in economic activity continued until the second quarter of 1975. At the trough, real GNP was about 8 percent below the peak set in the final months of 1973. Industrial production fell by 14 percent, and the capacity utilization rate in manufacturing declined from 83 to 66 percent. In the nine months ending in the second quarter of 1975, about 2.5 million jobs were lost. Since the labor force continued to expand, the total number of persons out of work rose from 5 million in the third quarter of 1974 to 8.2 million in the second quarter of 1975. During the same period, the unemployment rate climbed from 5.5 to 8.9 percent.

The recovery that got under way in the summer of 1975 was led by a modest rise (about 4 percent) in real consumer spending—which, in turn, was stimulated by the $20 billion reduction in personal income taxes

TABLE 1.   TRENDS IN OUTPUT, EMPLOYMENT, AND PRICES, 1959–1975

Category	1959	1961	1969	1974	1975
OUTPUT					
GNP (Current Dollars, $ Bil.)	483.7	520.1	930.3	1,397.4	1,477.5
Real GNP (1958 Dollars, $ Bil.)	475.9	497.2	725.6	821.2	797.7
Industrial Production					
(1967 = 100)	64.8	66.7	110.7	124.8	113.4
EMPLOYMENT (Thousands)					
Civilian Labor Force	68,369	70,459	80,734	91,101	92,658
Employment	64,630	65,746	77,902	85,936	84,787
Unemployment	3,739	4,713	2,832	5,165	7,871
Unemployment Rate (Percent)	5.5	6.7	3.5	5.6	8.5
PRICES					
GNP Deflator (1958 = 100)	101.7	104.6	128.2	170.2	185.2
Wholesale Price Index					
(1967 = 100)	94.8	94.5	106.5	160.1	174.8
Consumer Price Index					
(1967 = 100)	87.3	89.6	109.8	147.7	161.1

Source: U.S. Department of Commerce, Bureau of Economic Analysis. U.S. Department of Labor, Bureau of Labor Statistics.

adopted in the spring of 1975. As the latter year unfolded, the rise in spending by the household sector gathered strength; and a marked slackening in the pace of inventory liquidation as 1975 drew to a close was another source of support for total economic activity. However, the pace of recovery was moderate by historical standards. Although the pace of inflation was moderating rapidly in late 1975, the outlook was for a continuation of high levels of unemployment and a considerable backlog of excess capacity. This was clearly not an environment in which blacks and other members of minority groups—along with poor whites—could expect to prosper.

Trends in Labor Force, Employment, and Unemployment

In 1975, there were 10.5 million blacks [1] in the labor force. Blacks held 9.1 million jobs, and 1.5 million were unemployed. In the same year, the civilian labor force totaled 92.6 million. Total employment averaged 84.8 million, and 7.8 million persons were idle. Thus, in 1975, blacks made up 11.4 percent of the civilian labor force, 10.7 percent of total employment, and 18.6 percent of total unemployment. Behind these figures, however, is a picture of black participation in the labor market that has been both variable and distressing. The general dimensions of

Change				Average Annual Percentage Change			
1959–69	*1961–69*	*1969–74*	*1974–75*	*1959–69*	*1961–69*	*1969–74*	*1974–75*
446.6	410.2	467.1	80.1	6.8	7.5	8.5	5.7
249.7	228.4	95.6	−23.5	4.3	4.8	2.2	−2.9
45.9	44.0	14.1	−11.4	5.5	5.3	2.4	−8.7
12,365	10,275	10,367	1,557	1.7	1.7	2.4	1.7
13,272	12,156	8,034	−1,149	1.9	2.1	2.0	−1.7
−907	−1,881	2,333	2,706	−2.7	−3.0	12.8	52.4
−2.0	−3.2	2.1	2.9	−	−	−	−
26.5	23.6	42.0	15.0	2.3	2.6	5.8	8.8
11.7	12.0	53.6	14.7	1.1	1.5	8.5	9.2
22.5	20.2	37.9	13.4	2.3	2.6	6.1	9.1

the situation among blacks are generally known. However, it might be helpful to sketch the highlights in broad outline.

TRENDS IN THE BLACK LABOR FORCE

Before looking at the actual changes in the black labor force, long-term trends in the black participation rate [2] should be noted. During the last few years, the black participation rate has continued to decline. This decrease was more pronounced than long-run trends in participation would have warranted. Much of the decrease continued to be among adult men. Black workers in the experienced age group (twenty-five to fifty-four) continued to show declines in participation. Moreover, although decreases were particularly sharp during the 1970–71 recession, it seems reasonable to conclude that the period of economic stagnation during the last five years—combined with the rapid growth in the number of better educated young workers—may have produced an economic climate discouraging to adult black males, particularly those with few skills.

In general, participation rates for older black workers have declined in line with white rates. However, the 1969–74 period saw a sharp drop in participation among black men and women fifty-five to sixty-four years of age which was not experienced among their white counterparts.

Adult black women aged twenty to thirty-four kept their participation rate essentially unchanged during the last five years, and increases were experienced in the age groups twenty-five to thirty-four and thirty-five to forty-four. But these increases were not as fast as those registered by white women in the same age categories. The participation rates among black youths fluctuated substantially from year to year, but they generally remained below the rates of the 1960s. The participation rates for black teenagers were also significantly less than the rates for white teenagers.

During the sustained expansion of the national economy from 1961 through 1969, the black labor force rose in line with the total civilian labor force. So blacks as a fraction of the total remained unchanged at 11.1 percent. Among blacks, as well as among whites, adult women and youths of both sexes accounted for a larger share of the rise in the labor force during the 1960s than they represented at the beginning of the decade. But in the last five years, the black labor force expanded much more rapidly than the labor force as a whole. However, blacks' share of total employment remained essentially unchanged (at 10.8 percent), so the incidence of unemployment among blacks rose steadily.

TRENDS IN EMPLOYMENT

During the 1960s, blacks got a moderately larger share of the increase in employment than they had at the beginning of the decade. In 1961, they held 10.4 percent of the total, but they accounted for 12.8 percent of the expansion in jobs between 1961 and 1969. Within the black group, adult females got a relatively larger share of the expanded jobs than black men. This pattern paralleled that evident among whites. On the other hand, black youths made virtually no progress toward improving their relative employment position during the decade. This was in sharp contrast to the situation among white youths. In 1961, black teenagers had 0.6 percent of the total jobs, and in 1969, they held 0.8 percent. White youths expanded their share of total employment from 5.6 to 7.0 percent over these years.

TRENDS IN UNEMPLOYMENT

Between 1961 and 1969, the total number of workers without jobs dropped by 1.9 million. This reflected the recovery from the 1960–61 recession, as well as the substantial growth of the economy during the decade. Over these same years, unemployment among blacks declined by 400,000. This reduction was about in line with the decrease in joblessness in the economy generally, and blacks' share of total unemployment was roughly the same in 1969 (20.2 percent) as it was in 1961 (20.6 percent).

Between 1969 and 1974, the total number of workers without jobs rose from 2.8 million to 5.1 million. Blacks accounted for about one-fifth of this increase of 2.2 million—roughly the same as their share of total unemployment in 1969. The experience among sex and age groups within the black community was essentially the same as that among their white counterparts. The relative rise in joblessness among adult males was noticeably greater than that which occurred among both adult women and teenagers of both sexes. During 1975, under the impact of the worst recession since World War II, the level of total unemployment jumped to 7.8 million. Blacks accounted for about 16 percent of this increase of 2.8 million. In general, in terms of its demographic characteristics, this rise in unemployment represented an extension of the pattern that had prevailed during the preceding five years.

During the 1973–75 recession, the labor market experience of blacks differed substantially from that of their white counterparts. For example during the worst part of the recession, from September 1974 through April 1975, the total civilian labor force continued to expand. In contrast, the black labor force declined somewhat—with the decreases concentrated among adult males and teenagers of both sexes. During the same period, blacks lost their jobs at almost double the rate experienced by whites. For example, in September 1974, blacks held 10.9 percent of the total jobs. But during the succeeding seven months, they accounted for 21.7 percent of the recession-induced decline in employment. About 17.5 percent of the climb in total joblessness over this period was borne by the black community. Moreover, with the beginning of recovery during the summer of 1975, blacks were called back to their jobs at a somewhat slower pace than was the case among whites. Moreover, the actual level of unemployment among black teenagers was still on a rising trend at the end of the year.

For the economy as a whole, the total unemployment rate averaged 8.5 percent in 1975. For blacks, the rate was 13.8 percent, and for whites it was 7.8 percent. Thus, the black-white ratio was slightly less than the historic two to one. However, this was due to the severity and duration of the recession (which brought such an enormous increase in joblessness among whites, as well as among blacks) rather than to any basic relative improvement in the position of blacks in the economy. The unemployment rate among all teenagers averaged 19.9 percent in 1975, but it was 36.9 percent among black teenagers and 17.9 percent among their white counterparts.

As indicated above, as 1975 drew to a close, the worst recession the country has seen since the Great Depression was definitely over. But it was also clear that the nation would be faced with an exceptionally high rate of unemployment and a large backlog of unused plant capacity for a number of years. In the face of that outlook, it was also clear that the deep pessimism within the black community regarding its economic future was thoroughly justified.

TABLE 2. EMPLOYED PERSONS 16 YEARS AND OVER, BY OCCUPATION GROUP AND
COLOR, 1959, 1969, AND 1974 (THOUSANDS)

Occupation	1959				
	Total		Black		
	Num- ber	Per- cent Dist.	Num- ber	Per- cent Dist.	Per- cent of Total
TOTAL EMPLOYED	64,627	100.0	6,621	100.0	10.2
WHITE-COLLAR WORKERS					
Total	27,593	42.7	954	14.4	3.5
Prof. and Technical	7,140	11.1	304	4.6	4.3
Managers & Adm. (ex. farm)	6,936	10.7	163	2.4	2.4
Sales Workers	4,210	6.5	83	1.3	2.0
Clerical Workers	9,307	14.4	404	6.1	4.3
BLUE-COLLAR WORKERS					
Total	23,993	37.1	2,728	41.2	11.4
Craftsmen	8,554	13.2	389	5.9	4.5
Operatives	11,816	18.3	1,321	20.0	11.2
Nonfarm Laborers	3,623	5.6	1,018	15.3	28.1
SERVICE WORKERS					
Total	7,697	11.9	2,109	31.9	27.4
Private Household	1,948	3.0	973	14.7	49.9
Other Service Workers	5,749	8.9	1,136	17.2	19.8
FARM WORKERS					
Total	5,344	8.3	830	12.5	15.5
Farmers & Farm Managers	3,013	4.7	232	3.5	7.7
Farm Laborers & Supervisors	2,331	3.6	598	9.0	25.7

Source: U.S. Department of Labor, Bureau of Labor Statistics, *Manpower Report of the President,* 1975, Table A-15, p. 225, and Table A-16, p. 227.

Changing Structure of Black Employment

At this juncture, we can take a closer look at the principal changes in the composition of black employment in recent years. These changes can be seen in both the occupational and industrial distribution of black workers.

OCCUPATIONAL DISTRIBUTION

The extent of the occupational changes among black workers can be traced in Table 2. Advancement in the range of jobs held by blacks in the decade of the 1960s is quite noticeable. This is particularly true of the improvements in the highest paying occupations. Between 1959 and

	1969					1974			
Total		Black			Total		Black		
Number	Percent Dist.	Number	Percent Dist.	Percent of Total	Number	Percent Dist.	Number	Percent Dist.	Percent of Total
77,902	100.0	8,383	100.0	10.8	85,936	100.0	9,316	100.0	10.8
36,845	47.3	2,198	26.2	6.0	41,739	48.6	2,977	32.0	7.1
10,769	13.8	695	8.3	6.5	12,338	14.4	970	10.4	7.9
7,987	10.3	254	3.0	3.2	8,941	10.4	379	4.1	4.2
4,692	6.0	166	2.0	3.5	5,417	6.3	214	2.3	4.0
13,397	17.2	1,083	12.9	8.1	15,043	17.5	1,414	15.2	9.4
28,237	36.2	3,590	42.9	12.7	29,776	34.7	3,748	40.2	12.6
10,193	13.1	709	8.5	7.0	11,477	13.4	874	9.4	7.6
14,372	18.4	2,004	23.9	13.9	13,919	16.2	2,041	21.9	14.7
3,672	4.7	877	10.5	23.9	4,380	5.1	833	8.9	19.0
9,528	12.2	2,239	26.7	23.5	11,373	13.2	2,337	25.1	20.5
1,631	2.1	714	8.5	43.8	1,228	1.4	474	5.1	38.6
7,897	10.1	1,525	18.2	19.3	10,145	11.8	1,863	20.0	18.4
3,292	4.3	356	4.2	10.8	3,048	3.5	254	2.7	8.3
1,844	2.4	84	1.0	4.6	1,643	1.9	64	0.7	3.9
1,448	1.9	272	3.2	18.8	1,405	1.6	190	2.0	13.5

1969, the number of blacks in professional and technical positions increased by 129 percent (to 695,000) while the increase in the total was only 51 percent (to 10.8 million). Blacks had progressed to the point where they accounted for 6.5 percent of the total employment in these top categories in the occupational structure in 1969, compared with 4.3 percent in 1959. They got about 11 percent of the net increase in such jobs over the decade. During this same period, the number of black managers, officials, and proprietors (the second highest paying category) rose by almost three-fifths (254,000) compared to an expansion of 15 percent (8 million) for all employees in this category.

In the 1960s, black workers left low-paying jobs in agriculture and household service at a rate about 1.5 times faster than white workers. The number of black farmers and farm workers dropped by 57 percent (to

356,000) in contrast to a decline of about 38 percent (to 3.3 million) for all persons in the same category. The exit of blacks from private household employment was even more striking. During the decade of the 1960s, the number of blacks so employed fell by 27 percent (to 714,000); the corresponding drop for all workers was only 16 percent (to 1.9 million).

While blacks made substantial progress during the 1960s in obtaining clerical and sales jobs—and also registered noticeable gains as craftsmen—their occupational center of gravity remained anchored in those positions requiring little skill and offering few opportunities for further advancement. At the same time, it is also clear from the above analysis that blacks who were well prepared to compete for the higher-paying positions in the upper reaches of the occupational structure did make measurable gains during the 1960s. Nevertheless, compared with their overall participation in the economy (11 percent of total employment), the occupational deficit in white-collar employment—amounting to roughly 40 percent—remained quite large in 1969.

Data on occupational distribution of total employment by color in 1974 are also shown in Table 2. In general, these figures show the mixed experience of blacks in the last five years. Blacks' share of total jobs remained unchanged at 10.8 percent. However, between 1969 and 1974, they raised their share of professional and technical jobs. The number of blacks employed in white-collar jobs rose by 779,000—a gain of 35 percent. The number holding blue-collar jobs in 1974 was 158,000 above the 1969 level, an increase of only 4 percent. Within the blue-collar group, the rate of expansion was particularly slow in the case of operatives, and the number of nonfarm laborers actually declined over the five-year period. In both cases, the changes were mainly a reflection of the fact that total employment in the manufacturing sector (in which a sizable proportion of blacks is employed) expanded rather slowly between 1969 and 1974.

INDUSTRY STRUCTURE OF BLACK EMPLOYMENT

In 1968, about 24.2 percent of black job holders were employed in manufacturing. The corresponding proportion for total employment was 27.2 percent. By 1972, the corresponding figures were 24.1 percent for the total and 22.6 percent for blacks. Over the same four years, however, blacks' share of total jobs in manufacturing climbed slightly (from 9.6 to 9.9 percent).

The proportion of the black work force employed in transportation and public utilities rose somewhat between 1968 and 1972—from 4.3 to 5 percent. The proportion for all workers was essentially unchanged—at about 5.8 percent. However, a sizable divergence is evident in the trade field, in which 13.8 percent of blacks (in contrast to 20 percent of the total) found jobs in 1972. These fractions were essentially the same in 1968. A smaller (but still noticeable) divergence can be seen in the case of finance, insurance, and real estate—which accounted for 5.2 percent of total employment compared with 3.2 percent of black employment in 1972. Yet, these industries did become a somewhat more important source of black jobs during the four-year period. On the other hand, blacks were overly represented in services (23.9 percent of employed blacks versus 17.9 percent of the total) in 1972. In general, blacks tend to have a disproportionate share of the jobs in low-wage industries, and they tend to be underrepresented in high-wage industries.[3] For example, among the low-wage manufacturing industries are lumber, tobacco, textiles, and apparel. In all of these, blacks' share of the total jobs in 1972 was well above their share of all jobs in the private sector. In contrast, among the high-wage industries, only in primary metals; stone, clay, and glass; and transportation equipment (particularly automobile manufacturing) did blacks have an above-average share of the total jobs. Among the high-wage manufacturing industries in which blacks were noticeably underrepresented are fabricated metals, machinery (both electrical equipment and nonelectrical varieties), instruments, paper, printing and publishing, and rubber. They were similarly underrepresented in transportation and public utilities, wholesale trades, construction, and mining.

Between 1968 and 1972, blacks made some progress in migrating from low-wage to high-wage industries, but in several cases, they became even more heavily represented in low-wage sectors. For example, blacks' share of total jobs declined somewhat in lumber and furniture manufacturing, food processing, and services—all low-wage industries. They also expanded their share of employment in a number of high-wage sectors: electrical machinery, transportation equipment, paper, chemicals, petroleum, and transportation and public utilities. On the other hand, blacks' share of total employment rose in tobacco, textiles, and apparel, in which wages are below average. Their share eased off somewhat in printing and publishing and in wholesale trade, in which wages are above average.

Impact of the Equal Employment Opportunity Program

Over the last decade, blacks have given a great deal of support for the national policy aimed at creating equal employment opportunities launched in Title VII of the Civil Rights Act of 1964. This provision created the Equal Employment Opportunity Commission (EEOC) and the commission began operations on July 2, 1965. However, EEOC started life with a number of handicaps; it was not until 1972 that the commission got enforcement powers of its own. Once the new authority was implemented in March 1973, EEOC could initiate civil actions in federal courts to enforce the provisions barring job discrimination and

TABLE 3. TOTAL AND EEOC-REPORTED EMPLOYMENT, 1966 AND 1974 (NUMBERS IN THOUSANDS)

Occupation	1966					
	Total Employment[1]			EEOC-Reported Employment[2]		
	Total	Black		Total	Black	
	Number	Number	Percent of Total	Number	Number	Percent of Total
TOTAL EMPLOYMENT	67,325	6,487	9.6	25,573	2,087	8.2
WHITE-COLLAR	33,068	1,644	5.0	10,997	278	2.5
Prof. & Technical	9,310	551	5.9	2,834	68	5.3
Professional	–	–	–	1,693	22	1.3
Technical	–	–	–	1,141	46	4.0
Managers & Officials	7,405	207	2.8	2,084	17	0.8
Sales Workers	4,541	138	3.0	1,802	43	2.4
Clerical Workers	11,812	748	6.3	4,277	150	3.5
BLUE-COLLAR	26,950	3,300	12.3	12,615	1,357	10.8
Craftsmen	9,589	600	6.3	3,630	132	3.7
Operatives	13,829	1,782	12.9	6,507	701	10.8
Laborers	3,532	918	26.0	2,478	524	21.1
SERVICE WORKERS	7,308	1,544	21.1	1,961	452	23.0

Source: U.S. Department of Labor, Bureau of Labor Statistics, *Manpower Report of the President*, April, 1975, Tables A-15, p. 225; A-16, p. 227, and G-10, p. 347.
[1] Excluding private household and farm workers.
[2] Reported to U.S. Equal Employment Opportunity Commission by firms with 100 or more employees.

to remedy instances of their violation. Coverage of the statute was extended to employees of state and local governments and their instrumentalities, employees of educational institutions, and firms or labor organizations with fifteen or more workers or members. Additional protection was also provided federal government employees.

Armed with this new authority and an enlarged budget, EEOC in the last few years accelerated its drive against employment discrimination—concentrating on sex and language bias, as well as on racial barriers. It achieved a landmark settlement of its suit against AT&T in January 1973, which called for cash payments (mainly to blacks and white women) in excess of $50 million in compensation for past discrimination and as bonuses for transferring to better-paying jobs. The commission has also worked out agreements in trucking, steel, and other industries which will yield greatly improved job opportunities for blacks in the years ahead.

			1974		
Total Employment [1]			EEOC-Reported Employment [2]		
Total	Black		Total	Black	
Number	Number	Percent of Total	Number	Number	Percent of Total
81,660	8,588	10.5	31,603	3,484	11.6
41,739	2,977	7.1	14,668	868	5.9
12,338	970	7.9	3,833	180	10.5
—	—	—	2,387	73	3.1
—	—	—	1,446	107	7.4
8,941	379	4.2	3,127	88	2.8
5,417	214	4.0	2,714	149	5.5
15,043	1,414	9.4	4,994	451	9.0
29,776	3,748	12.6	14,515	2,043	14.1
11,477	874	7.6	4,227	293	6.9
13,919	2,041	14.7	7,413	1,165	15.7
4,380	833	19.0	2,875	585	20.3
10,145	1,863	18.4	2,420	573	23.7

MIXED PATTERN OF JOB EXPANSION

Given the efforts of EEOC to broaden job opportunities for blacks and other minorities (and more recently for women), one can naturally ask just what has been the impact of the campaign. Unfortunately, no direct answer can be given. But the indirect evidence does suggest that the commission's activities are having generally favorable results. Employers, trade unions, and others covered by the statute are required to report the racial and sex composition of their work forces to the commission at least once each year. So far, EEOC has required annual reports from those with 100 or more employees. On the basis of these reports, one can get a fairly good idea of the changing composition of jobs held by blacks compared to others. Table 3 shows total and black employment in EEOC-reporting firms by major occupational categories, for 1966 and 1974. Corresponding figures for all nonfarm employment reported by the Bureau of Labor Statistics (BLS) in the U.S. Department of Labor are also shown.

Several conclusions stand out in these data. Black employment in EEOC-reporting firms rose much faster than employment in the economy as a whole. For instance, blacks accounted for 23 percent of the growth in jobs in EEOC-reporting firms versus 15 percent in the total. However, within the white-collar category, only clerical workers and sales workers recorded relatively larger gains on EEOC-reported payrolls (42 percent versus 21 percent and 12 percent versus 9 percent, respectively). In the case of professional and technical workers, EEOC figures show blacks getting 11 percent of the increase in jobs versus 14 percent for black professionals and technicians in the economy at large. The lag was especially noticeable among managers and officials. In the country as a whole, blacks accounted for 11 percent of the expansion; their share in EEOC reporters was only 7 percent. In contrast, blacks got a much larger share of the new craft and service jobs in EEOC-reporting firms—*e.g.*, 27 percent of craft jobs versus 15 percent for all firms and 26 percent of service jobs versus 11 percent for all employers combined. In the case of operatives, blacks got 51 percent of the rise in jobs reported by EEOC firms while in the total economy, the increase in such jobs held by blacks was nearly three times as large as the increase in the total. In the case of laborers, blacks in EEOC firms accounted for 15 percent of the rise in employment—while a decline in the number of laborers in the economy at large offset about 10 percent of the increase in employment in this category.

On the basis of these figures, I conclude that the companies reporting under the EEOC requirements are opening jobs to blacks at a rate much faster than is true for all employers in the country as a whole. At the same time, however, it appears that the expansion is much slower in the upper reaches of the occupational scale than it is among job categories at the lower end. Thus, the task of occupational upgrading for blacks remains considerable.

RACE, SEX, AND EQUAL OPPORTUNITY

In recent years, the black community has been concerned about what appears to be a counter-move in the campaign to enhance equal opportunity. This counter-move appears in a variety of forms, but the main thrust is frequently expressed in charges of "reverse discrimination" against whites—especially against white men. But blacks are also becoming apprehensive over the extent to which the strong drive for equal opportunity on the part of white women might have an adverse effect on blacks—especially on black men.

The first concern extends well beyond the specific competition for jobs. It is also manifested in the spreading controversy over admissions standards for colleges and universities and in the debate over staffing patterns in institutions of higher education. It is argued by some that "open admissions" policies designed to expand opportunities for blacks and others to get a college education have lowered standards and are a threat to the quality of higher education. In a similar vein, some critics feel that federal government guidelines aimed at increased employment and upgrading of women and members of minority groups on college and university faculties are setting targets which can only be reached by lowering standards. As seen by the black community, these criticisms are leading to a narrowing of the goals of equal opportunity and—if allowed to continue—will lead to a significant slowing in the pace of progress.

Blacks' concerns over the foregoing developments can be documented but not measured. But the question of whether white women are gaining jobs at the expense of black men can be quantified to some extent. For this purpose, the data collected by the EEOC are helpful. In 1966, white women held 28 percent of the 25.6 million jobs reported by the EEOC firms shown in Table 3. Black men held 5.7 percent of the total. By 1974, total EEOC-reported employment had risen to 31.6 million jobs. White women's share of the total had risen to 30.1 percent (a gain of 2 percentage points), and the share of black men had climbed to 6.5 percent of the total (a gain of only 0.8 percentage points). Over the same time span, the share of total jobs held by white men decreased from 60.7 to 53.4 percent. The share held by black women rose from 2.5 to 4.1 percent. Members of minority groups other than blacks (American Indians, Orientals, and Spanish-speaking groups) raised their share of the total from 3.1 to 5.4 percent. Thus, the share of jobs held by white men declined over the eight-year period, and their loss was represented as relative gains by minority groups other than blacks, white women, black women, and black men—in that order.

Much of the focus is really on the competition for white-collar jobs—particularly for those at the top of the occupation ladder. Between 1966 and 1974, white men's share of total white-collar jobs declined by 6.5 percentage points to 53.8 percent of the total. The fraction of such jobs held by white women rose by 1.3 percentage points to 40.4 percent. Black women's share rose by 2.2 percentage points to 3.8 percent of the total. The fraction held by black men increased by 1.2 percentage points to 2.1 percent of the total. The share held by other minority groups rose by 1.8 percentage points to 3.8 percent of all white-collar jobs. But the most striking changes occurred in the distribution of professional jobs. In this case, the fraction of such jobs held by white men decreased by 16.6 percentage points—to 67 percent of the total in 1974. A substantial proportion of this loss appeared as an increase of 12.8 percentage points in the share of such jobs held by white women—raising their proportion to 25.9 percent of the total. The shares of black men and black women each rose 0.9 percentage points, and they each accounted for about 1.5

percent of the total. In 1974, white men held 83 percent of the managerial jobs on the payrolls of EEOC-reporting firms. This was a decrease of 6 percentage points since 1966. About half of this relative loss (2.8 percentage points) appeared as a gain in the position of white women—raising their share of the total of such jobs to 12 percent. The fraction held by black men moved up by 0.5 percentage points to 2.1 percent of the total. The fraction held by black women rose by 0.2 percentage points to 0.7 percent of the total. Other minority groups raised their fraction by 1.2 percentage points to 2.2 percent of the total.

In conclusion, the above data suggest that—at the margin—white women increased their share of the higher-paying jobs at a rate slightly faster than their representation in total employment. In contrast, all other groups—black men, black women, and other minorities—experienced relatively more modest improvements. While white men saw their share of total employment (and especially among the better-paying occupations) decline slightly over the eight-year period, they still command the heights of the occupational ladder with little or no challenge. Consequently, it is in that direction that blacks must look as they seek to improve their occupational status in the years ahead.

Blacks in Public Sector Employment

The foregoing discussion has dwelt on trends in black employment in the private sector. At this point, we should focus on the mixed picture in the public sector. Historically, a larger proportion of employed blacks (especially of those in professional positions) has been on the public payroll than has been true for the population as a whole. For example, while blacks represented about 10 percent of total employment in nonfarm occupations in private industry in 1974, they accounted for 16 percent of all civilian employees in the federal government. Moreover, while federal employment represented 2.8 percent of the total jobs in the economy in 1974, about 4.8 percent of the blacks in civilian jobs were on the federal payroll.

Behind these overall statistics is an even heavier reliance by blacks on the public sector for a disproportionate share of the better jobs they hold. The extent of this reliance was fully documented in the 1960 and 1970 Census of Population. In 1960, employment in public administration at the federal, state, and local level accounted for about 4.9 percent of total employment. The percentage of blacks so employed was roughly the same, 5 percent. However, while just 6 percent of all professional and technical workers were employed by public agencies, 7.3 percent of black workers in the same occupations were employed by such agencies. By 1970, public administration represented 5.5 percent of total employment, but the proportion for blacks had risen to 6.6 percent.

For black workers, public sector jobs tend to pay much better than the jobs they hold in the private sector compared with the situation among white workers. For example, in 1974, the average black government employee earned $6,464 compared with the average of $5,125 earned by blacks on private payrolls. The government jobs were paying about 26 percent more on the average. The average pay of white workers on government payrolls was $8,600 in 1974, compared with $7,533 in the private sector. In this case, the government jobs were paying 14 percent more. In public service, average compensation of blacks was 75 percent of that of whites. In the private sector, blacks' compensation was only 68 percent of that of whites. Finally, while black workers earned 6.8 percent of the total income in 1974, their share of total private sector earnings was 6.6 percent—and their share of total earnings in the public sector amounted to 10 percent.

The reasons for this much greater reliance of blacks on public sector employment are clearly understood. Partly because of the existence of a racially segregated school system in the United States for such a long time, black public school teachers and administrators found relatively greater opportunity within the parallel system. In addition, for political reasons (especially in the North and West), blacks historically have gotten a share of the local public service jobs. At the federal level, and especially so in recent years, blacks have found a much more hospitable environment in the public sector than was true in private industry. The official effort to expand equal opportunity during the last decade brought particularly striking results in the federal government—at least in terms of the lower and middle grades of the classified federal service.

But as I reflect on these data, I find them more disturbing than comforting. In the years ahead, the principal expansion of employment is likely to be in the private sector. If blacks are to share fully in this expansion, they must make accelerated progress in private sector employment. This is especially true with respect to the better-paying occupations.

Blacks and the Distribution of Income

During the last five years, the distribution of money income in the United States has become more unequal, and economic equity has deteriorated. This is a reversal of the trends evident during the preceding decade. A surface review of the data on income distribution might suggest that relative income shares have remained essentially unchanged since the end of World War II. However, a closer examination of the latest evidence identifies a marked tendency toward inequality among a number of segments of the population during the first half of the 1970s.

In general, over the last five years, income has been redistributed so as to favor whites versus blacks; the better off versus the poor, and the newer regions of the country versus the old. The key factors producing this result can be readily identified: the strong expansion of the nation's economy during the 1960s opened a wide range of opportunities for blacks, poor people, and the least skilled to participate more fully in the mainstream of economic activity. Correspondingly, they got a somewhat larger share of total income. The same was true of those regions of the country (especially the South) from which blacks were migrating in substantial numbers.

In contrast, during the last five years—under the combined impact of high inflation rates and slower economic growth—these disadvantaged groups have fallen further behind the more fortunate members of society. Moreover, the outlook for a more equal distribution of income over the rest of this decade is far from bright. Partly because of higher energy prices and a reduced rate of capital formation—but above all because of the overall thrust of national economic policy—the growth rate of the American economy out to the 1980s will probably fall far below its potential. Under these circumstances, the drift toward greater inequality may continue. These principal points are amplified further in this section.

INCOME DISTRIBUTION IN THE UNITED STATES

One of the most common ways to assess inequality in the distribution of income is to calculate the share of total money income before taxes received by each fifth of families—having first ranked the families by the size of their total income.[4] These calculations have been made for families in the United States, by race of head.

In general, the observed pattern of income distribution implies that lower income black families receive an even smaller proportion of total money income than do lower income white families in periods of reduced economic growth. Some of the greater sensitivity of the income of black families to cyclical slowdowns may be explained by the fact that a rapidly increasing proportion of black families is headed by females. For example, in 1975, about 35.3 percent of all black families were headed by females compared with 10.5 percent of all white families. So proportionately, nearly 3.5 times as many black families as white families were headed by women. The figure was 2.5 times in 1960. In addition, the average number of earners in black families is below that for white families. In 1975, about 39.8 percent of all white families had two or more earners while the corresponding percentages for black families was 35.8 percent.

Thus, although black families have made some progress in improving their income position relative to whites, black income still lags far behind the income of white families—given the distribution of the two groups in the nation's population. In addition, averages for blacks as a whole may disguise a deteriorating situation for lower income black families.

AMOUNT AND SOURCES OF INCOME

In 1974, total money income before taxes received by families and individuals in the United States amounted to $922.2 billion. Of this total, whites received $846.2 billion, and blacks and other racial minority groups received $76 billion. So, while whites constituted 88.1 percent of the total number of families and individuals reported, they received 91.8 percent of aggregate income. In contrast, blacks and other racial groups accounted for 11.9 percent of all families and individuals, but they got only 8.2 percent aggregate income.

In absolute terms, the income gap remains quite large. For example, in 1974, the black population in the United States was estimated at 24 million by the U. S. Bureau of the Census—which also put the total population at 211 million. Thus, blacks represented 11.1 percent of the total. (It should be noted that these figures refer to blacks only rather than to blacks and other racial minorities.) In the same year, blacks' income amounted to $62.9 billion, representing 6.8 percent of the $922.2 billion received in the nation as a whole. So, compared with the situation in either 1960 or 1969 (when blacks' share was 6.2 percent and 6.4 percent, respectively), blacks had improved their income position slightly by 1974. On the other hand, if they had also received 11.1 percent of total income in 1974—thus matching their share of the total population—their cash receipts in that year would have amounted to $102.4 billion —or $32.5 billion more than they actually received. The explanation of this short-fall is widely known: a legacy of racial discrimination and deprivation has limited blacks' ability to acquire marketable skills while barring them from better paying jobs.

Income sources other than earnings provided about 17 percent of total receipts for blacks and about 16 percent of white receipts. However, the detailed sources differed markedly in several instances. Two sources were quite close; Social Security and railroad retirement receipts represented 6.3 percent of the total for blacks and 5.6 percent for whites. Unemployment and workmen's compensation represented identical fractions for both groups (2.8 percent). On the other hand, private pension funds were a slightly less important source of income for blacks than for whites— 1.4 percent versus 1.9 percent of the total, respectively.

But the major divergence among blacks and whites with respect to a specific income source is found in the case of public assistance and welfare. In 1974, this source provided $3.7 billion (or 5.9 percent) of the total income of blacks. The figures for whites were $6.4 billion—or only 0.8 percent of the total. So, in 1974, about $10.2 billion of public assistance and welfare payments were received by families and individuals in the United States. Blacks received 36 percent of the total welfare payments—compared with 6.8 percent of total incomes.

The explanation of this heavier reliance on public assistance by blacks is widely known, but it might be helpful to reiterate the reasons: the incidence of poverty in the black community is roughly double that among whites, and—obviously—welfare payments are made to the poor and not to the rich. Moreover, the principle component of welfare outlays is aid to families with dependent children (AFDC). The typical AFDC family is headed by a female, and the proportion of such families is greater among blacks than among whites. In recent years, black families have made up about half of all AFDC families, but they have accounted for less than their proportionate share of all the families receiving aid to the blind, aged, and disabled.

REGIONAL DISTRIBUTION OF INCOME

Between 1959 and 1974, the South and West were the fastest growing regions of the country. While a substantial number of blacks moved out of the South to other sections of the country during these same years, the South continued to account for over half of the total black population in the country. In fact, a sharp slowdown in the rate of out-migration of blacks from the South occurred over the last five years. For example, in 1959, 60.3 percent of the black population lived in the South. The fraction had declined to 53.5 percent in 1969—but in 1974, the proportion was still 53.2 percent. The South also raised slightly its share of the total white population in the country—from 27.2 in 1959 to 27.8 percent in 1969, and to 29 percent in 1974. In terms of the total population, the South's share rose from 30.7 percent in 1959 to 30.8 percent in 1969, and to 31.8 percent in 1974.

Reflecting these population gains, as well as a high rate of regional economic development, the South made noticeable gains in its share of the nation's total money income between 1959 and 1969. Again this was an outcome one would expect—given the faster pace of economic growth in the region compared with the rest of the country. Simultaneously, an outcome that was not equally expected is the degree to which blacks in the South shared in the overall redistribution of income.

It was noted above that the net migration of blacks from the South virtually came to a halt over the last five years. So blacks in the South represented about the same proportion (6.1 percent) of the nation's total population in both 1969 and 1974. Between these two years, the share of the nation's total income received by blacks in the South rose from 3 to 3.2 percent. In contrast, blacks and other racial minorities in the North and West represented about 5.3 percent of the nation's total population in both years—but their share of total income expanded from 3.9 percent in 1969 to 5 percent in 1974. Consequently, while blacks in the South continued to experience relative improvement in their income position, the pace of progress slowed appreciably in the last five years.

This outcome is a direct reflection of the sluggish economic conditions that prevailed in the nation as a whole during much of this period. While increased opportunity for blacks in the South has clearly induced more young blacks to remain in the region than would have been the case in the past, the slower growth of jobs in the rest of the country has also dampened their incentives to leave. In the past, the out-migration of many lower income blacks contributed to the rise in per capita incomes in the South. With more such persons remaining in the region—where average incomes are lower than they are in the rest of the country—this has resulted in relatively less improvement in the income position of southern blacks.

Long-Term Outlook for Employment and Income

At this point, we should look ahead to the kind of economic horizon—and the prospects for black employment—which might prevail at the end of this decade. It might be recalled that in early 1976, the federal government put in the public domain a revised set of forecasts and projections that suggested it will be necessary for this country to endure a slower rate of economic growth and a higher level of unemployment than we might like—if we are to make headway in fighting inflation during the rest of this decade. Working against the background of an average unemployment rate of 8.5 percent in 1975, the administration concluded that a rate of inflation of about 4 percent by 1981 (apparently its target) would be compatible with an unemployment rate of 5 percent in that year. If the actual unemployment results are less promising than the administration anticipates, the consequences will be very bad for the nation at large—and disastrous for the black community. If the higher national rate were to prevail at the end of this decade, blacks would have little chance to resume the progress (checked by two recessions) toward closing the jobs and income gaps they suffer vis-a-vis whites. Since early 1975, I have been urging the federal government to provide more stimulus to encourage a more vigorous recovery from the worst recession we have had since the Great Depression. I have been particularly distressed at the reluctance of the Federal Reserve System to use monetary policy more actively to promote an increased availability of credit and lower interest rates.

I understand the basis for the federal government's hesitation: it is deeply concerned with inflation and is anxious to avoid contributing to the revival of inflation at a double digit pace. I agree that inflation is a serious and continuing problem, and the implementation of public policy must be cautious. However, we still have an enormous backlog of unused human and material resources, and this will give us ample room for the expansion of production for quite some time before output begins to press against capacity. If such a policy were followed, the main beneficiaries would be poor whites, blacks, and members of other minority groups on the edges of the national economy who now face considerably less than a hopeful prospect for the remainder of the present decade.

Notes

1. A longer analysis of this subject has been made available as a special report of the National Commission for Manpower Policy entitled *The Economic Position of Black Americans: 1976.*

2. Most of the statistics relating to blacks as used in this discussion refers to "Negroes and other races." Blacks constitute about 92 percent of the persons in this statistical category used by the U.S. Bureau of the Census.

3. The participation rate is the total labor force expressed as a percentage of the noninstitutionalized population.

4. "The Social and Economic Status of the Black Population in the United States, 1975," *Current Population Reports,* Special Studies, Series P-23, no. 54, July 1975.

5. A comprehensive discussion of this subject can be found in *The Economic Report of the President, 1974,* chapter 5, "Distribution of Income," pp. 137-80.

Robert J. Lampman

7

Employment
versus Income Maintenance

Among our evolving national goals are (1) the attainment of high employment as indicated by a low unemployment rate, (2) the offsetting of income losses arising out of such stated contingencies as unemployment, old age, disability, and family dissolution, and (3) the reduction and eventual elimination of income poverty. Closely related to the above are the goals of (4) helping people buy such essentials as food, health care, housing, and education, and (5) achieving a fair distribution of the burden of taxes. All five of these purposes have a distributional content and reflect interest—albeit a diffused and inchoate interest—in wider sharing of opportunities and risks and income.

This chapter is centered on goals 2 and 3, but it will be noted that there is a necessary overlap and interaction among all five of the goals. Thus, unsatisfactory performance with reference to the employment goal contributes to income loss and to income poverty, and slow progress against income poverty levels adds to pressure on government to help people buy essential goods. Further, policies aimed at several goals may blur at the edges to the extent that they involve subsidy to income. For example, job creation may subsidize wages via the employer, and food stamps may be a subsidy via the grocer, but both may have outcomes similar to a cash income supplement as far as a particular family is concerned.

The question most particularly addressed here, namely, employment

ROBERT J. LAMPMAN *is William F. Vilas Research Professor of Economics and Fellow, Institute for Research on Poverty at the University of Wisconsin. Presently a member of the board of directors of the Manpower Demonstration Research Corporation, he has also been a staff member of the Council of Economic Advisers (1962–63).*

versus income maintenance, implies a substitutability of one for the other
and a choice between them. The choice is, perhaps, more of one and less
of another. What particular policies on the employment front will diminish the needs for what particular kinds of income maintenance, and what
particular income maintenance policies will obviate the necessity for
certain changes in the labor market? How do the costs and benefits of
the alternatives compare? In this chapter, we have not resolved all these
questions, but we do attempt to present an overview of the existing income maintenance system as it relates to the labor market and to define
the issues involved in choices of more income maintenance or more job
creation.

The Rationale and Scope of Cash Transfers

Employment is, of couse, the main source of income for most people
most of the time. About 75 percent of national income can be identified
as labor income, including wages and salaries and the self-employment
earnings of managers and professionals. The remaining 25 percent is
property income in the form of profits, rent, and interest. Most consumption is paid for out of current earnings, although a nontrivial
amount comes out of borrowing against future earnings and dissaving
what was accumulated out of past earnings. Some consumption, for
example, food purchased with food stamps, is financed by government
and takes the form of what we identified above as "helping people buy
essentials." Moreover, some part of consumption is paid for by cash
transfer payments which are diverted to selected households via taxation
from the stream of current labor and property income.

These cash transfers, which now amount to about 10 percent of national income, constitute what is sometimes called an income maintenance system. This term of relatively recent usage refers to a set of public
and private institutions designed to replace or supplement earnings and
thereby to add to the purchasing power of some consumers. Among these
institutions are social insurance, public assistance, and private pension
and supplementary unemployment insurance plans. Their development
reflects a rejection of the harsh doctrine of individual responsibility for
income loss and income inadequacy, and an acceptance of social responsibility for wider sharing of income. Accompanying this doctrinal shift is
the decline in the roles of the extended, three-generation family and of
private charity.

Social insurance started in this country with industrial accident insurance in 1911, and grew in the 1930s to include retirement, survivors' and
unemployment benefits. More recently it has been extended to pay cash
benefits for income loss due to nonoccupational disability and benefits
in kind to cover costs of health care. Public assistance has its roots in
general, undifferentiated relief in colonial America, out of which emerged
measures for prevention, rehabilitation, and alleviation targeted to spe-

cific groups of veterans, disabled and aged persons, and broken families. Today, public assistance includes cash assistance for the aged, blind, and disabled under the aegis of the new (1974) Supplemental Security Income (SSI) program, and for broken families via Aid to Families with Dependent Children (AFDC). The latter program concentrates its benefits on families headed by women, although a companion measure legislated in 1961—AFDC for Unemployed Fathers—and now in effect in twenty-four states makes it easier for two-parent families to collect some benefits. At the bottom of the system there remains today, as a vestigial remnant of the colonial system, what is called general assistance, to which the federal government does not contribute.

Both social insurance and public assistance have a strong categorical philosophy, under which the level and duration of benefits vary with the identified cause of income loss or deficiency. Some causes go unrecognized in the standard set of nation-wide laws. That is, long-term unemployment, short-term and partial disability, and low income due to low-wage or irregular employment are not in themselves the basis for valid claims for either insurance or assistance benefits.

Income maintenance has grown steadily in recent decades to cover more risks and more people and to pay higher benefits and is now "big business." In 1974, this system paid out cash benefits of $112 billion to about 50 million people. (The exact number of beneficiaries is difficult to estimate since some people receive more than one benefit.) See Table 1. About a third of all households received a benefit from one or more of these transfer programs. With the recession and inflation of 1975, these cash transfers grew more rapidly than usual and in July of that year were running at an annual rate of $140 billion.

Cash Transfers Respond to Personal and Social Disasters

These benefits are designed to respond to personal or family crises associated with loss of a job, retirement, loss of health, and loss of a family breadwinner. However, social insurance and public assistance respond in rather different ways. Social insurance is generally aimed at replacing a modest fraction of the income lost by those who have had a firm attachment to the labor force. Thus, unemployment insurance (UI) benefits, which vary considerably among the states, are about 50 percent of wages and are restricted to those who have recently worked fourteen to twenty weeks in covered employment. There is, however, a tilt in the benefit formula, so that wage-replacement tends to be above 50 percent for low-wage workers and below that for high-wage workers. Because not all employments are covered, and because not all unemployed people have a record in covered employment, and because benefits only run for a stated period—usually thirteen to twenty-six weeks, but longer now under temporary extended UI—only about half of those counted as unemployed draw UI benefits and the portion of all wages lost because of

TABLE 1. CASH BENEFITS AND NUMBERS OF RECIPIENTS OF "INCOME MAINTE-
NANCE" PUBLIC PROGRAMS, GROUPED BY RISK, 1974

Item	Cash Benefits (in billions of dollars)	Recipients (in millions) of persons)
Total	112.4	n.a.
1. Insurance for retirement and disability [a]	64.8	28.5
Assistance for aged, blind, and disabled (Supplemental Security Income)	5.3	3.7 [b]
Workmen's Compensation	4.0	n.a.
Temporary disability insurance	0.9	n.a.
2. Insurance for survivors	21.0	10.2
Aid to Families with Dependent Children	7.9	11.0 [b]
3. Unemployment insurance	6.7	2.7 [c]
4. General assistance	0.9	0.9 [b]

Source: Social Security Bulletin, December 1975, pp. 26ff.

[a] The division between these benefits and those for survivors is estimated from table M-13 in source below.

[b] Average monthly number.

[c] Average weekly number. Dependents not included. This number reached a peak of 4.6 million in March, 1975.

unemployment which is replaced by UI is typically only about 25 percent. Replacement rates for earnings lost due to disability, retirement, and premature death also vary by prior earnings and tilt in favor of the low-wage earner. The aggregate replacement rate associated with these hazards is on the order of one-third. Social insurance typically does not take full account of nonwage income or assets of the covered worker nor of income or needs of other family members in determining benefits.

Public assistance formulas are not designed in terms of replacement of income loss, but rather are calculated to bring actual income—which may include a social insurance benefit—up to a stated level of need of the family unit. This means that income after a disastrous event may either exceed or fall far short of the family income before the event. Legislative bodies tend to be more generous in setting some benefit levels—particularly for aged, blind, and disabled persons—than others—particularly for mothers with dependent children. Public assistance benefits are usually calculated after taking account of all current family income and also of assets.

While cash transfers respond to personal disaster, it is also appropriate to view them as responding to the national economic catastrophe of recession. In the years 1970-72, an increase of 1 percentage point in the national unemployment rate yielded an average loss of income of 2 percent for families at the poverty line, but a loss of only 1 percent of income for families with incomes five times as high as the poverty line. Cash transfers offset 9 percent of the income loss for high-income families, 37 percent for low-income families headed by males, and 56 percent for low-income families headed by females.[1]

This offsetting of income losses due to recession through income maintenance is a way of stabilizing the economy, *i.e.*, of restoring purchasing power to mitigate the downturn. With recovery, the aggregate level of income maintenance benefits declines as other sources of income increase. When a recession hits, social insurance—particularly UI—and public assistance—particularly general assistance—automatically, *i.e.*, without action by the Congress, pay out more benefits. All transfers tend to have a countercyclical pattern since people tend to retire earlier, to claim a disability more promptly, and to postpone a marriage longer in a recession than in more prosperous times. Congress may, in a discretionary manner, add to the stabilizing power of the income maintenance system, as it did in temporarily extending the duration of UI benefits in December 1974. It is also true, of course, that both at national and state levels, discretionary changes can go the other way. In 1975, for example, Massachusetts repealed a cost-of-living adjustment for AFDC and SSI benefits.

Income maintenance benefits can also serve to protect some part of the population against the ravages of inflation. However, it is not clear how they can, as in the case of a recession, make a contribution to the solution of the national problem. Wage-related benefits tend to rise with wages, which may rise with inflation. However, legislation is required if benefit formulas are to be adjusted to take account of inflation. Recently, retirement benefits under social security were so adjusted, but in such a way as to overcompensate those beneficiaries who earn part of their covered wages in an inflationary period. Federal SSI benefits are indexed to rise with the general price level, as are food stamps. However, AFDC benefits are not so indexed and their adjustment for inflation is left to the states.

Cash Transfers Reduce Income Poverty

One may view the income maintenance system and its growth as adding strength to our resolve to reduce income poverty. In 1974, 24.3 million people, or 11.6 percent of the population, were below the Social Security Administration guidelines set at $5,008 for a family of four persons. In 1959, 21 percent of the population was similarly poor.

The fundamental ingredient of poverty-reduction is real economic growth, or increase in per capita capacity to produce. It appears that a 1 percent increase in per person output at a stable unemployment rate will reduce the number in poverty by about 500,000. Cutting the unemployment rate can contribute to poverty reduction independent of economic growth. A 1 percentage point lowering of the unemployment rate will take about 700,000 persons out of poverty, all other things remaining the same. Demographic change is another factor that influences the rate of poverty-reduction. Recent years have brought several such changes that have been adverse to this goal. In particular, the proportion of all persons living in female-headed households, which are especially prone to poverty, rose from 12.3 to 15.1 percent between 1965 and 1972. In the same period, the proportion of the population who are aged rose somewhat and the labor force participation of aged men fell from 28 to 24 percent. (It is hard to establish what part of these changes may have been induced by the increased generosity of income maintenance benefits.)

Aside from economic growth, lower unemployment, and favorable demographic change, a leading way to reduce income poverty is discretionary change in income maintenance. This year marks the end of a decade of particularly rapid growth of income maintenance and other social welfare expenditures. The latter term includes public expenditures for health care, veterans' programs, education, nutrition, housing, emergency employment, manpower training and other social services. More than half of these expenditures yield noncash or in-kind benefits, but they are supportive of the five goals listed at the outset of this chapter. Total social welfare expenditures rose from 12 percent of GNP in 1965 to 20 percent in 1975. See Table 2. This reflects a growth rate of 8 percent per year in constant per capita dollars. In fiscal 1975, the growth rate—in large part due to recession and inflation—was 7.1 percent, while in the 1950–65 period these expenditures grew at only about half that rate.

TABLE 2. SOCIAL WELFARE EXPENDITURES UNDER PUBLIC PROGRAMS, SELECTED FISCAL YEARS, 1955 THROUGH 1975 (AMOUNTS IN BILLIONS OF DOLLARS, EXCEPT PERCENTAGES)

	1950	1955	1960	1965	1970	1975
Total Social Welfare Expenditures	$23.5	$32.6	$52.3	$77.2	$145.8	$286.5
Social insurance	4.9	9.8	19.3	28.1	54.7	123.4
Public aid	2.5	3.0	4.1	6.3	16.5	40.5
Health and medical programs	2.1	3.1	4.5	6.2	9.8	16.6
Veteran's programs	6.9	4.8	5.5	6.0	9.1	16.7
Education	6.7	11.2	17.6	28.1	50.9	78.4
Housing	—	0.1	0.2	0.3	0.7	3.0
Other social welfare	0.5	0.6	1.1	2.1	4.1	7.9
Total social welfare expenditures as percent of GNP	8.9	8.6	10.6	11.8	15.3	20.1

Source: Alfred M. Skolnik and Sophie R. Dales, "Social Welfare Expenditures, 1950–75," Social Security Bulletin, vol. 39, no. 1, pp. 3–19.

These social welfare expenditures are strikingly pro-poor in their overall impact. One careful estimate is that both in 1965 and 1972, 42 percent of these expenditures went to, or were spent on behalf of, the fifth of the population who would have been poor in the absence of cash transfers. See Table 3. However, individual programs vary considerably in their

TABLE 3. SOCIAL WELFARE EXPENDITURES OF ALL LEVELS OF GOVERNMENT, BY TYPE, WITH PERCENTAGE SPENT ON PRETRANSFER POOR, 1972 [a]

	Total Expenditures (in billions of dollars)	Percentage Spent on Pretransfer Poor
Total	$181.7	42
Cash transfers	80.1	53
Social security and railroad benefits	40.4	58
Public employee retirement	11.7	38
Unemployment insurance	6.8	21
Workmen's compensation	3.8	33
Public assistance	10.8	87
Veteran's benefits	6.2	43
Temporary disability	0.4	21
Noncash benefits	101.6	35
Nutrition	3.7	70
Housing	1.8	55
Health	24.6	56
Welfare and OEO services	5.3	72
Employment and manpower	3.9	72
Education	62.2	19

Source: Robert Plotnick and Felicity Skidmore, *Progress Against Poverty: A Review of the 1964–1974 Decade,* New York, Academic Press for the Institute for Research on Poverty, 1975, pp. 56–57. Reprinted by permission of Academic Press, Inc.

[a] The concepts and classifications used in this table differ in several regards from those used in Tables 1 and 2.

emphasis on the poor. Public assistance paid out virtually all of its benefits to the poor, but unemployment insurance devoted only 21 percent of its benefits to that group. Cash transfers, or what we are here calling income maintenance, amounted to $80 billion in 1972, and 53 percent of that amount or $42 billion went to the pretransfer poor.

This $42 billion, given the fact that some pretransfer poor got more than enough cash transfers to take them over the income-poverty line for their family size, resulted in a posttransfer poor number of 12 percent of the population, in contrast to the 19 percent counted as poor pretransfer.[2] It is a shocking fact that in spite of the enormous increase in cash transfers between 1965 and 1972 (from $37 billion to $80 billion in current dollars), the percentage of the population in posttransfer poverty only fell from 15.6 to 11.9 percent. This is due to the failure of pre-transfer poverty to decline much at all, in fact by only about a million persons. At the same time, the pretransfer income deficit, that is, the difference between actual earnings and poverty line earnings, rose from $29 billion to $34 billion in 1972 dollars. Most demographic subgroups showed little change in the frequency of pretransfer poverty. However, families headed by nonwhite males under sixty-five had a big fall, while families headed by white females under sixty-five had a substantial increase in that frequency.

In spite of the slow reduction of pretransfer poverty during the 1965–1972 period, there was, as previously mentioned, some progress against poverty in the posttransfer terms. Cash transfers moved 33 percent of pretransfer poor households out of poverty in 1965, and moved 44 percent in 1972. While 69 percent of the group received a transfer in 1965, 78 percent did so in 1972. This percentage varied considerably by demographic group, however. Less than half of the poor able-bodied fathers, couples without children, and unrelated individuals received a transfer. This fact is often cited as evidence of unfair treatment by the cash transfer system.

The effectiveness of the cash transfer system in relieving poverty for some groups in 1972 is indicated by Table 4.

TABLE 4. ANTI-POVERTY EFFECTIVENESS OF CASH TRANSFERS, BY DEMOGRAPHIC GROUPS, 1972 (NUMBERS IN THOUSANDS)

	Pretransfer Poor Households	Pretransfer Poor Households Made Non-poor by Cash Transfers	
		Number	Percent
All Households	17,640	7,682	44
With aged heads	8,643	5,461	63
With non-aged male heads, with children	2,011	464	23
With non-aged female heads, with children	2,210	503	23
With non-aged heads, with no children	4,776	1,254	26

Source: Robert D. Plotnick and Felicity Skidmore, *Progress Against Poverty*, Table 6.4, p. 147. Reprinted by permission of Academic Press, Inc.

Closer analysis reveals that blacks are less likely than whites to receive enough cash transfers to take them out of poverty. Those living in the South, those with limited education, and unrelated individuals are also less likely than the average to move out of poverty via cash transfers. The number of posttransfer poor declined from 21 percent of the population in 1959 to 13 percent in 1968. It then declined much more slowly to 11 percent of the population in 1973 and rose to almost 12 percent in 1974. The poverty-income gap remaining after cash transfers was cut by only a billion dollars between 1965 and 1972 and stood at $12.5 billion in 1972. This amount equals about 1 percent of GNP, a relationship which indicates how close we are to the elimination of income poverty.

It can be argued that we are, in fact, closer to that goal than the money income figures indicate. One scholar estimates that after adjusting for underreporting of incomes (which is particularly large for cash transfers), intrafamily transfers, and taxes paid, the poverty income gap was really only $9 billion in 1972. Further, he finds that if one takes account of noncash transfers in the form of food, housing, and health care (which increased from $9 billion in 1968 to $16 billion in 1972), then the poverty income gap was only $5 billion.[3] Following this line of reasoning, and noting the advent of SSI and the expansion of food stamps in 1974, one can conclude that the goal of eliminating income poverty as stated by President Johnson in 1964 had been virtually achieved before the onset of the current recession.

How Were the Poor Related to the Labor Market in 1974?[4]

After receipt of cash transfers, 24.3 million persons were income poor in 1974. The composition of this group differed from the rest of the nation in a number of ways. It was disproportionately located in the South (44 percent) and in what have been designated as "poverty areas" (44 percent). It was relatively poorly educated, with 32 percent of family heads having 8 years or less of schooling. It was also disproportionately nonwhite (31 percent). About half of all the poor were single women or in family units headed by women. One-fifth of the group were unrelated individuals. Half of the poor families were headed by a person out of the labor force.

The frequency of poverty was two or more times as high as the overall average of 11.6 percent for the following groups: unrelated individuals, female heads, Negroes, families with five or more children, farmers and farm laborers, and families where the head did not work during the year. Interestingly, the frequency of poverty was below the national average for families headed by a person sixty-five years of age or older. And for families where the head was unemployed, the frequency of poverty was only slightly above the average at 16.1 percent.

The composition of the poverty population has changed significantly since 1965. Particularly, the aged have declined in numbers, while unrelated individuals and female heads have increased. The latter two groups have increased relative to the total population, but the aged have been taken out of poverty in large numbers by cash transfers. With regard to location, the poor are now more heavily concentrated in metropolitan areas; the share in such areas rose from 47 to 59 percent.

It is important to envision "the poor" as not static either in terms of aggregate numbers or of composition. Some people leave poverty every year and some enter it. We say that poverty declines when more leave than enter. Hence, it is misleading to speak of "the poor," just as it is to speak of "the unemployed," as if it were a permanent class. The University of Michigan Survey Research Center followed 5,000 households over a five-year period. Of those households that were poor in 1967, only 32 percent were poor for the following four years, 42 percent were nonpoor for at least one year but with no consistent pattern, and the remaining 26 percent were not poor after 1967, although many of them did not rise far above the poverty-line. Many nonaged families moved in and out of poverty in the five-year period, in most cases because of a change in family composition, the incurring of disability, or the passing of age sixty-five.

We noted above that poverty was not strikingly higher among the unemployed than among the population at large. Also, among the poor, families with an unemployed head made up only 9 percent of the total (compared to 5 percent in the total population). So, unemployment is not the most distinguishing characteristic of the poverty population. Looking at the figures another way, one is impressed by how many of the poor are employed. Out of 5.1 million poor families, 3.2 had at least one earner in 1974; 1 million had two or more earners. While another 1.5 million worked part of the year, 1.2 million poor family heads worked the full year. Of the latter group, only 643,000 gave unemployment as the reason for not working; the remainder cited such reasons as disability and family responsibilities.

Table 5 displays the reasons for not working given by low-income persons 14 years old and over and by a subclass of the poor, namely, unrelated individuals. The table shows that the poor differ from the nonpoor chiefly with respect to disability and school attendance. Low-income persons who did not work for reasons other than school, illness, or family responsibilities represent only about 5 percent of all poor persons of working age.

The numbers cited are without regard to sex or age of family head. They are, however, markedly different for families headed by men and those headed by women. Half of 2.4 million female-headed poor families had at least one earner; 0.3 million female heads worked the full year and 0.7 million worked part of the year. Of the latter group, 196,000 gave unemployment as the reason for less than full-year work. Table 6 compares the work experience of poor and nonpoor mothers with children under eighteen. In contrast to female heads, 75 percent of all poor, male family heads worked during the year; 51 percent worked full-time, year around. In about 90 percent of the poor families headed by a male who is not ill, disabled or retired, the man worked at sometime during the year.

TABLE 5. WORK EXPERIENCE OF ALL PERSONS 14 YEARS OLD AND OLDER, AND
ALL UNRELATED INDIVIDUALS, BY LOW-INCOME STATUS IN 1973

Work Experience	All Persons 14 Years Old and Older		All Unrelated Individuals	
	Total	Below Low-Income Level	Total	Below Low-Income Level
Total (in millions)	157.3	15.4	18.3	4.7
Percentages of Total				
Worked last year	69	40	62	35
Did not work	34	60	38	65
Main reason for not working				
Ill or disabled	5	14	10	23
Keeping house	17	23	13	19
Going to school	7	12	1	5
Unable to find work	1	2	0	0
Retired	5	7	11	13
Other	0	2	1	3
In armed forces	1	0	0	0

Source: U.S. Bureau of the Census, *Current Population Reports,* Series P-60, No. 98,
January 1975, Tables 13 and 31.

One group of the poor in whose work effort there is special interest
are the so-called "welfare mothers" on AFDC rolls. In any recent month
about 3 million women with 7 million children have been in this status.
In 1974, they received $8 billion in AFDC cash benefits. At any moment
in time, 15 percent of the welfare mothers are working outside the home;
almost half have previously been employed. This group's involvement
with the job market is characterized in one study as "extensive but inter-
mittent." Half of the families have earnings at some time during the
year, and over a three-year period, three-fifths of the family heads worked
at one time or another, and 35 percent worked for one-third or more of
the period.[5]

According to the study cited above,

> Turnover in the welfare population is high. Most families going on welfare
> leave the program within a few years. While there is substantial movement
> from welfare to non-welfare status, the latter often being attained as a con-
> sequence of re-employment, there also is substantial welfare recidivism. . . .
> Thus while there is much short-term success in removing families from de-
> pendency, long-term success is much less likely. . . . As might be expected,
> variations in length of spells on welfare are associated with differences in
> family structure and labor market experience . . . (and in generosity of the
> welfare program they face.) Generosity may take the form of high guarantees,
> low tax rates, or lenient administration. . . . (pp. 28-30)

TABLE 6. "WORKING MOTHERS"—WOMEN WITH OWN CHILDREN UNDER 18 YEARS
OLD BY LOW-INCOME STATUS IN 1973, AND WORK EXPERIENCE

Work Experience of Mother	All	Below Low-Income Level
Wives of family and sub-family heads		
Total (in millions)	25.5	1.4
Percent who worked last year	53.0	34.0
Full year, full-time	18.0	5.0
Female family and sub-family heads		
Total (in millions)	4.7	2.0
Percent who worked last year	65.0	43.0
Full year, full-time	31.0	8.0

Source: U.S. Bureau of the Census, *Current Population Reports,* Series P-60, No. 98,
January 1975, Table 34.

The authors believe that

> Moderate liberalization of welfare programs does not run the risk of elimi-
> nating work among the poor in general. Work and welfare will continue to
> go together, both serially and simultaneously. But liberalization may induce
> more cutbacks among some workers, as returns to work are delayed, overtime
> and moonlighting reduced and voluntary job separations increased. (p. viii)

Benefits for Those Expected to Work

The clearest confrontation between unemployment and income
maintenance is, of course, in unemployment insurance. UI is designed to
cope with short-run involuntary unemployment of experienced workers.
Eligibility turns on a work test with a proviso that a beneficiary need
accept only "suitable work." There is always a certain amount of controversy about whether benefits, which are tax-free, are too high relative
to wages, particularly in those states where benefits are adjusted for
numbers of dependents, and also in those cases where the beneficiary is
a secondary worker. The manner in which benefits are reduced in
recognition of part-time work is claimed by some to be a disincentive
to full-time employment. Moreover, the fact that some unemployed
persons can simultaneously draw UI benefits along with either supplementary unemployment benefits or food stamps means that they may
have little monetary incentive to seek another job.[6]

In recent recessions, Congress has temporarily extended UI to cover
longer-term unemployment. This would seem to violate the original
rationale for the UI eligibility restrictions, its benefit structure, and its
emphasis upon job search. One can certainly raise questions as to whether
extended UI is the most imaginative use of funds to meet the needs of
long-term unemployed people. One clear alternative to extended UI is
AFDC-UF.

About 10 percent as many "welfare fathers" are on AFDC-UF rolls as are mothers on AFDC. This program, although offered with federal matching funds, is now in effect in only twenty-four states. Eligibility is carefully guarded; a father must be totally unemployed for a month after having worked in each of several recent quarters, and until a 1975 U.S. Supreme Court ruling he had to have exhausted UI benefits. He must meet a relatively strict work test and if he works as much as 100 hours in a month, he loses eligibility. Even taking account of these conditions, it appears that only about 15 percent of those categorically eligible for this program and residing in states where it is available are participating in the program. This contrasts with an AFDC participation rate of about 80 percent.[7]

There are, then, numerous controversies about AFDC-UF and UI. It seems that the closer we get to a program intended to supplement the incomes of people who are ordinarily expected to work, the more strife-ridden are the policy choices. Disabled people—if they are permanently and totally disabled—and aged people are not expected to work, although income maintenance laws do not totally discourage their work. Female heads of families face an ambivalent social attitude. On the one hand, AFDC was adopted in 1935 and the survivors' part of social security was added in 1939 for the purpose of encouraging mothers to stay home and take care of their children. More recently, attitudes have been changing on this score. By providing, in 1962, for deductibility of work expenses, including the cost of child care, and, in 1967, for the deductibility of the first thirty dollars and one-third of additional earnings, Congress indicated it wanted to encourage welfare mothers to work. It further emphasized this point in 1972 by requiring mothers whose youngest child is over five years of age to take a work test and to undergo training if it is available.

Female heads without children in their care and able-bodied, nonaged males are expected to work. UI benefits are restricted to the minority of the short-term unemployed who have substantial work experience and hence are denied to many young people and many secondary workers. This can be rationalized on the grounds that, in many cases, especially where the worker does not have dependents, short-term unemployment is not a cause of major hardship. Many persons experience unemployment in a year but do not as a result of that fall into poverty. Cash benefits after exhaustion of UI are grudgingly made available to a handful of fathers under AFDC-UF and general assistance. Only in a recession do we relent and extend UI benefits to cover large numbers of the long-term unemployed.

One major piece of social legislation—the food stamp program—modifies the stands taken on other programs with respect to expectations of work. This program, as amended in 1974, is a federally-funded, nation-wide program. It does not distinguish between male and female heads of families, nor does it separate adults with children from those without children, nor those with prior work experience from those with no work experience, nor those with short-term from those with long-term unemployment. For that matter, it does not deny benefits to those who are currently employed. It does feature a work test, as well as an assets test. It is a universal negative income tax with benefits payable in kind. Food stamp bonus values are scaled to family size and to total family income net of certain expenses. Currently, this program is larger than many of our cash benefit programs and is paying out $5 billion worth of benefits to about 20 million people. Even so, it appears that less than half of those eligible are in fact drawing food stamp benefits.

Is it possible that the adoption and the growth of food stamps herald a major change in the historic pattern of denying benefits to those who are expected to work and, hence, a decline of concern for careful categorization of beneficiaries of income maintenance? Or does the incongruity simply mean that the voters do not think of food stamps as income maintenance and, therefore, as not subject to the same standards? We will return to this question and some of its implications later, but first let us look briefly at efforts being made to find jobs for the unemployed.

While cash benefits are relatively sparse for those who are expected to work, the nation has made a considerable effort to help people prepare for and find jobs. A vast array of educational services at primary, secondary, and postsecondary levels are available. These include the services of technical and vocational training. Moreover, specialized training and retraining with federal funding has been offered via the Manpower Development and Training Act, the Work Incentive Program, the Economic Opportunity Act, and the Comprehensive Employment and Training Act. Some of these funds have gone to on-the-job training.

Vocational guidance through the schools and employment counseling and labor market information through the Employment Service are also offered. Efforts have been made to reduce race and sex and age discrimination in the labor market and to improve the geographic mobility of labor. Public funds also go into such employment-related services as child care for the children of working mothers and vocational rehabilitation for disabled workers.

Finally, modest efforts at job creation have been made, with tax breaks for private employers who hire "hard to employ" persons, and with "emergency employment" in public service. Thus far, funding has been very limited for this sort of intervention in the labor market, but there are live possibilities for a more extensive three-pronged provision of public service employment. These would develop (1) a nation-wide set of "sheltered workshops" for severely handicapped workers, (2) transitional employment for hard-to-employ people such as ex-offenders and high school dropouts, and (3) temporary employment for those who are cyclically or structurally unemployed. Many people favor such an employment emphasis over continued expansion of income maintenance. The argument is over "labor-market reform" versus "welfare reform."

Policy Choices on Employment and Income Maintenance

National economic policy is motivated by concern for high employment. By fiscal and monetary methods, we seek to minimize unemployment, subject to the constraint of avoiding run-away inflation. Education, training, and labor market services encourage would-be workers to fit themselves for jobs that may be available. Those who are successful in the work place gain social status, which reinforces the economic returns from work.

At the same time, we have moved far in recent decades to provide an impressive set of benefits in cash and in kind, which may be received without an equivalent exchange of work in the current period. As discussed above, a subset of these benefits are made available in the event of a loss of earnings or are conditioned to rise if earnings fall below certain levels. To finance these benefits, we have imposed substantial tax burdens on income and consumption. This movement has continued despite sometimes bitter controversy over whether it is contradictory to, or subversive of, the goal of high employment. Does the availability of social welfare benefits—or do the taxes levied to pay for them—discourage people from seeking and holding jobs?

The desire to minimize such discouragement may explain why the great bulk of social welfare expenditures are addressed to the aged and the disabled, *i.e.*, to people who are not expected to work, and why such expenditures on behalf of able-bodied, nonaged persons and their children are relatively small. It appears that only a sharp increase in unemployment due to recession moderates anxiety over public financing of idleness on the part of those expected to work. What seems like an acceptable income maintenance system at 4 percent unemployment, seems unduly harsh at 8 percent unemployment. Recession highlights the fact that our regular cash benefits are designed to replace only a small part of total income lost to either short or long-term unemployment. It further calls attention to the fact that chronically low earnings have not been, until recently, in themselves a basis for income supplementation.

Public opinion polls show a strong preference for employment over income maintenance for those able to work. To some extent, this is merely fuel for stronger aggregative measures to maintain a strong private demand for labor. But the same low ranking for income maintenance follows if the question is asked: would you prefer a guaranteed job or a guaranteed income for those who are able to work? Nonetheless, legislators decline to go very far down the guaranteed job road. This, too, may change if the present high levels of unemployment persist for several years.

Rather than adding cash benefits for unemployed and low-income workers, and rather than moving strongly in creating jobs in public service employment, Congress elected, starting in 1965, to increase in-kind benefits. This important drift in the balance of types of benefits—featuring food stamps, medical care, and housing—and the fact that some families simultaneously received several benefits—raise questions about the equity of the combined set of benefits. Thus, both the recession and recent changes in the system of related benefits dictate the need for reconsideration of the relationship between employment and income maintenance.

In the last ten years, an increasing number of people have questioned the conventional wisdom of categorical eligibility for income maintenance benefits. At one extreme, some have argued for abolition of all existing social insurance and public assistance and in-kind benefit schemes and replacement of them by a single needs-based assistance program or a negative income tax. (It is interesting to note that for the previous hundred years or more, progressive thought on welfare questions encouraged increased categorization.) Others have sought to narrow or widen existing categories or to create new ones.

Much of the controversy about categorization centers on AFDC and the belief that at least some part of its present beneficiaries should be expected to work. One way to divide the category would be along the line of the mother's "expected wages net of child-care costs." [8] Alternatively, Congress could eliminate cash benefits for this category and replace it with extensive public provision of child care services, including care during school vacation periods. However, one should note that such care, according to federally set standards, costs over $2,000 per child per year, and there are equity issues to resolve in deciding who should be eligible for this subsidized service. At present, reimbursement of day care expense is a principal reason for the high break-even points of AFDC, which go as high, in some states, as $10,000 of earnings. Child care costs are also deductible under the income tax.

Rather than narrowing eligibility for AFDC, some want to widen it to include intact families headed by able-bodied men. The federal adoption of AFDC-UF in 1961 was, of course, a step in this direction, and further steps, including mandating it for all states, could be taken. Whether we want to take these steps and thereby impose relatively high disincentives on family heads who are clearly expected to work is not easily answered in the affirmative. Another proposal that brings us up to the same question is to abolish both AFDC and AFDC-UF and introduce a single, new program for all families with children. This is what President Nixon proposed under the title of Family Assistance Plan in 1969. Congress debated this plan and revised versions of it for three years, but failed to adopt it.

Since 1972, however, a number of things have happened which indicate some shifts of thinking. One is the flowering of the noncategorical food stamp program, which, as we mentioned earlier, reaches not only male-headed families, but also childless couples and single persons. This amounts to a negative income tax (NIT) with benefits in kind. It has a relatively low guarantee—about $2,000 for a family of four—but a relatively low rate of fall in benefits as other income rises—*i.e.*, benefits fall thirty cents for every extra dollar of income—so the break-even level of earnings is well above the poverty line. This program does several remarkable things. (The key terms of NIT design are discussed below.) First, it narrows the difference in treatment accorded equally poor AFDC families in high-benefit and low-benefit states. These differences used to be on the order of six to one before food stamps. Now they are only two to one. Second, it reduces the disparity between transfers available to equally poor male and female-headed families. Third, it breaks down the inhibition against transfers to people who do not fit in previously established categories. Food stamps are not far removed from money and could be cashed out, and the funds could be rolled into a noncategorical cash-benefit scheme with coverage even wider than that proposed by President Nixon.

Another straw in the wind, which indicates noncategorical thinking, is the refundable earned income credit for low-wage-earners with children. This was first recommended by Senator Russell Long, and later adopted in the Tax Reform Act of 1975, under the title of "earned income credit." This allows a worker to reclaim 10 percent of earnings up to $4,000 of earnings, and a declining percentage to $8,000 of earnings. This may be characterized as an earnings subsidy, or a NIT with a zero guarantee, a less than zero implicit tax rate up to $4,000, and a rate of 10 percent thereafter. Unlike most negative income tax plans, the Long version does not make any adjustment for family size. It is similar to the British Family Income Supplement of 1971.

Another factor working for change is the effect recession-with-inflation has had on state and local government treasuries. The federalization of assistance to the aged, blind, and disabled via SSI—a part of the Nixon welfare initiative which was legislated in 1972 and put into effect in 1974 —has been of help to the states and localities, and this has encouraged their support of federalization of AFDC. So, the precedents supplied by food stamps and the earned income credit, along with the financial plight of state governments may point the way to a new type of income maintenance for those people who are expected to work.

Any proposal to introduce a new income-conditioned benefit for those expected to work must confront issues of equity and incentive. How high should one set the guarantee, *i.e.*, the benefit payable at the zero level of other income for each family size? How fast should benefits fall as earnings increase? (This is sometimes referred to as the offset or implicit tax rate. If benefits fall $500 as earnings rise $1,000, the rate is 50 percent.) The answer to those two questions will determine the break-even point, or the earnings level at which benefits fall to zero. (Hence, if the guarantee is $1,000 and the implicit tax rate is 50 percent, then the break-even point is $2,000.) Numerous subsidiary questions must be answered, having to do with definition of the family unit (whose income must be reported?), definition of income (what earnings, property income, and transfer benefits must be reported, and what exemptions, and deductions will be allowed?), and the accounting period (should it be a month, as in AFDC, or a year, as in the income tax?).

Much research effort has gone into the question of how responsive work effort would be to various levels of guarantee and of tax rate. The first experimental inquiry into this question was the so-called New Jersey Study, which placed a sample of families headed by working-age men on a variety of negative income tax plans and compared their changes in hours of work over a three-year period with changes observed in a control group. The leading finding of that study was that in the experimental families, considered as a group, male family heads reduced hours worked by 6 percent, and wives by 30 percent. A conservative reading of the experiment is that it gives tentative support to the idea that work reductions are not likely to be very great among male family heads under a negative income tax with a moderate guarantee and a moderate tax rate. Hence, supporters of NIT for male-headed families find the outcome of the experiment to their liking.

To keep the implicit tax rate down for beneficiaries of a negative income tax turns out to be more difficult than might at first be imagined. For one thing, the tax rate in the benefit structure combines with tax rates in the social security payroll tax and in the income tax. Further, these rates combine with or add to the rate at which benefits fall in the several income-conditioned, in-kind transfers. The latter include food stamps, medicaid, public housing, rent allowances, child day care, legal services, and basic opportunity grants for higher education. (It should be noted that higher income families often benefit from income tax provisions dealing with expenditures on that list.) Hence, some account must be taken of the possibility that an NIT recipient facing an NIT rate of 50 percent might simultaneously receive several of these benefits (as some AFDC families now do) and experience a combined marginal tax rate on earnings in the range of 100 percent. This possibility can be minimized by cashing out some of the in-kind benefits and incorporating them in the NIT guarantee, by counting some of the benefits, *e.g.*, housing benefits, as income, and thereby discouraging their use, and by converting some of the benefits, *e.g.*, medicaid, to universally available or nonincome-conditioned benefits.[9]

The problem of introducing such a cash benefit has become more difficult with more in-kind benefits and with recent income tax changes. To do a fully satisfactory job of welfare reform, one must change not only AFDC and AFDC-UF, but in-kind benefits and the income tax as well. A carefully worked out scheme for meeting all these issues recently came out of the Congressional Joint Economic Committee (JEC).[10] This particular plan features a guarantee of $3,600 for a family of five, a 50 percent tax on earnings, and income tax reductions in the income range of $7,200 to $25,000. The net cost to the federal government after abolishing AFDC and food stamps is estimated at $15 billion. Thirty-four million people, aside from those continuing on SSI, would be eligible for cash benefits without a work test, and another 5 million would enjoy income tax cuts. State and local governments will absorb some of the $15 billion as the federal government takes over a larger share of welfare costs. It should be emphasized that many of the 34 million persons are children, and many families will draw small cash benefits since they will have earnings or social insurance benefits which take them near to the break-even point. Many variations on this particular plan can, of course, be devised, some costing more and some less. The main choices have to do with categorization and the tie-ins with other existing benefits. A major problem is to limit disincentives to work.

It is sometimes suggested that public service employment (PSE) is a direct alternative to such income maintenance reforms as that offered by JEC. It is true that PSE offers income to some of the people in the 34 million indicated above, and it does it without imposing an implicit tax rate on its beneficiaries. In that sense it is rivalrous with the negative income tax approach. However, it is more accurate to say that the two approaches are complements, rather than alternatives, since they are directed to quite different purposes.

The special problem to which income maintenance reform is directed is the inadequacy of income support now offered for "noncategorical" low-income persons. The low income in the target cases arises out of short- and long-term unemployment, and also out of the low wage rates of some who are usually employed. PSE may or may not reach many of those in this NIT target group. Similarly, PSE may or may not reach many of those in the target groups of the existing income maintenance system. However, sheltered workshops would provide an alternative for some now drawing disability benefits; and transitional work experience for the "hard-to-employ" would attract some volunteers or selectees off the AFDC rolls. These two phases of PSE, which are concerned more with therapy and training than with income maintenance, could be designed to reach few or many of the large pool of AFDC and SSI beneficiaries.

A third phase of PSE aims at providing temporary jobs to the cyclically and structurally unemployed. As we noted above, most unemployed persons are not eligible for UI benefits. In some versions, this phase of PSE is better compared to alternative macroeconomic policies aimed at simply increasing the overall demand for labor than to income maintenance aimed at selected categories, all members of which are entitled to even-handed treatment. In other versions, PSE is seen as a variant of revenue sharing designed to benefit state and local governments. Suppose we now had in place a PSE program which provided a million temporary jobs for the cyclically unemployed and that this actually resulted in a decline in unemployment of one million. What income maintenance programs could we then abolish? What income maintenance reform effort could we then abandon? The answers are doubtless the same as the answer to the question: what changes would we make in income maintenance institutions if unemployment fell for any reason from, say, eight million to seven million persons? Obviously, a great deal would be left for income maintenance to do even if we had such a plan to provide a million jobs. Exactly how much would be left depends on who gets those jobs, whether any now employed are displaced, and whether the job-takers would otherwise have claimed income maintenance benefits.

PSE has problems, which are common in social welfare expenditures, of equity and incentive. Who should be eligible for—or required to take —PSE jobs? Should the emphasis be upon those who have the greatest need or those who can make the greatest contribution to output? Should priorities be set to assure that some of the jobs go to long-term unemployed, heads of families, veterans, minority group members, youthful workers, and those in still other categories? Then there is the issue of wages. Should they be higher than welfare benefits to attract people off the welfare rolls, or lower than the minimum wage to avoid diverting workers out of the private sector? What about the work to be done? If it is socially valuable, can it be turned off when the recession abates? If it is not socially valuable, will the morale of the workers suffer? Finally, to what standards of achievement are managers of PSE to be held? Perhaps the standard should simply be that of doing something no income maintenance program can do, namely, providing a socially useful job that did not exist before. If designed to answer these questions in a reasonable manner, PSE will merit support and will ease the role of income maintenance.

The broad range of policy choices reviewed above do not lend themselves to a neat summary in terms of employment versus income maintenance. We presently have a complex and interlocking set of macro- and micro-policies, preventive and alleviative measures, cash and in-kind benefits, tax laws, and labor market regulations, all bearing on several related goals having distributional content. The particular ways in which cash income maintenance is designed—especially as it touches people who are expected to work—may well influence employment behavior. An effort to provide more cash transfers to the "working poor" should integrate cash with noncash and tax benefits. But such an effort cannot by itself improve job opportunities. Hence, creative policy to increase employment is necessary to success in maintaining and improving incomes.

Notes

1. Edward M. Gramlich, "The Distributional Effects of Higher Unemployment," *Brookings Papers on Economic Activity*, September 1974. This study

was based on a panel of 2,930 families. It recognizes income loss from un-employment, withdrawal from the labor force, shorter hours of work, and work at lower wage rates because of the recession.

2. In the remaining part of this section I rely heavily for facts on changes in poverty on the following two books: Robert D. Plotnick and Felicity Skid-more, *Progress Against Poverty: A Review of the 1964–1974 Decade* (New York: Academic Press for the Institute for Research on Poverty, 1975); and Michael C. Barth, George L. Carcagno, and John L. Palmer, *Toward an Effective Income Support System: Problems, Prospects, and Choices* (Madi-son, Wisconsin: Institute for Research on Poverty, 1974).

3. Timothy R. Smeeding, "The Anti-Poverty Effectiveness of In-Kind Trans-fers," forthcoming in *Proceedings of the American Economic Association, 1976.* Cf. Edgar K. Browning, *Redistribution and the Welfare System* (Wash-ington: American Enterprise Institute for Public Policy Research, 1975).

4. This section is largely drawn from Bureau of the Census reports cited in Tables 5 and 6.

5. Barry L. Friedman and Leonard J. Hausman, "Work and Welfare Patterns in Low Income Families," mimeographed (Waltham, Mass.: Brandeis Uni-versity, June 1975), p. 38.

6. Raymond Munts and Irwin Garfinkel, *The Work Disincentive Effects of Unemployment Insurance,* Kalamazoo, Upjohn Institute for Employment Insurance, 1974.

7. Russell M. Lidman, "Why Is the Rate of Participation in the Unemployed Fathers' Segment of Aid to Families with Dependent Children So Low?" Institute for Research on Poverty Discussion Paper, 1975.

8. See Daniel H. Saks, *Public Assistance for Mothers in an Urban Labor Mar-ket,* Princeton, Industrial Relations Section, Princeton University, 1975, Chapter 6. Friedman and Hausman, *op cit.,* pursue this same question, but find that labor market problems of welfare mothers are not clearly linked with particular demographic characteristics. They say that "People with the same characteristics have widely varying labor market experiences. Thus we are unable to develop a set of simple rules that eliminate the need for case by case discretion." (p. viii)

9. For a full review of these problems and of alternative ways to deal with them, see Barth, *et al., op. cit.;* the 20-volume *Studies in Public Welfare,* Subcommittee on Fiscal Policy of the Joint Economic Committee, Congress of the United States (Washington D.C.: Government Printing Office, 1973 and 1974); and *Integrating Income Maintenance Programs,* edited by Irene Lurie (New York: Academic Press for the Institute for Research on Poverty, 1975).

10. The JEC plan is presented in volume 20 of *Studies in Public Welfare;* it is entitled *Income Security for Americans: Recommendations of the Public Welfare Study,* and dated December 5, 1974.

8

Some Time Dimensions
of Manpower Policy

A decade ago many writers argued that work was on its way out. Automation promised to perform the dull and repetitive tasks in factories and ultimately to perform most services as well. In the new leisured world, life could be devoted to learning and contemplation; or conversely, the sociologists warned, freedom from work could result in a meaningless existence for mankind. Five years later, by contrast, many of the same writers worried not about the quantity but about the quality of work. Disenchantment with one's job was allegedly widespread, with alienation from work leading to absenteeism, alcoholism, and drug addiction.

By 1975 unemployment had reached its highest level in forty years, and public attention shifted back to the question of job scarcity. For while it is true that *Work is Here to Stay, Alas,*[1] the numbers of jobs available do not match the numbers of job seekers at current rates of pay. Within this context, certain policy questions are inevitable. How much job creation should be initiated? What is the role of manpower training when experienced workers are being laid off? And not surprisingly, what is the appropriate distribution of work over the labor force?

Introduction: The Allocation of Jobs
in an Era of Unemployment

As in past recessions, the persistence of high levels of unemployment raises the question of whether a reallocation of work over a larger num-

JUANITA M. KREPS *is Vice President and James B. Duke Professor of Economics at Duke University. In addition to leading textbooks on economics she has written extensively in the areas of labor and manpower. Her most recent books are* Sex in the Market Place *and* Women and the American Economy *(for the American Assembly).*

ber of persons might not reduce the incidence of unpaid idleness.[2] Work sharing through the introduction of a workweek of four eight-hour days has surfaced as the most popular proposal, combined in one instance with a recommendation that unemployment insurance funds be used to make up some of the fifth day's lost earnings. Part-time work is being urged as both a means of increasing the number of jobs and a way to meet the needs of particular groups: teenagers, retirees, and mothers of small children. In certain European countries, interest in greater flexibility in working arrangements has gained ground, in part because of slack economic conditions and rising unemployment.

To some economists, an analysis of the relation between hours of work and level of unemployment is a useless exercise; to others, work-sharing arrangements are a cop-out. The former argue from the weight of evidence that attempts to increase the numbers of jobs by reducing the workweek through whatever devices are available—penalties for overtime, for example—are not generally effective in reducing unemployment. Industry will persist they contend, in finding the most effective combinations of labor and capital; the long-run demand for labor may be decreased, not increased, by requirements for time-and-a-half pay. Moreover, the rise in fringe benefits as a proportion of all labor costs makes hiring additional workers less and less appealing. The latter group of economists, who object to work sharing on the basis that it fails to provide an acceptable solution to the problem of unemployment, believe that through fiscal measures the economy should be stimulated sufficiently to generate full-time jobs for those who wish them, budget deficits notwithstanding.

In a broader perspective, however, it is important to note that the drive to reduce working hours usually gains force in periods of heavy unemployment, and to speculate on the probable effect of the current recession on the amount of time the worker will spend on the job. Significant changes were made in work schedules during the depression of the 1930s, through the passage of legislation specifying premiums for all hours over forty per week and providing benefits during retirement; similar actions may well be considered appropriate in the present era which exhibits some of the same, albeit less severe, problems. Indeed, a high unemployment rate may continue to be the catalyst for allocating more time to nonwork pursuits. Once working time is reduced, earlier work schedules are seldom reestablished. Workers who resist an increase in free time at the expense of income until the pressure for jobs leads to a change of policy may nevertheless quickly adjust after a shorter workweek (or worklife) is established. Hence a four-day workweek, or a month's annual vacation, or retirement at age sixty-two, could become the norm in the same manner as the forty-hour week or retirement at age sixty-five. In short, cyclical pressures to reduce working time accentuate the long-run decline brought about by productivity growth and its income effect on the consumption of leisure.

Inducements to reduce the time any one person spends at work are not new; premium overtime pay and loss of Social Security benefits are standard policies designed in part to spread work. There is no restriction on moon-lighting, however, nor any significant move to increase the number of part-time jobs offered by industry. The links between part-time work, lower weekly hours in general, and expanded employment are not easy to predict. If the normal workweek were reduced to thirty-two hours, for example, the meaning of part-time work (which is now defined as less than thirty-five hours) would be changed. Once workers generally observed a thirty-two-hour week, the incentive to moonlight would surely grow. Thus, the adoption of shorter workweeks could result in more multiple job holders. Yet when the economy is operating at a level too low to provide full employment, and social policy cannot or does not generate enough additional jobs to make up the balance, what is appropriate manpower action? Can forced idleness be translated into education and job training, for example? If so, what are the necessary changes in income maintenance programs? Are there circumstances in which shorter working time for the employed improves job prospects for the unemployed?

Consideration of the time dimensions of manpower policy constitutes but one aspect of comprehensive planning. Set in the perspective of current levels of unemployment, the issues raised are of both short and long-run significance. In the immediate future, work sharing will continue to be suggested as a source of new jobs. It is well to recognize that reduced working time is often offered as a means of alleviating unemployment, and to respond to that policy suggestion. In a longer time frame, the question of how much work each of us does in a lifetime has great importance for human welfare. Beyond some level of material well-being, the growth of free time becomes as important as the growth of income. The allocation of nonworking time among families, moreover, may be at least as uneven as the distribution of income.

Long-run structural changes in the economy—changes which reapportion time from work to nonwork pursuits—should be distinguished from those adjustments which workers make to the resulting patterns set for the workplace. Trends in productivity, as determined by technology, labor force size and quality, and natural resources, lead to gradual changes in the economic environment which in turn shift the aggregate demand for labor and its composition. Growth in output per man-hour during the twentieth century has reduced the demand for employment in farming and manufacturing, for example, and workers have moved from these sectors into services. In the process of such industrial and occupational shifts, however, other adjustments have occurred: hours on the job have declined, longer educational periods have been sustained, retirement has become an important lifestyle, women have entered and men, young and old, have left the workforce. The precise form of the adjustment varies from one era to another; we opted for shorter workweeks during the first third of the twentieth century, longer vacations during the second, and most recently, lengthened retirement. But the exploration for the long-run movement toward reduced working time turns on the growth in productivity, rather than a heightened desire for leisure *per se.*

The fact that productivity may generate greater free time as well as goods is not always recognized, in part, perhaps, because free time carries no dollar value and, like nonmarket work, it is excluded from measures of economic growth. Yet the worth of nonworking time needs to be taken into account, not only to provide an accurate appraisal of the long-run impact of increased productivity on the quality of life, but also because of the manner in which public and corporate policy affects the utility of free time. For example, workers may have strong preferences for certain forms of leisure, while not caring at all for others; each additional hour of free time, moreover, can be compared with the income not earned during that hour. As productivity and real wages rise, free time becomes more expensive. One recent study found that the relative preference for compensation options ran as follows: extra vacation, which exceeded the second alternative of a pay increase; a pension increase (which increased with age, not surprisingly); somewhat less enthusiasm for family dental plans, early retirement, and a four-day workweek; and almost no endorsement of shorter workdays.[3]

Just as the worth of nonworking time is likely to be overlooked, so too, is the fact that the free time accruing to the family (as opposed to the family head) may not be growing in line with the overall reduction in working hours; the opposite may have occurred. For while weekly hours on the job have declined, vacations have grown, and the male's working years as a proportion of his life have fallen, the female's market work has grown sharply. In a family in which the wife takes a full-time job, yet homework continues to be done by the family members, there has probably been a loss of nonworking time; married women who add market work to their household tasks are likely to be working longer hours than they did half a century ago. Thus, the significant increase in leisure time as depicted by the declining average market workweek may be a myth for the family as a whole.

Certainly the hours of labor supplied by married women have increased. Unless there has been a proportionate decrease in their home work and in their husband's working time, the family's total work effort has increased and leisure time declined. As a result the utility of additional free time could be increased relative to further income, suggesting that work reductions would be warmly received—or in any event, that in the future the family (particularly the two-earner family) may favor work reductions over income increases, as productivity grows. In brief, the growth in labor force activity of married women with children should shift the terms of the family's leisure/income trade-off in favor of free time.

As background for further consideration of these questions, the section following reviews the long-run record of growth in productivity and decline in working hours. Economists' interpretations of the relationship between the rise in real wages and the amount of labor offered have occasionally conflicted, but an inverse relationship is clearly evident and adequately explained in terms of male labor force behavior. Whether the same response will ensue from a work force that is rapidly changing in age, sex, and educational composition, is a question to which little attention has been directed.

Higher Productivity, Lower Work Time

With few interruptions real output per man-hour has risen steadily during the twentieth century, bringing with it both higher living standards and a reduction in time spent on the job. Between 1910 and 1948 the private sector increase averaged 2 percent annually, as the index of productivity per man-hour rose from 47.6 to 100.2 during the period.[4] In the prolonged prosperity following World War II, the average increase was greater—3 percent per year from 1949 to 1973 [5]—although in certain recent years productivity changes have been quite low or even negative. In 1969, for example, productivity rose less than one-third of 1 percent. In 1970 the increase was 1 percent, while 1974 saw a decline of 2.6 percent.[6]

Economic theory suggests that a rise in real wage rates leads the worker to offer more hours of labor. But this increase may be more than offset by the worker's tendency to want more of all goods, including leisure, now that his wages are increasing; as a result, rising real wage rates can be associated with declining work effort.[7] The long-run decline in time spent at work is consistent with this theoretical formulation.

WAGE RATES AND THE SUPPLY OF LABOR: EARLIER VIEWS

Earlier analyses of the relationships between the wage rate and the quantity of labor offered were less conclusive, however. The English mercantilists believed that the supply curve of labor was inversely related to the wage rate, reasoning that man would work only long enough to provide sustenance. According to Thomas Manly, higher wages meant "the men have just so much more to spend in tipple and remain now poorer than when their wages were less. . . ." [8] Josiah Child observed of the poor that ". . . In a cheap year they will not work over 2 days a week, their humor being such that they will not provide for a hard time but just work so much and no more as may maintain them in that mean condition to which they have become accustomed." [9]

Even at the time Adam Smith was developing his economic views, it was widely believed that increases in wages would diminish the supply of effort.[10] Smith attempted to combat the prevailing views of the mercantilists by arguing that high wages evoked a greater amount of effort than low wages. He observed that "Where wages are high, accordingly, we shall always find the workmen more active. . . ." He further noted that the majority of workmen, when liberally rewarded, were likely to overwork and threaten their health.[11] J. B. Say repeated Smith's position that a liberal wage encouraged industry.[12]

Malthus argued, as one might expect, that a negative relationship existed between wages and hours worked. When subsistence could be maintained with two or three days' labor per week, the worker would be content with that subsistence level.[13] Jevons' views, which emphasized the irksomeness of work, were not too different from those heard among today's writers. An increase in output and wages per hour, he wrote, would be accompanied by a reduction in hours worked; with a higher wage, the worker would gain more satisfaction from free time than from the consumption of additional wage goods. He made an exception for professionals, however, on the grounds that their work was less unpleasant.[14]

Alfred Marshall agreed with the positions held by Smith and Say, concluding that ". . . increased renumeration causes an immediate increase in the supply of efficient work." [15] Following Jevons, he noted that additional hours of work could become burdensome, however. Relaxation and leisure were coming to be valued more highly, with a resulting downward pressure on working hours. Chapman followed a similar line of reasoning noting that the strain from additional hours of work increased; as wages increased, the value of leisure was enhanced.[16] Pigou apparently accepted the thesis that wages and hours worked were negatively related. He reasoned that a tax on income increased the marginal utility of money but not the marginal disutility of work; the effect of an income tax was therefore to increase the number of hours worked.[17]

WAGE RATES AND THE SUPPLY OF LABOR: RECENT ANALYSES

In twentieth century discussions of the labor supply, opinion has also been divided. Consideration has frequently centered on the effects of taxation (positive or negative) on work incentives. An income tax, it is frequently argued, reduces work effort; by contrast, sales taxes diminish consumption and may actually encourage persons to work more in order to maintain consumption levels.[18] G. F. Break holds, however, that the supply of labor is either not very responsive, or responds inversely to the movement of wages; that the income tax has little disincentive effect on the amount of work offered. For many reasons, he points out, workers continue to maintain their work efforts despite the inroads made by taxes: heavy family commitments, including a high divorce rate; increasing demand for consumer durables; greater urbanization and its effect on consumption; and decreasing flexibility in individual working schedules.[19] Earlier, James Duesenberry noted that many consuming units demanded a certain level of living that they felt must be maintained. The pressure of this commitment tended to force workers to observe particular work schedules at any given wage rate, thus making the supply curve inelastic; or else to demand a certain level of income, which could be maintained with fewer hours of work as wage rates increased.[20]

Numerous economists have noted the long-run decline in the length of the male's work year and observed that this decline has been associated with the rise in average income in industrialized nations. Clarence Long found that a 1 percent rise in income resulted in a 0.27 percent decline in hours worked in the United States in 1890–1950, a 0.34 percent decline in Canada in 1921–1941, a 0.39 percent decline in Great Britain in 1911–1951, and a 0.92 percent fall in Germany in 1895–1950.[21] "Decreases in hours were not systematically associated with increases in income, at least in the short-run;" depression and war played a part, with rising incomes creating a "conducive social, political, and economic atmosphere." [22] Again, the impact of cyclical factors on the long-run shift in working time should be noted. In retrospect, what appears to be a smooth and quite gradual decline in hours spent on the job was in reality more of a step-like progression downward, with cyclical shocks to the economy inducing changes in working patterns that then became permanent. Among males, the decline in work effort took the form of reduced hours per week rather than a decline in labor force participation, particularly in the first third of the century.

Other studies, notably the earlier works of Paul Douglas,[23] have found similar evidence that the wage rate was inversely related to the time spent at work. T. A. Finnegan's study more than a decade ago showed that adult males with higher hourly earnings worked fewer hours per week than those with lower rates of pay.[24] Winston concluded from international data that there is a significant correlation between income and the aggregate allocation of effort to income acquisition, and that the values of the estimated relationship are strikingly similar to those from earlier studies using intercity and industry cross-sectional data on occupational subgroups within societies.[25] Of the variables other than income that explain the allocation of effort, the author found the most important to be the state of aggregate demand as indicated by the level of unemployment.

Study of the labor force behavior of males—in particular, their work response to changes in real wages—no longer provides an adequate basis for estimating the labor supply function. As Long has shown, the labor market activity of married women has provided an offset to the declining activity rates and hours of work of males. Given the woman's traditional alternative of nonmarket work, it is reasonable to suppose that her labor supply is more responsive to wages than that of the man, and that the inclusion of other groups of secondary workers (teenagers, retirees) changes the nature of the aggregate supply of labor. Noting the importance of this change in labor force composition, contemporary writers point to an additional dimension of the labor/leisure trade-off: the role of investments in human capital. When the alternatives to work are broadened to include such investments of time, along with the option of nonmarket work, particularly by secondary workers, the time dimensions of manpower policy become more complex.

For one example of the way in which the composition of the work force affects policy decisions, consider the debate over family income maintenance. As Cain and Watts pointed out:

> It is not . . . the private income tax that is most likely debated today regarding the labor-supply effects. The positive income tax is no longer widely believed to have serious consequences for work effort—although one may rightly question the evidence for this. It is now those who face the lowest positive-income tax rates, or even no income tax at all, who are the focus of the greatest interest and controversy.[26]

By providing incomes that are sometimes higher than the lowest earnings, and by withdrawing transfers when recipients acquire paying jobs, the welfare system has provided disincentives to work. Attempts to eliminate these disincentives and to reduce the inequities between low income workers and welfare families have led to many proposals for reform. The Family Assistance Program, for example, would have extended income maintenance to all families whose incomes fell below a certain minimum. The immediate threat of such proposals is always posed: will people continue on the job if they are guaranteed incomes without work? In reporting the empirical results of several recent estimates of labor supply, Cain and Watts lay out the possible outcomes of an income maintenance policy. Real output could be reduced if income guarantees lowered work effort; the amount of income-related benefits would rise if lower earnings resulted from reduced labor supply; benefits would not replace all earnings of workers, and hence the net increase in the incomes of families would be smaller than the benefits. On the other hand, the authors note two important offsets to any loss of market goods: one, some of the time not spent at work could be used for human capital growth and two, nonmarket production would increase.[27]

Diversion of effort from market into home work, particularly where there are small children, or into further education or training, would seem to be an acceptable by-product of the guaranteed income, particularly in periods of heavy unemployment. An income scheme that would encourage additional nonmarket work or educational endeavor would reduce both the short and the long-run costs of unemployment. And since unemployment rates are particularly high for teenagers and women, programs designed to encourage these alternative uses of time may have special appeal. It is important to examine more closely the range of options in the use of time by reviewing some of the current shifts in labor force composition and the ways in which these shifts may ultimately affect worker preference.

THE LONG-RUN DECLINE IN HOURS AT WORK

As the preceding review of opinion suggests, productivity gains have enabled workers to buy more free time as well as more goods and services. Time free of market work has appeared in the form of shorter workdays, fewer workdays per year, and recently a decline in the number of working years. Earlier estimates show that the average male worker gained 1,220 nonworking hours per year during the period 1890 to 1960. This increase in time away from work was allocated in roughly the following manner: a reduction in the workweek of 1,100 hours, as the average workweek declined from 61.9 hours to 40.7 hours; an increase in paid holidays amounting to 32 free hours per year; an increase in paid vacations which accounted for a decline of 48 hours per year; and a further 40 hour decline due to increase in paid sick leave.[28] An additional 9 nonworking years in youth and in old age raise significantly the male's nonworking time during his lifespan.

The proportion of productivity gains being allocated to leisure appears to have declined in recent years. Clark Kerr estimates that prior to 1920, half of productivity increases were taken in the form of additional leisure, whereas the 1920 and 1950 portion was about 40 percent.[29] Peter Henle concludes that the leisure share of growth in output per man-hour dropped to 11 percent from 1940 to 1960,[30] a decline that seems to be continuing. Geoffrey Moore and Janice Hedges estimate that workers took only about 8 percent of the productivity advances in leisure during the decade of the 1960s.[31]

The forms in which nonwork time is taken also appears to be changing. Our estimates of increase in annual leisure between 1890 and 1963 showed that 90 percent of this gain came as reduced hours per workweek. However, recent increases in nonworking time have been largely in the form of additional paid holidays and vacation time. In his report on the gain in leisure between 1940 and 1960, Henle noted that over 50 percent of the growth in annual leisure was due to six additional days of paid vacation and an increase of four paid holidays.

> Perhaps the most significant development was that more than half the total gain in paid leisure resulted from increased vacation and holiday time, rather than from a reduction in the work week. This is a definite shift from the pattern of earlier years and seems to indicate that leisure time preferences are running more to additional whole days each year rather than additional minutes each day.[32]

The pattern of allocating a significant proportion of leisure gains to additional whole days continued into the 1960s. During that decade, 20 hours of the 50 hour increase in nonworking hours per year came in the form of vacation and holidays. By the end of the 1960s, over two-thirds of all workers in the private nonfarm economy received a paid vacation and the total number of weeks that workers spent on vacation increased by almost 50 percent between 1960 and 1969. The average length of vacation rose from 1.8 to 2.2 weeks for full-time workers.[33] Paid leave (except sick leave) represented 5.6 percent of the total employee compensation for all industries in 1972 and 6.5 percent of the total in manufacturing.[34] H. Gregg Lewis' earlier analysis of the components of leisure during the first half of the twentieth century pointed out the tendency to bunch leisure time into hours and days spent at home, and the reluctance of workers to choose much "at work" leisure. He concluded that the cost and taste factors were quite stable, and thus that the forms of leisure would probably observe roughly the same proportions in the future.[35] The move toward larger blocks of time at the beginning and end of worklife, and the continued growth in vacation time, are compatible with his interpretation.

The long-run decline in average hours worked has been influenced by structural shifts in both the demand for and supply of labor. On the demand side, a decline in the relative importance of agriculture and other occupations that have traditionally involved long working hours, has helped to lower average weekly hours. In addition, the rapid rise of the service sector with its propensity for part-time jobs has made available jobs that call for fewer than the standard forty hours per week. The rising work activity of women has increased the proportion of workers who prefer part-time schedules; of all workers who choose to work part-time, 69 percent are women.[36] The combination of greater numbers of working women and a changing occupational and industrial composition of the economy has stimulated the decline in average hours of work per week. However, the workweek for full-time workers has declined more slowly than the average for all workers; the average workweek of 46 hours for full-time workers in 1955 had declined less than an hour—to 45.1 hours—by 1970.[37]

"The Pervasive and Awkward Scarcity of Time" [38]

At the individual level, the distribution of time appears to be much more equitable than that of income or wealth or personal attractiveness; each of us is given that same twenty-four hours a day and with few exceptions, most of us will live to old age. Yet the amount of time we spend at work and at play varies widely. Within a family, working time differs across an even broader range, depending on whether one or two adults enter the work force, on the number (and quality) of children and hence the amount of home work required, on the stage of the life cycle, and on the taste for leisure.

Nor is there always a wide range of choice as to how one spends the allotted time. A workweek of forty hours may be required if one is to work at all; retirement may be compulsory; no job may be available; school may be required. Far from being able to continue on the job as long as he would like, the amount and timing of work available to the individual is constrained by custom, regulations, and the demand for labor. The gift of twenty-four hours a day can seldom be translated into the precise quantities of work and leisure that would maximize one's satisfactions.

Formulating the critical questions concerning the aggregate allocation of time between work (in both the market and the home) and nonwork pursuits, and the distribution of work over the age groups and between the sexes, is basic to the consideration of many aspects of social policy, income maintenance, tax issues, and educational expenditures. What do we need to know about the way working and nonworking time has come to be apportioned as we enter the last quarter of the twentieth century? And what do we expect to happen to current patterns of time use, given the demographic and economic trends already in motion? In particular, what are the implications of major shifts in the distribution of market work between men and women, and between age groups?

An important distinction may be drawn between the amount of free time which accrues to the individual in the work force, as a result of rising productivity and real income, and that available to the family given the rising labor force activity of women. While there can be no doubt that the former has grown throughout the century, the status of the latter is in some doubt. When the individual worker, typically a male, gets shorter working hours, his family gains free time unless he takes a second job. But with the entrance of his wife to the labor force, the family loses time and household services, even if the workweek of the paid labor force continues its gradual decline. Moreover, the uses of whatever free time is available surely varies, depending on whether it is the male's or female's time. Among those who are married, the male's alternative to market work is largely leisure, the female's, home work. It follows that the impact of additional free time on the well-being of the family depends to a substantial degree on who gains the freedom from market work.

To identify the questions it is useful to examine briefly the changes that are occurring in the allocation of market work by age and sex, and to ask whether similar reallocations of work may not have to take place in the home as well. The male's use of time will surely vary, depending on whether he is the sole support of a family or one of two family wage earners. The female's work expectations have been revolutionized during the past three decades. Young adults enter the labor force much later and older people leave their jobs much sooner than heretofore. Within these decisive movements, market work appears in a different perspective; work is more evenly shared between the sexes, more concentrated in the middle years, and more productive because of added education. The alternative uses of time need also to be reexamined, since so much of the lifespan falls outside the workplace. Indeed, further lengthening of the periods before and after worklife will call for a volume of transfers for education and retirement that are sustainable only through far greater tax collections than have been required in the past.

WORKLIFE CHANGES AMONG MEN AND WOMEN [39]

The labor force participation rates of married women more than doubled from 1900 to 1940, and then almost tripled again between 1940 and 1970. By contrast, the levels of market work of single men and women have seen a gradual decline during most of this century. As a result, married women have come to be an ever larger portion of all workers; by 1974, the category of "married women, husbands present" had reached 22.5 percent of the total labor force. Since the participation rate of each cohort of women exceeds that of its predecessor and since, within an age group, there is no evidence of a decline in the overall participation rate during or after the childbearing years, it is clear that married women now expect continuous worklives, with very short absences from their jobs.

The labor force activity of married men has moved in the opposite direction. The work rate of married men aged sixteen and over, wife present, has fallen from 92.6 percent during the past three decades. While labor force rates for men aged twenty to fifty-four remained relatively stable,[40] a systematic decline has occurred for older and younger males. The decline has been fastest for the sixty-five and over age group, where the rate has dropped from 54.5 percent in 1947 to 24 percent in 1974; most of this decline occurred prior to 1965. A steady though less rapid decline has also occurred for men aged fifty-five to sixty-four, whose work rates have fallen 10 percentage points in the last twenty years. Since the late 1940s, a very slight decline has been evident for married men in the forty-five to fifty-four age group.

Early retirement, both voluntary and involuntary, occasioned in part by older men's relative disadvantage in educational level and the availability of improved retirement benefits, have accelerated the withdrawal of males from the labor force. In addition, a rise in public and private health benefits has permitted older men to leave the work force with disability pensions. The Parnes data on white males aged forty-five to fifty-nine show that among men who reported no health problems there was a decline of only 1 percentage point in labor force participation between 1966 and 1969; however, the work rate of males who developed health problems during the period dropped by 16 percentage points.[41]

HUMAN CAPITAL AND TIME ALLOCATION

The expanded work rates of women, offset by reduced labor force activity of young and older men, raises questions as to the volume and sex distribution of investments in human capital. It is clear that among married women, the higher their educational attainment, the greater the level of labor force participation. For wives with four or more years of college, the 1972 work rate is 54.8 percent, as contrasted with a rate of only 32.4 percent for those having less than a high school education. This pattern holds when presence and age of children are held constant. When there are no children under age eighteen in the family, the college-educated woman's work rate is 65.8 percent, while that of nongraduates of high school is only 28.5 percent. Although average educational attainment for females has risen only slightly in the past two decades, it is nevertheless true that each cohort of women (and men) is better educated than its predecessor. Increasing enrollments of women in higher education, particularly in graduate and professional schools, indicates stronger career commitments and an increased willingness to invest in women's education.

Additional education affects male labor force participation in the same manner. Although there has been much less variation in work activity of males of different educational attainments, Bowen and Finnegan found a significant correlation between educational level and participation rate, after controlling for variables such as age, marital status, color, and other income. In their sample of males in urban areas in 1960, the adjusted population rates ranged from 90.3 percent of the males with less than four years of schooling to 99.1 percent for those with seventeen or more years of school.[42] There is a strong positive correlation between years of education and labor force participation among older males; the rates vary from 71 to 87 percent, with the sharpest declines in work activity during the past decade being for men with the least education.

Findings by Taubman and Wales [43] and other investigators have called into question the economic gains to education promised by earlier writers. They found that additions to lifetime earnings from education are lower than previously estimated, and that much of the increment is attributable to the screening effect of schooling. The impact of such conclusions on the level of investments in education is yet uncertain, although the shortage of jobs for recipients of certain postbaccalaureate degrees has already resulted in declining graduate enrollments. But while total college enrollments have leveled off, primarily because of fewer students of college age, women's proportion of all students (particularly in graduate and professional schools) has grown sharply.

Shortage of jobs for youth generally has an offsetting effect, *i.e.*, that of inducing them to continue in school. Extensions of the period of schooling during recessions, particularly, helps to hold down measured unemployment, meanwhile improving the human capital base for future work roles. The increased use of time for education and training has the effect of adding to the stock of capital in much the same manner as the purchase of physical plant and equipment; both investments yield returns of varying rates. But whereas investments in physical capital are usually made by business on the basis of an expected private return, investments in education are made primarily by the public sector and the individual. The returns, moreover, which accrue in part to the society in the form of greater contributions, including tax revenues, and in part to the individual in the form of higher lifetime earnings, do not always appear competitive with those in physical capital; the consumption component of education alone tends to cause some understatement of its return. On the other hand, the estimated costs of investments in human capital, which usually include foregone earnings, may be overstated by the assumption that a paying job is an alternative to schooling when in fact no such option is available.

Given the excess of nonworking time during periods of substantial unemployment, the costs of education and job training are quite low. The student's time, the most expensive ingredient of the educational service, is virtually costless. Similarly, for the experienced worker off the job, most of the training costs—income transfers made through unemployment insurance—are already provided. In short, human capital investment costs are lowest when paid work is not an alternative to training, *i.e.*, when nonworking time cannot immediately be converted into work and earnings.

A FOURTH DIMENSION: NONMARKET WORK

Inclusion of schooling as a third dimension of time use broadens the framework of analysis beyond the work/leisure division usually postulated. Few people (least of all the students) would argue that education is a form of leisure; its inclusion in the growth of leisure gives an upward bias to these estimates or conversely, overstates the rate of decline in working time. In addition to formal education, investments in on-the-job training are equally important, Mincer concludes, and have been increasing since 1939.[44] Since on-the-job training displaces work, more time spent in such training means that actual working hours decline even when recorded weekly hours are unchanging. A three-activity model shows less leisure, fewer hours of work, and a continuing growth in the amount of time spent in education and training.

When home work is added as a fourth acivity, the pattern of time use becomes even more complex. For although household production has been greatly simplified by technology and reduced family size, a great deal of adult time continues to be spent on home work. When a married woman with a family takes a market job, who performs the services she formerly rendered? What happens to the family's free time? As in the case of excluding schooling from the calculations of the growth in nonworking time, failure to enter an estimate of the losses of free time associated with the wife's entrance to the work force leads to an overstatement of aggregate leisure. The extent to which the loss of free time that occurs from women's higher work rates is offset somewhat by an increased freedom from work on the part of young and older men; the extent of this offset is not known. But the concentration of work in one stage of the life cycle would be burdensome, even if such an offset were provided at other stages, and the utility of nonworking time may be far less in later years than in middle years.

If all time not spent in market activities is considered free time, then certainly the influx of married women into the labor force has meant a decline in leisure for them. Previously, however, such women were not idle. Thus when home work is included in the model some trade-off occurs between the added market work, and the home work of the woman and the free time of her family. Several alternatives are available to the family as it seeks to maintain its previous level of consumption of home-produced goods. First, the wife can continue her level of home work and therefore give up leisure time for income. Second, other family members may reallocate some of their time to home work, giving up some of their free time. Finally, the family may purchase goods and services previously produced by the wife in the market with some or all of the wife's earnings.

Kathryn Walker and William Gauger examined the reallocation of time of family members following the entrance of the wife into the labor force.[45] They found that in an average week, employed wives devoted two hours less time to household activities than wives who did not work outside the home. Thus much of the time spent on market work was deducted from their free time; hours spent on home work generally declined by less than 30 percent for wives with market jobs. Husbands spent an average of 1.5 hours per day on household tasks; however, "the time contribution of the husband did not relate to the wife's hours of employment." [46] Clearly, women entering the labor market suffer a sudden reduction in their free time as market work is added to home work.

In the future, it seems likely that the two-earner families will want larger proportions of their growth in productivity in the form of free time. The husband may seek less market work due to income effects from his wife's wages, while the wife may seek reduced market work time while still maintaining her career. In addition, the wife may attempt to modify her total working hours by transferring household responsibilities to the husband. If she is successful, future trends in nonmarket working time will bring increases in free time for women as they try to regain their previous leisure; in contrast, married men whose wives are working will give fewer hours to paid work but additional time to work in the home.

Time as a Balance Wheel

Nonmarket work, as well as longer periods of education and training, counterbalance to some degree the freedom from work generated by rising productivity. What appears in the statistics as a steady decline in working hours thus overstates the availability of the contemplative time that de Grazia equates with leisure. Despite the offset of nonmarket work, however, it is important to note that the worker who retains his job during a recession may have fewer paid hours available to him than he would like; that in addition to unemployment, involuntary reductions in hours worked are an important cost of a recession. Study has indicated that in some sectors of the labor force, hours lost through reductions in the working time of those retaining their jobs exceeded the hours lost by persons who became unemployed.[47] The burden of involuntary part-time work or shortened workweeks falls on much the same group as unemployment: the unskilled, young workers, the uneducated, and minorities. Moreover, it is clear that in line with earlier indications, the cyclical impact on hours during the most recent recession was greater in the downturn than in the recovery: "The rate of involuntary part-time work rises sharply during economic declines but falls more gradually after recovery begins." [48] Through the long-run, the cumulative effect of such growth in the residual of involuntary part-time work lends further weight to the importance of time as a balance wheel.

Social policy could of course encourage additional education throughout life as a further use of the growth in output per man-hour; or force some reduction in the workweek by legislating premium pay for hours over, say thirty-five per week; or offer retirement pensions prior to age sixty-two. Within the range of possible actions designed to increase the nonworking time of the employed, presumably in order to increase jobs and lower the number of persons unemployed, some would be preferred to others, as earlier discussion has indicated. In general, the creation of part-time jobs for those who prefer them and the extension of education over the lifespan seem to be more widely acceptable than the alternatives.

But in the short-run the limits within which policy can redivide paid work may be quite narrow, and in most instances work-sharing efforts are likely to be made at the expense of efficiency. As Melvin Reder has argued, reducing the hours of the more productive worker in order to create jobs for the less productive is difficult to defend. Moreover, the number of jobs is not fixed except in the short-run: to concentrate on some immediate reallocation of existing jobs rather than looking to sources of growth and job creation is to deny the validity of much of economic analysis. Indeed, Samuel Gampers' pronouncement that "So long as there is one man who seeks employment and cannot obtain it, the hours of labor are too long," if taken literally, would achieve full employment at some fraction of present working schedules, all the more because the availability of jobs clearly increases the number of job seekers.

The unemployment figure, which merely counts the numbers not working but looking for work at a given time, is but one component of the potential labor that would come onto the market if additional jobs were available at going rates of pay. The National Urban League argues

that its "Hidden Unemployment Index," which includes the unemployed, half the part-time workers who want to work full-time, and the
discouraged workers, revealed an actual jobless rate of 15 percent early
in 1976. Since wage rates are downwardly rigid, neither the unemployed
nor the peripheral workers who are outside the labor force are brought
into paid jobs in the absence of an economic stimulus that creates new
jobs. The wage rate, postulated in classical economics as the equilibrating
force through which unemployment would be reduced to zero, is now
generally fixed by agreement or legislation.

One interesting question is whether the equilibrating function im-
puted to the wage rate by earlier economists may not have been performed in part by working time and further, whether the significance of
working time as a balance wheel may not have become more and more
important as wages became less subject to reduction. In order to compare
the impact of these alternative policies—a lowering of wages versus a
reduction in working time—it is necessary to specify whether or not the
reduction is in response to an increase in output. Assuming no change
in productivity, downward flexibility of working hours allows the individual worker to increase his free time with no loss of money wage. But
such a reduction in hours raises costs, whereas reduced wages would
lower costs. If productivity is rising, however, downwardly flexible hours
allows the worker to gain free time (and possibly higher wages as well,
depending on the size of the productivity gain) at no rise in costs. Since
wages would not fall in such growth periods, the only question has to
do with the division of economic growth between wages and free time.
Through the long-run a decline in the proportion of productivity gains
have been translated into leisure for those with jobs. Expansions in output thus required additional workers, whose time on the job is similarly
short.

Time may become a more significant factor in achieving an equality
between the numbers of job seekers and the demand for labor as the
fixing of wages becomes more institutionalized. Certainly the time dimension will be more critical because if wages are fixed or economic
growth is slowed a high level of unemployment persists. If extended
unemployment insurance payments assume the role of more or less permanent income maintenance, as it has in the immediate past, the question of what use to make of the unemployed's time becomes more critical.
Can this form of idleness be turned to other forms: education, job
training, public works? Given the reluctance to encourage higher growth
because of inflationary threats or environmental considerations, nonworking time may increase more rapidly than in recent decades.

Turning from the macroeconomic questions to those of the individual
worker, economic analysis of life cycle behavior has recently emphasized
a number of issues long neglected in the literature. Ghez and Becker
point out that time, being a scarce resource, family decisions not only on
how much work they will offer in the market but also on their demand

for many goods—recreational, health, education—are as constrained by time as income. They show that the number of hours worked is positively related to the price of time over the life cycle, with the greatest amount of time spent at work when productivity is highest. Their theoretical formulation provides a framework for analyzing human capital investment over the life cycle, the relation between consumption and age, the timing of marriage and children.[49]

Increased attention to the time component of consumption as well as production will help to clarify alternative policy considerations, frequently those in the manpower field. But manpower planners are not allowed the luxurious assumption that a family can choose that combination of work and leisure that maximizes its welfare over the life cycle. Rather, the manpower problem is one of finding ways to maintain the worker's productive capacity through the worklife, and to insure that such capacity matches the needs of the labor market. During recent decades, the time required to maintain one's productive effiiciency has increased and the time actually spent at work for pay has declined—further evidence that working time serves as a balancing mechanism—while the match between labor force quality and market demand has been uneven.

Although the overriding concern in an era of unemployment is job creation, the long-run problem of accommodating to a growing work force and rising productivity via changes in working time will persist. There can be little doubt that time spent at work, particularly by those in declining industrial sectors, will continue to decrease under the pressure of finding jobs for all the job seekers. Labor unions have always understood the time dimension, and have looked to decreasing hours as a solution to unemployment. AFL President William Green posed the question in 1932 as follows: "Is there any reasonable, sensible-minded man who can believe we could equip industry with machinery and provide [employment] six days per week and eight hours per day . . . for every man and woman willing to work?"[50] But there has been limited understanding of the need to adjust earnings to the new work schedules if reduced hours are to allow for additional jobs, and even less recognition of the fact that such changes in working time occur only gradually, offering no immediate solution to unemployment. The pace of the change in working time may well increase in the years ahead, however, as a result of demographic patterns and broad shifts in the composition of the labor force.

In view of pending legislation that will establish the government as an employer of those workers otherwise unable to find jobs, the question of working time becomes particularly significant. Would these workers be hired at forty hours per week? Or would the government offer a shorter workweek in order to spread its expenditure over a larger number of the unemployed, or in order to effect some downward pressure on the workweek in the private sector? Massive public employment at say, thirty-five hours per week would probably hasten the decline in overall working schedules. Indeed, such legislation could give a major impetus to the long-run trend toward lessened work, which would be the first public use of time as a balance wheel in four decades.

Beyond such uses of work patterns in public works, policy leverages for influencing the allocation of time out of work and into nonwork pursuits are not easy to implement. Industry has generally favored work-life reductions through early retirement, which allows upward mobility of the work force. The costs are high, however, for either the firm or the retiree, or both. Worker response to a reduced workweek is mixed, but uniformly negative if earnings are reduced accordingly. Negotiated sabbaticals and retirement programs have been more widely accepted, but have not generated additional jobs. Major or sudden changes in working time are therefore improbable. But the pressure to increase nonworking time will surely persist if unemployment remains high, particularly if transfers via unemployment insurance continue to point up the present high cost of taking working time in this form.

Notes

1. Sar A. Levitan and William B. Johnston, *Work is Here to Stay, Alas* (Salt Lake City: Olympus Publishing Co., 1973).

2. For analyses of the question, see Joseph W. Garbarino, "Fringe Benefits and Overtime as Barriers to Expanding Employment," *Industrial and Labor Relations Review,* April 1964, pp. 426-42; Robert M. Macdonald, "The Fringe Barrier Hypothesis and Overtime Behavior," *Labor and Industrial Relations Review,* July 1966, pp. 562-69; and Reply, pp. 569-72; Ronald G. Ehrenberg, "The Impact of the Overtime Premium on Employment and Hours in U.S. Industry," *Western Economic Journal,* June 1971, pp. 199-207. See also Myron Joseph, "Hours of Work Issues," *Technology and the American Economy,* Appendix volume II, National Commission on Technology, Automation, and Economic Progress, 1966, pp. 325-47; and his citations on the historical pattern of working hours; Clyde E. Dankert *et al., Hours of Work* (New York: Harper and Row, 1965), especially the articles by Frederick Meyers, David Brown, and Melvin W. Reder; H. Gregg Lewis, "Hours of Work and Hours of Leisure," Industrial Relations Research Association, *Annual Proceedings,* 1957, pp. 10-16.

3. J. Brad Chapman and Robert Otterman, "Employee Preference for Various Compensation and Fringe Benefit Options," *The Personnel Administrator,* November 1975, pp. 30-36.

4. Bureau of Labor Statistics, *Trends in Output per Man-Hour in the Private Economy, 1909–1958,* bulletin no. 1249, 1959.

5. William Eisenberg, "Measuring the Productivity of Non-financial Corporations," *Monthly Labor Review,* November 1974.

6. Jerome Mark, "Productivity and the Costs in the Private Economy," *Monthly Labor Review,* June 1975.

7. Lionel Robbins, "On the Elasticity of Demand for Income in Terms of Effort," *Economica* 10, June 1930, pp. 123-29. For estimates of income and substitution parameters made by several recent authors, see Glen G. Cain and Harold W. Watts, *Income Maintenance and Labor Supply* (Chicago: Rand-McNally, 1973), esp. pp. 330-40. Subsequent references to earlier analyses are taken from Joseph J. Spengler, "Product-Adding versus Product-Replacing Innovation," *Kyklos*, X (Fasc. 3 1975), pp. 267-77. See also Juanita M. Kreps and Joseph J. Spengler, "The Leisure Component of Economic Growth," *Technology and the American Economy, op. cit.*, pp. 368-70.

8. Thomas Manly, "Usury at 6 Percent," an article published in 1661; as quoted in Paul Douglas, *The Theory of Wages.* (New York: The Macmillan Company, 1934), p. 210.

9. Josiah Child, *A New Discourse on Trade* (6th ed.), p. 12, as quoted in Paul Douglas, *op. cit.*, p. 270.

10. See Edgar S. Furniss, *The Position of the Laborer in a System of Nationalism.* New York, 1920, chapters 6 and 7, and Lujo Brentano, *Hours and Wages in Relation to Production.* New York, 1894, pp. 2-7.

11. Adam Smith, *An Inquiry into the Nature and Causes of the Wealth of Nations.* Modern Library Edition, 1937, pp. 81-82.

12. J. B. Say, *Traité d'économie politique,* Paris, 1841, book II, ch. 7, sec. 4.

13. T. 'R. Malthus, *An Essay on the Principles of Population,* London, 1826, pp. 368, 379, 424-25, 525.

14. W. S. Jevons, *The Theory of Political Economy,* 5th ed., Edinburgh, 1864, pp. 142-44, 328, 330, 339-48.

15. Alfred Marshall, *Principles of Economics,* London: Variorium edition, 1961, pp. 140-43, 526-629, 680-96, 720-74.

16. S. J. Chapman, "Hours of Work," *Economic Journal,* XIX (1909), pp. 354-73.

17. A. C. Pigou, *A Study in Public Finance,* London, 1929, pp. 83-84 and *The Economics of Stationary States,* London, 1935, pp. 163-64.

18. See W. A. Morton, "A Progressive Consumption Tax," *National Tax Journal,* vol. 4, June 1951.

19. G. F. Break, "Income Taxes and Incentives to Work," *American Economic Review,* 47, September 1957.

20. James Duesenberry, *Income, Saving, and the Theory of Consumer Behavior,* Cambridge, 1949.

21. Clarence Long, *The Labor Force Under Changing Income and Employment,* Princeton, 1958, pp. 272-73.

22. *Ibid.,* p. 271.

23. Douglas, *op. cit.;* also, Erika H. Schoenberg and Paul H. Douglas, "Studies in the Supply Curve of Labor," in *Landmarks in Political Economy,* vol. I, Earl J. Hamilton *et al.,* eds., Chicago, 1962, pp. 229-61.

24. T. A. Finnegan, "Hours of Work in the United States: A Cross-Sectional Analysis," *Journal of Political Economy,* 70, October 1962, pp. 452-70.

25. Gordon C. Winston, "An International Comparison of Income and Hours of Work," *Review of Economics and Statistics,* 48, February 1966, pp. 28-38.

26. Cain and Watts, *op. cit.,* pp. 3-4.

27. *Ibid.,* pp. 4-5.

28. Kreps and Spengler, *op. cit.,* pp. 355-65.

29. Clark Kerr, "Discussion," *American Economic Review,* May 1956, p. 219.

30. Peter Henle, "Recent Growth of Paid Leisure for U.S. Workers." *Monthly Labor Review,* March 1962, p. 256.

31. Geoffrey Moore and Janice Hedges, "Trends in Labor and Leisure," *Monthly Labor Review,* February 1971, p. 11.

32. Henle, *op. cit.,* p. 257.

33. Moore and Hedges, *op. cit.,* pp. 5-6.

34. Bureau of Labor Statistics, *Employee Compensation in the Private Non-farm Economy,* 1972, BLS Bulletin No. 1873, 1975.

35. H. Gregg Lewis, *op. cit.*

36. Department of Labor, *Manpower Report of the President: 1975.*

37. Moore and Hedges, *op. cit.,* p. 5.

38. "In the world of common-sense experience the only close rival of money as a pervasive and awkward scarcity is time." Wilbert Moore, *Man, Time, and Society,* New York, 1963, p. 4.

39. Parts of this section are drawn from Juanita Kreps and Robert Clark, *Sex, Age, and Work: The Changing Composition of the Labor Force.* (Baltimore: Hopkins Press, 1976).

40. See Joseph Gastwirth, "On the Decline of Male Labor Force Participation," *Monthly Labor Review,* October 1974, pp. 44-46. He concludes that more than half the decline for males of this age group from 1955 to 1969 resulted from more liberal benefits and less stringent requirements for unemployment insurance, welfare payments, and disability payments.

41. U.S. Department of Labor, *The Pre-Retirement Years,* Manpower Research Monograph 15, vol. 3 (Washington: U.S. Government Printing Office, 1972), p. 23.

42. Bowen and Finnegan, *op. cit.,* p. 296.

43. Paul Taubman and Terence Wales, *Higher Education and Earnings* (New York: McGraw-Hill, 1974).

44. Jacob Mincer, "On-the-Job Training: Costs, Returns, and Some Implications," *Journal of Political Economy,* October 1962.

45. Kathryn Walker and William Gauger, *The Dollar Value of Household Work.* (Ithaca, N.Y.: New York State College of Human Ecology, Cornell University, 1973).

46. *Ibid.,* p. 4.

47. See citations provided by Robert W. Bednarzik, "Involuntary Part-time Work: A Cyclical Analysis," *Monthly Labor Review,* September 1975, especially George L. Perry, "Labor Force Structure, Potential Output, and Productivity," *Brookings Papers on Economic Activity,* no. 3, 1971; and Stuart O. Schweitzer and Ralph E. Smith, "The Persistence of the Discouraged Worker Effect," *Industrial and Labor Relations Review,* January 1974, pp. 249-60.

48. Bednarzik, *op cit.,* p. 16.

49. Gilbert R. Ghez and Gary S. Becker, *The Allocation of Time and Goods Over the Life Cycle* (New York: National Bureau of Economic Research, 1975).

50. Quoted in Clyde E. Danker, "Automation, Unemployment, and Shorter Hours," in Dankert, *op. cit.,* p. 163.

Index

Abramovitz, Moses, 21, 8-32, 93, 103
Ackley, Gardner, 70, 80
AFDC (Aid to Families with Dependent Children), 160, 173, 175, 178-81
AFDC for Unemployed Fathers, 165, 174-75, 178
Age-sex proportions of unemployed, 40-41, 46-48
American Telephone & Telegraph Company, 152
Andersson, R., 104
Antidiscrimination, 130-33, 139-40
Area Redevelopment Act of 1961, 30, 91
Automation, 92, 93, 96, 184

Balanced budgets, 60-62
Balance of payments, 8, 17-19, 20, 22, 65-67, 71
Becker, Gary S., 200
Bell Telephone System, 135
Benefit-cost studies, 102
Bergmann, Barbara R., 4, 120-40
Birth rates, 9, 14
Blacks
  changing structure of employment, 148-51
  discrimination, 120-40, 151-56
  education, 96, 127
  Equal Employment Opportunity Program, impact of, 151-56
  income distribution, 121, 122, 157-61
  industry structure of employment, 150-51
  labor force trends, 144-46
  occupational distribution, 122-24, 148-50
  public sector employment, 156-57
  societal status, 124-27
  unemployment, 8, 9, 29, 68, 120, 123-24, 136, 144, 146-47
  welfare and, 159-60
Blinder, Alan S., 129
Bowen, W. G., 196
Break, G. F., 189
Bretton Woods system, 65
Brimmer, Andrew F., 4, 142-62
British Family Income Supplement of 1971, 179
Budget balancing, 60-62
Burns, Arthur, 21
Business cycle stabilization, 15-17

Cain, Glenn G., 191

Canada, unemployment in, 11, 38
Cash transfers, see Income maintenance
Chapman, S. J., 189
Child, Josiah, 188
Civil Rights Act of 1964, 94, 103, 121, 123, 131, 151
Clark Committee, 29, 30
Collective bargaining, 78, 87, 106, 112
Commission on Civil Rights, 132
Community Action Agencies, 95
Community Work and Training Program, 95
Comprehensive Employment and Training Act (CETA) of 1973, 1, 2, 100-2, 108, 110, 176
Comprehensive Manpower Programs, 100
Concentrated Employment Program (CEP), 100
Congressional Office of Placement and Office Management, 132
Consumer price index, 14, 17-18
Cooperative Area Manpower Programs System (CAMPS), 99
Corporations, 43, 63
Cost-push inflation, 18
Council of Economic Advisers (CEA), 39, 45-46, 59, 60, 62, 63, 65-70, 91, 92, 94, 111, 113
Creeping unemployment, 92
Crime, 120, 121

Decategorization, 99-102
Decentralization, 99-102
Demand management
  changing views on employment policy and, 28-32
  conflicts and constraints in practice of, 10-26
  cycle stabilization versus full-employment growth, 15-17
  Eisenhower Administration, 21-22
  fiscal and monetary instruments, competing functions of, 19-20
  inflation and balance of payments, 17-19
  Johnson Administration, 23-24
  Kennedy Administration, 22-23
  limitations of traditional, 85-90
  manpower policies and, 85-116
  Nixon Administration, 24-25
  postwar employment and price record, 10-15
  Truman Administration, 20-21

Devaluation, 24, 67, 79
Discrimination, 5, 29, 120-40, 151-56
Dollar, 18, 65-67
Douglas, Paul, 190
Dual labor market theory, 96, 98, 106
Dusenberry, James, 190

Earned income credit, 179
Eckstein, Otto, 70
Economic Opportunity Act, 94, 176
Education, 29, 96, 98, 127, 155, 196-97
   vocational, 99, 100, 103, 176
Eisenhower Administration, 3, 17, 19, 21-
   22, 60, 92
Elementary and Secondary Education Act
   of 1965, 94
Emergency Employment Act (EEA), 1971,
   2, 108, 109
Emergency Jobs and Assistance Act of
   1974, 108, 110
Employment Act of 1946, 2, 8, 27, 37-39
Employment policies, conflicting goals of,
   59-81
   balance of payments, 65-67
   budget balancing, 60-62
   competition, promotion of, 78
   inflation-unemployment trade-off, 62-65,
      71, 73, 75
   manpower training, 77-78
   pinpointed job creation, 75-77
   price-reducing measures, 78-79
   structural unemployment, 67-70
   wage-price restraints, 79-81
Employment Service, 91, 176
Employment subsidies, 85, 114-16
Equal Employment Opportunity Commission (EEOC), 122-23, 131, 133, 135,
   151-56
Equal Pay Act, 131
Exchange rates, 66, 67, 71, 79
Excise taxes, 57, 74, 78
Experience rating, 111, 112

Family Assistance Plan, 178, 191
Federal Reserve System, 18, 20, 22, 161
Federal Supplemental Benefits, 113
Feldstein, Martin, 50-51, 111
Finnegan, T. A., 190, 196
Fixed exchange rates, 66
Flanagan, Robert, 103
Flexible exchange rates, 67, 71
Food stamp program, 71, 175-76, 179
Ford Administration, 2, 45, 55, 71, 72-75,
   80
Forecasting, 16
Foreign investments, 66, 67, 71
Foreign trade, 66
Four percent target unemployment rate,
   11-13, 46, 54, 60, 65, 81, 91, 92
France, unemployment in, 11, 38-39
Frictional unemployment, 26-27, 62, 70
Functional finance, theory of, 15

Gauger, William, 198
General Accounting Office, 132
General assistance, 165, 167
Germany, unemployment in, 11
Ghez, Gilbert R., 200
G.I. Bill, 28
Ginzberg, Eli, 1-7, 28, 78, 103
GNP (gross national product), 42, 44, 61,
   62, 72, 73, 103, 143
Gold, 22, 23, 65-67
Gompers, Samuel, 199
Gordon, R. A., 30
Great Depression, 27
Great Society, 70
Green, William, 201

Hall, Robert, 97, 98
Hawkins-Humphrey   Full   Employment
   Bill, 2
Health, Education and Welfare, Depart-
   ment of, 99, 131
Hedges, Janice, 192
Heller, Walter W., 60-62, 63, 69
Henle, Peter, 192
Hidden unemployment, 200
Hill-Burton Act, 28
Home work, 197-98
Houthakker, Hendrik, 78

Immigration, 9
Income distribution, blacks and, 157-61
Income maintenance, 4-5, 16, 112, 113, 115,
   163-82, 191, 200
Income shares, 63
Income taxes, 78, 79, 189
Inflation, 8, 14, 17-19
   Eisenhower Administration, 21-22
   Ford Administration, 72-75, 80
   Kennedy Administration, 22-23
   Nixon Administration, 24, 71-72
   semi-, 105, 114
   true, 87
   Truman Administration, 20
   -unemployment trade-off, 18-19, 42-49,
      52-54, 62-65, 71, 73, 75-77, 86-89, 94,
      103
   wage-price restraints, 79-81
In-kind benefit schemes, 178
Interest rates, 20, 23, 74, 161
Internal Revenue Service, 133
International monetary system, 8, 18
Inventory investment, 15, 16
Investment tax credit, 66
Involuntary unemployment, 27
Italy, unemployment in, 11, 38-39

Japan, unemployment in, 11, 38-39
Jevons, W. S., 189
Job Corps, 95
Job creation, 75-77, 85, 107-11, 176
JOBS (Job Opportunities in the Business
   Sector), 95, 115, 116

Jobs, character of, 51-52
Johnson Administration, 3, 23-24, 64-66, 70, 94
Joint Economic Committee (JEC), 29, 39, 180-81

Kennedy Administration, 3, 17, 19, 22-23, 30, 59-70, 92
Kerr, Clark, 192
Keynes, John Maynard, 27
Keynesian economics, 85-89, 92
Khrushchev, Nikita, 70
Korean War, 8, 14, 18, 20
Kosters, Marvin, 107
Kreps, Juanita M., 4, 5, 184-202

Labor, Department of, 99
Labor force
  age-sex composition of, 40-41, 46-48
  growth of, 9
  hidden reserve, 14
  postwar changes in composition of, 12
  women in, 12-14
  youth in, 12-14
Labor unions, 43, 63, 105, 111, 201
Lampman, Robert J., 4, 163-82
Leisure, 185-87, 189, 192-94, 197-99
Lewis, H. Gregg, 193
Liberty Mutual Insurance Company, 133-35
Life chances, redistribution of, 138-39
Lindbeck, A., 103
Long, Clarence, 190
Long, Russell, 179

Macroeconomic policy, full employment and, 37-58
  age-sex composition of labor force, 46-48
  inflation barrier, 42-43
  inflationary expectations, 52-54
  limits of, 40-42
  Phillips Curve, 43-45, 52, 53
  voluntary unemployment, 48-52
Malthus, Thomas, 189
Manly, Thomas, 188
Manpower Development and Economic Opportunity Administration, 100
Manpower Development and Training Act of 1962, 30, 92, 100, 108, 176
Manpower Report of the President (1970), 30-31
Marriage rates, 14
Marshall, Alfred, 189
Marston, S. T., 111
Meidner, R., 104
Mincer, Jacob, 197
Minimum wage, 85, 86, 88, 105-7
Monopoly, 78
Moon-lighting, 186
Moore, Geoffrey, 192
Motivation, 95
Myrdal, Gunnar, 70

National Commission for Manpower Policy, 1-7, 100, 101, 113
National employment policy, issue of, 2
National Urban League, 199-200
Natural rate of unemployment, 53-54, 88
Negative income tax (NIT), 178, 179-81
Neighborhood Youth Corps Program, 95
New Careers program, 95
New Jersey Study, 180
Nixon Administration, 2, 24-25, 31, 61-62, 65, 71-72, 80, 100, 178
Noninflationary unemployment rate, 48, 51, 52, 54

Occupational segregation, 122-24, 127, 133-37
Office of Economic Opportunity, 99
Office of Federal Contract Compliance, 131
Oil prices, 24
Okun, Arthur M., 2, 59-81
Oligopoly, 78
On-the-job search, 96
On-the-job training, 99, 103, 128, 176, 197
OPEC (Organization of Petroleum Exporting Countries), 72
Operation Mainstream, 95
Operation twist, 66

Palme, Olof, 90
Part-time work, 3, 13, 185, 186, 199
Payroll taxes, 78
Perry, George, 46-48, 52
Phillips Curve, 43-45, 52, 53, 88, 90, 113
Pigou, A. C., 189
Pinpointed job creation, 75-77
Poverty, 30, 120, 121, 167-72
Price and wage controls, 56, 57, 71, 72, 79-80, 105
Price stability, 14, 20, 42, 62-64, 66, 72, 93
Private pension funds, 159
Productivity, 88, 199, 200
  American approach, 91-105
  Swedish approach, 90-92, 99, 103-4, 110
  work time and, 188-93
Progressive taxation, 16
Property tax, 74
Public assistance, 159-60, 164-82
Public Employment Program (PEP), 108, 109
Public service employment (PSE), 56, 85, 86, 88-89, 107-11, 176, 178, 181-82, 201-2
  blacks in, 156-57
Public works bill (1976), 2

Quit rates, 95-98, 105, 106

Racial wage differentials, 103
Railroad retirement receipts, 159
Real wage insurance, 80-81
Recessions, 14, 19-21, 59, 72, 142, 143, 147, 177

Reder, Melvin, 199
Retirement, 76, 186, 187, 195, 202
Retraining, 29
Revenue-sharing, 100
Ruttenberg, Stanley, 99

Sales taxes, 79, 189
Say, J. B., 189
Schulze, Charles, 63
Seasonal unemployment, 26
Self-employment, 13
Semi-inflation, 105, 114
Seniority, 98, 116, 136, 137
Sex roles, 139
Short-time benefits, 114
Shultz, George P., 31
Simon, John, 71
Slichter, Sumner, 106
Smith, Adam, 188-89
Smith-Hughes Vocational Education Act, 91
Social insurance, 164-82
Social Security, 94, 159
Societal status, influence of, 124-27
Solow, Robert M., 2, 37-58, 87, 89, 95, 96, 98, 110, 112
Special Unemployment Assistance, 113
Stagflation, 43, 114
Steel industry, 63
Stewart, Charles, 114
Structural unemployment, 27, 29, 62, 67-70, 77, 92, 95, 96, 97
Subsidies, 57-58, 114-16
Supplemental Security Income (SSI) program (1974), 165, 167, 181
Sweden
    productivity approach to, 90-92, 99, 103-4, 110
    unemployment in, 11, 38-39

Taubman, Paul, 196
Taxes, 19, 20, 23, 94
    excise, 57, 74, 78
    income, 78, 79, 189
    negative income, 178, 179-81
    payroll, 78
    progressive, 16
    property, 74
    sales, 79, 189
Tax Reform Act of 1975, 179
Technological unemployment, 92, 93, 96
Theobald, Robert, 67
Training Within Industry program, 91
True inflation, 87
Truman Administration, 20-21, 60
Turnover rates, 14, 29, 77, 97, 105

Ulman, Lloyd, 4, 85-116
Unemployment
    age-sex proportions, 40-41, 46-48
    blacks, 8, 9, 29, 68, 120, 123-24, 136, 144, 146-47

Unemployment (*cont.*)
    compared to foreign countries, 8, 10-11, 38-39
    creeping, 92
    dual labor market theory, 96, 98
    Eisenhower Administration, 3, 21-22, 60, 92
    Ford Administration, 45, 55, 72, 73, 75
    Four percent standard, 11-13, 46, 54, 60, 65, 81, 91, 92
    frictional, 26-27, 62, 70
    hidden, 200
    -inflation trade-off, 18-19, 42-49, 52-54, 62-65, 71, 73, 75-77, 86-89, 94, 103
    involuntary, 27
    Johnson Administration, 3, 23-24, 64, 94
    Kennedy Administration, 3, 22-23, 30, 59, 60, 92
    minimum wage cutting and, 105-7
    motivation and, 95
    natural rate of, 53-54, 88
    Nixon Administration, 24, 71, 72
    noninflationary rate of, 48, 51, 52, 54
    postwar record, 10-15
    prewar views about, 26-28
    public job creation and, 107-11
    quit rates, 95-97, 112
    search theory, 96, 98
    seasonal, 26
    structural, 27, 29, 62, 67-70, 77, 92, 94, 95, 97
    technological, 92, 93, 96
    Truman Administration, 20-21, 60
    unskilled workers, 8, 29, 68
    voluntary, 26-27, 48-52, 95, 112
    weighted rate of, 47
    women, 9, 12-13, 29, 40-41, 47, 94, 120, 123-24
    work sharing and, 185-86
    youth, 8, 9, 12-13, 29, 40-41, 47, 51-52, 54, 68-69, 71, 94, 95, 105, 106-7, 147
Unemployment insurance (UI), 9, 11, 71, 85, 86, 88-89, 111-14, 159, 165-66, 169, 174, 175, 185, 200, 202
United Kingdom, unemployment in, 11, 38-39
Urban blight, 120, 121

Vietnam War, 8, 14, 18, 40, 59, 64, 65, 80, 94
Vocational education, 99, 100, 103, 176
Vocational Rehabilitation Act of 1963, 94
Voluntary unemployment, 26-27, 48-52, 95, 112

Wachter, Michael, 48
Wage and price controls, 56, 57, 71, 72, 79-80, 105
Wage and price guidelines, 56
Wage equalization, 90-91, 99
Wage-price guideposts, 63-64, 80
Wage rates, 121-22, 188-91, 200

Wage subsidies, 57-58, 114-16
Wales, Terence, 196
Walker, Kathryn, 198
Watts, Harold W., 191
Weighted unemployment rate, 47
Welch, Finis, 107
Welfare, 9, 120, 121, 159-60, 164-84
West Germany, unemployment in, 38-39
Whyte, W. F., 126-27
Winston, Gordon, C., 190
Wiseman, Michael, 108, 109, 110
Women, 6-7, 9, 12-14
   discrimination, 120-40
   education, 196
   home work, 197-98
   occupational segregation, 122-24
   sex roles, 139
   societal status, 124-27
   unemployment, 9, 12-13, 29, 40-41, 47,
      94, 120, 123-24

Women (*cont.*)
   wage rates, 121, 122
   worklife changes, 194-95
Work Experience and Training Program,
   95
Work Incentive Program (WIN), 94, 95,
   101, 108, 115, 176
Workmen's compensation, 159
Work sharing, 185-86
Workweek, 75-77, 184-94, 199-202
World War II, 18, 20

Youth, 6-7
   education, 196-7
   unemployment, 8, 9, 12-13, 29, 40-41,
      47, 51-52, 54, 68-69, 71, 94, 95, 105,
      106-7, 147
Youth Minimum Wage, 107

Zero unemployment, 2

About The American Assembly

The American Assembly was established by Dwight D. Eisenhower at Columbia University in 1950. It holds nonpartisan meetings and publishes authoritative books to illuminate issues of United States policy.

An affiliate of Columbia, with offices in the Graduate School of Business, the Assembly is a national educational institution incorporated in the State of New York.

The Assembly seeks to provide information, stimulate discussion, and evoke independent conclusions in matters of vital public interest.

AMERICAN ASSEMBLY SESSIONS

At least two national programs are initiated each year. Authorities are retained to write background papers presenting essential data and defining the main issues in each subject.

A group of men and women representing a broad range of experience, competence, and American leadership meet for several days to discuss the Assembly topic and consider alternatives for national policy.

All Assemblies follow the same procedure. The background papers are sent to participants in advance of the Assembly. The Assembly meets in small groups for four or five lengthy periods. All groups use the same agenda. At the close of these informal sessions, participants adopt in plenary session a final report of findings and recommendations.

Regional, state, and local Assemblies are held following the national session at Arden House. Assemblies have also been held in England, Switzerland, Malaysia, Canada, the Caribbean, South America, Central America, the Philippines, and Japan. Over one hundred institutions have co-sponsored one or more Assemblies.

ARDEN HOUSE

Home of the American Assembly and scene of the national sessions is Arden House, which was given to Columbia University in 1950 by W. Averell Harriman. E. Roland Harriman joined his brother in contributing toward adaptation of the property for conference purposes. The buildings and surrounding land, known as the Harriman Campus of Columbia University, are 50 miles north of New York City.

Arden House is a distinguished conference center. It is self-supporting and operates throughout the year for use by organizations with educational objectives.

AMERICAN ASSEMBLY BOOKS

The background papers for each Assembly are published in cloth and paperbound editions for use by individuals, libraries, businesses, public agencies, nongovernmental organizations, educational institutions, discussion and service groups. In this way the deliberations of Assembly sessions are continued and extended.

The subject of Assembly programs to date are:

1951—United States-Western Europe Relationships
1952—Inflation
1953—Economic Security for Americans
1954—The United States' Stake in the United Nations
  —The Federal Government Service
1955—United States Agriculture
  —The Forty-Eight States
1956—The Representation of the United States Abroad
  —The United States and the Far East
1957—International Stability and Progress
  —Atoms for Power
1958—The United States and Africa
  —United States Monetary Policy
1959—Wages, Prices, Profits, and Productivity
  —The United States and Latin America
1960—The Federal Government and Higher Education
  —The Secretary of State
  —Goals for Americans
1961—Arms Control: Issues for the Public
  —Outer Space: Prospects for Man and Society
1962—Automation and Technological Change
  —Cultural Affairs and Foreign Relations
1963—The Population Dilemma
  —The United States and the Middle East
1964—The United States and Canada
  —The Congress and America's Future
1965—The Courts, the Public, and the Law Explosion
  —The United States and Japan
1966—State Legislatures in American Politics
  —A World of Nuclear Powers?
  —The United States and the Philippines
  —Challenges to Collective Bargaining
1967—The United States and Eastern Europe
  —Ombudsmen for American Government?
1968—Uses of the Seas
  —Law in a Changing America
  —Overcoming World Hunger
1969—Black Economic Development

　—The States and the Urban Crisis
1970—The Health of Americans
　—The United States and the Caribbean
1971—The Future of American Transportation
　—Public Workers and Public Unions
1972—The Future of Foundations
　—Prisoners in America
1973—The Worker and the Job
　—Choosing the President
1974—The Good Earth of America
　—On Understanding Art Museums
　—Global Companies
1975—Law and the American Future
　—Women and the American Economy
1976—Nuclear Energy
　—Manpower Goals
　—Capital Needs in America

Second Editions, Revised:

1962—The United States and the Far East
1963—The United States and Latin America
　—The United States and Africa
1964—United States Monetary Policy
1965—The Federal Government Service
　—The Representation of the United States Abroad
1968—Cultural Affairs and Foreign Relations
　—Outer Space: Prospects for Man and Society
1969—The Population Dilemma
1972—The Congress and America's Future
1975—The United States and Japan

About the National Commission for Manpower Policy

The National Commission for Manpower Policy was established by Title V of the Comprehensive Employment and Training Act of 1973. In creating the Commission, the Congress found that the responsibility for manpower and related programs was so "diffused and fragmented" that it was impossible to develop rational manpower priorities. Further, the Congress noted that a "coherent, flexible, national manpower policy" was necessary to the resolution of other economic and social problems. Accordingly, the National Commission for Manpower Policy was created to examine the myriad of issues involved in the development, deployment, and employment of the nation's human resources and, further, to recommend to the President and the Congress what the nation's manpower policies, goals, and programs should be.

The eighteen members of the Commission include the heads of six federal agencies: the Secretaries of Defense, Agriculture, Commerce, Labor, Health, Education, and Welfare, and the Administrator of Veterans Affairs; and eleven public members appointed by the President from among representatives of industry, labor, commerce, and education; persons served by manpower programs; and elected officials who have responsibility for operating such programs. The importance of assessing and addressing manpower issues at all three levels of government—federal, state, and local—was acknowledged by the President when he appointed a governor, mayor, and county executive to the Commission.

The Commission is a permanent statutory body with a director and an independent staff to execute its broad mandate. In addition to advising Congress on how to strengthen national manpower policy and programs, the Commission is responsible for assessing and recommending how the many federal manpower and manpower-related programs can be better coordinated. Further, the Commission is charged with independently determining the extent to which the recent decentralization of manpower programs to the states and localities are succeeding and the extent to which community needs are being met. Finally, the Commission is responsible for assessing how the nation's efforts to reduce dependence on foreign energy sources will affect employment and manpower.

An additional responsibility, one which the Commission has chosen for itself, is the need to inform not only the nation's policy-makers but also those who are directly affected by the nation's manpower policies: the public at large. To that end, the Commission has prepared and widely distributed a number of reports. Information on these reports and copies of them may be obtained through the Commission offices (Suite 300, 1522 K Street, N.W., Washington, D.C. 20005).

HD
5724
,J67

Jobs for Americans

CITY - COLLEGE LIBRARY
1825 May St. Ft. Brown
Brownsville, Texas   78520

Brownsville - Texas Southmost College